JUMP Math 4

Book 4 Part 1 of 2

T0302622

Contents

jump math™

MULTIPLYING POTENTIAL.

JUMP Math
One Yonge Street, Suite 1014
Toronto, Ontario M5E 1E5
Canada
www.jumpmath.org

Writers: Dr. John Mighton, Dr. Sindi Sabourin, Dr. Anna Klebanov, Dr. Sohrab Rahbar, Julie Lorinc
Editors: Dimitra Chronopoulos, Debbie Davies-Wright, Ewa Krynski
Layout and Illustrations: Linh Lam, Gabriella Kerr
Cover Design: Blakeley Words+Pictures
Cover Photograph: © LuckyOliver.com

ISBN 978-1-927457-12-2

Fifth printing June 2023

Printed and bound in Canada

A note to educators, parents, and everyone who believes that numeracy is as important as literacy for a fully functioning society

Welcome to JUMP Math

Entering the world of JUMP Math means believing that every child has the capacity to be fully numerate and to love math. Founder and mathematician John Mighton has used this premise to develop his innovative teaching method. The resulting resources isolate and describe concepts so clearly and incrementally that everyone can understand them.

JUMP Math is comprised of Teacher Resources, Digital Lesson Slides, student Assessment & Practice Books, assessment tools, outreach programs, and professional development. All of this is presented on the JUMP Math website: **www.jumpmath.org**.

The Teacher Resource is available on the website for free use. Read the introduction to the Teacher Resource before you begin using these materials. This will ensure that you understand both the philosophy and the methodology of JUMP Math. The Assessment & Practice Books are designed for use by students, with adult guidance. Each student will have unique needs and it is important to provide the student with the appropriate support and encouragement as they work through the material.

Allow students to discover the concepts by themselves as much as possible. Mathematical discoveries can be made in small, incremental steps. The discovery of a new step is like untangling the parts of a puzzle. It is exciting and rewarding.

Students will need to answer the questions marked with a in a notebook. Grid paper notebooks should always be on hand for answering extra questions or when additional room for calculation is needed.

Contents

PART 1

Unit 1: Operations and Algebraic Thinking: Patterns

Unit 2: Number and Operations in Base Ten: Place Value, Addition, and Subtraction

Unit 3: Operations and Algebraic Thinking: Rounding

Unit 4: Number and Operations in Base Ten: Multiplication

Unit 5: Operations and Algebraic Thinking: Division

Unit 6: Measurement and Data: Metric Units, Perimeter, and Time

Unit 7: Geometry: Shapes

PART 2

Unit 1: Operations and Algebraic Thinking: More Patterns

Unit 2: Number and Operations in Base Ten: Remainders

Unit 3: Operations and Algebraic Thinking: Word Problems

Unit 4: Number and Operations—Fractions: Fractions

Unit 8: Measurement and Data: US Customary Units and Area

Unit 9: Geometry: Angles

OA4-1 Increasing Sequences

Find the **difference** between 15 and 12 by counting on your fingers.

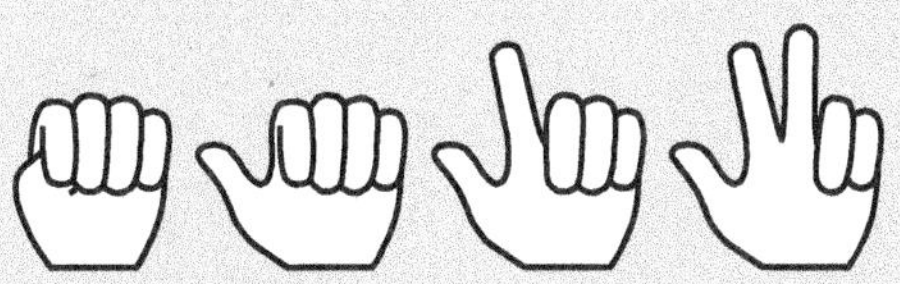

Say: 12 13 14 15

When you say 15, you have 3 fingers up. So the difference or gap between 12 and 15 is 3.

1. Find the difference between the numbers by counting up. Write your answer in the circle.
(If you know your subtraction facts, you may find the answer without counting.)

a) 2 ◯ 5
b) 3 ◯ 8
c) 6 ◯ 8
d) 4 ◯ 9
e) 12 ◯ 16
f) 13 ◯ 17
g) 21 ◯ 26
h) 37 ◯ 39
i) 26 ◯ 29
j) 32 ◯ 37
k) 24 ◯ 29
l) 44 ◯ 47
m) 51 ◯ 55
n) 46 ◯ 49
o) 28 ◯ 32
p) 34 ◯ 39
q) 89 ◯ 91
r) 62 ◯ 71
s) 87 ◯ 89
t) 59 ◯ 63

BONUS ▶

u) 96 ◯ 101
v) 97 ◯ 102
w) 98 ◯ 104
x) 117 ◯ 122
y) 219 ◯ 223
z) 146 ◯ 151
aa) 99 ◯ 108
bb) 99 ◯ 107

2. Why is 17 ◯ 85 harder to solve than 81 ◯ 85?

____

____

____

What number is 4 **more than** 16? (Or: What is 16 + 4?)

You can find the answer by counting on your fingers. Say 16 with your fist closed, then count up from 16 until you have raised 4 fingers.

16 17 18 19 20

The number 20 is 4 **more than** 16.

3. Add the number in the circle to the number beside it. Write your answer in the blank.

a) 5 (4) ____ b) 8 (2) ____ c) 7 (3) ____ d) 3 (4) ____

e) 17 (5) ____ f) 18 (4) ____ g) 14 (8) ____ h) 19 (6) ____

i) 30 (8) ____ j) 27 (9) ____ k) 34 (7) ____ l) 32 (5) ____

m) 67 (2) ____ n) 85 (5) ____ o) 42 (3) ____ p) 68 (4) ____

q) 54 (6) ____ r) 63 (5) ____ s) 98 (4) ____ t) 93 (8) ____

BONUS ▶

u) 132 (5) ____ v) 378 (4) ____ w) 499 (3) ____ x) 997 (5) ____

4. Fill in the missing numbers.

a) ____ is 4 more than 6 b) ____ is 6 more than 5 c) ____ is 5 more than 7

d) ____ is 1 more than 19 e) ____ is 6 more than 34 f) ____ is 5 more than 18

g) ____ is 8 more than 29 h) ____ is 7 more than 24 i) ____ is 8 more than 37

BONUS ▶

j) ________ is 5 more than 168 k) ________ is 9 more than 793

l) ________ is 3 more than 699 m) ________ is 4 more than 79,498

Continue this number pattern: 6 , 8 , 10 , 12 , ?

Step 1: Find the **difference** between the first two numbers.

6 , 8 , 10 , 12 , ? (difference: 2)

Step 2: Check that the difference between the other numbers in the pattern is also 2.

6 , 8 , 10 , 12 , ? (differences: 2, 2, 2, 2)

Step 3: Add 2 to the last number in the sequence.

6 , 8 , 10 , 12 , *14*

5. Extend the following patterns. Start by finding the gap between the numbers.

a) 1 , 3 , 5 , ____ , ____

b) 0 , 2 , 4 , ____ , ____

c) 3 , 7 , 11 , ____ , ____

d) 2 , 6 , 10 , ____ , ____

e) 1 , 4 , 7 , ____ , ____

f) 5 , 9 , 13 , ____ , ____

BONUS ▶

g) 1 , 11 , 21 , ____ , ____

h) 5 , 12 , 19 , ____ , ____

i) 21 , 24 , 27 , ____ , ____

j) 86 , 88 , 90 , ____ , ____

6. Aya reads 5 pages of her book each night. Last night she was on page 72.

What page will she reach tonight? Tomorrow night?

72	____	____
last night	tonight	tomorrow

7. Nick reads 3 pages of his book each night. Last night he was on page 51.

What page will he reach tonight? __________ Tomorrow night? __________

OA4-2 Decreasing Sequences

What number must you subtract from 22 to get 18?

Evan finds the answer by counting backward on his fingers.

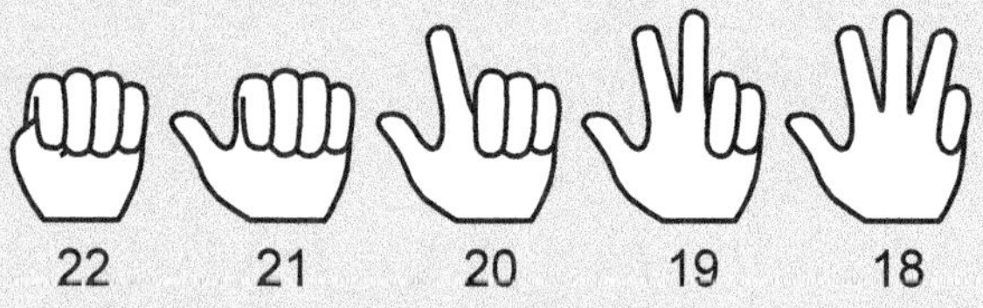

He could use a number line to help:

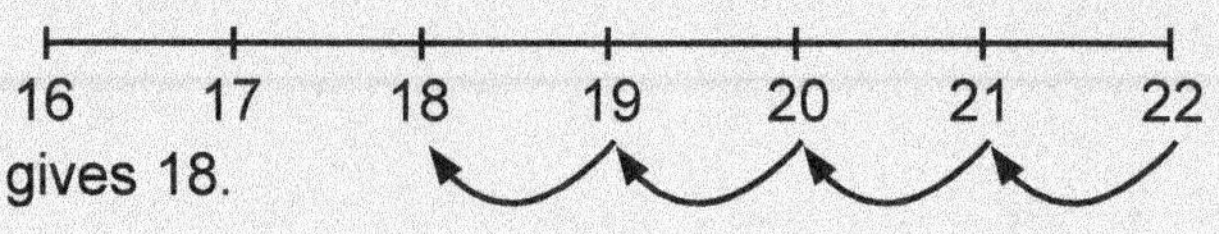

Evan has raised 4 fingers. So 4 subtracted from 22 gives 18.

1. What number must you **subtract** from the greater number to get the lesser number?

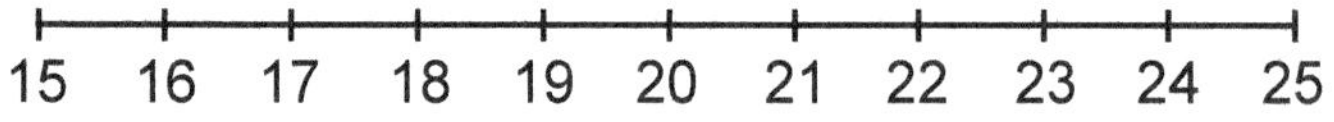

a) 23 (*−3*) 20 b) 24 ( ) 19 c) 21 ( ) 16 d) 22 ( ) 15

e) 24 ( ) 17 f) 19 ( ) 16 g) 23 ( ) 17 h) 25 ( ) 19

2. Find the gap between the numbers by counting backward on your fingers.

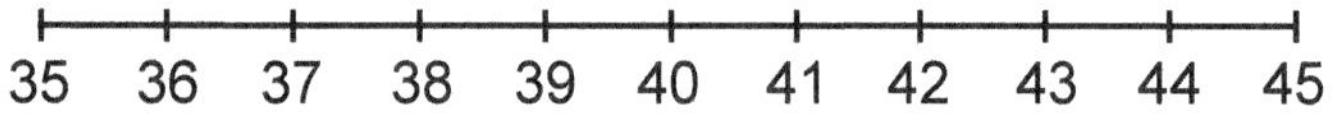

a) 42 (*−4*) 38 b) 41 ( ) 39 c) 42 ( ) 37 d) 38 ( ) 37

e) 41 ( ) 37 f) 40 ( ) 36 g) 42 ( ) 35 h) 43 ( ) 35

3. Find the gap between the numbers by counting backward on your fingers (or by using your subtraction facts).

a) 86 ( ) 81 b) 58 ( ) 52 c) 50 ( ) 48 d) 80 ( ) 78

e) 52 ( ) 47 f) 67 ( ) 63 g) 45 ( ) 36 h) 62 ( ) 56

i) 58 ( ) 51 j) 101 ( ) 97 k) 82 ( ) 76 l) 97 ( ) 89

What number is 3 **less than** 9? (Or: What is 9 − 3?)

Keitha finds the answer by counting on her fingers.

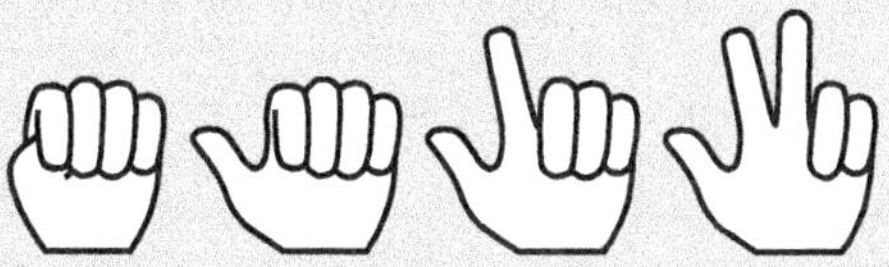

9 8 7 6

The number 6 is 3 **less than** 9.

4. Subtract the number in the circle from the number beside it. Write your answer in the blank.

a) 3 (−2) _____ b) 12 (−3) _____ c) 8 (−4) _____ d) 9 (−1) _____

e) 8 (−5) _____ f) 10 (−4) _____ g) 5 (−1) _____ h) 9 (−2) _____

BONUS ▶

i) 28 (−4) _____ j) 35 (−6) _____ k) 57 (−8) _____ l) 62 (−4) _____

5. Fill in the missing numbers.

a) _____ is 4 less than 7 b) _____ is 2 less than 9 c) _____ is 5 less than 17

d) _____ is 4 less than 20 e) _____ is 4 less than 32 f) _____ is 5 less than 40

In a **decreasing sequence**, each number is less than the one before it.

Let's extend the pattern in this decreasing sequence. 11 , 9 , 7 , _____ , _____

Step 1: Find the gap. 11 (−2) 9 (−2) 7 (−2) _____ (−2) _____

Step 2: Extend the pattern. 11 (−2) 9 (−2) 7 (−2) *5* (−2) *3*

6. Extend the following decreasing sequences.

a) 10 , 9 , 8 , _____ , _____ b) 14 , 12 , 10 , _____ , _____

c) 23 , 22 , 21 , _____ , _____ d) 24 , 21 , 18 , _____ , _____

OA4-3 Increasing and Decreasing Sequences

1. Extend the patterns, using the gap provided.

Example 1: 6 (+1) 7 , 8 , 9

Example 2: 8 (−2) 6 , 4 , 2

a) 5 (+5) 10 , ____ , ____ , ____

b) 1 (+3) 4 , ____ , ____ , ____

c) 3 (+3) 6 , ____ , ____ , ____

d) 12 (−2) 10 , ____ , ____ , ____

e) 12 (+2) 14 , ____ , ____ , ____

f) 25 (−5) 20 , ____ , ____ , ____

2. Extend the patterns by first finding the gap.

Example: 3 , 5 , 7 , ____

Step 1: 3 (+2) 5 (+2) 7 , ____

Step 2: 3 , 5 , 7 (+2) 9

a) 5 , 8 , 11 , ____ , ____

b) 2 , 4 , 6 , ____ , ____

c) 6 , 10 , 14 , ____ , ____

d) 1 , 3 , 5 , ____ , ____

e) 21 , 24 , 27 , ____ , ____

f) 12 , 17 , 22 , ____ , ____

g) 25 , 23 , 21 , ____ , ____

h) 59 , 54 , 49 , ____ , ____

3. Ahmed has a box of 24 pears. He eats 3 each day.

How many are left after 5 days? ______

24 , ____ , ____ , ____ , ____ , ____

4. Emma has $17. She saves $4 each day. How much money has she saved after 4 days?

OA4-4 Pattern Rules

1. Continue the sequence by *adding* the number given.

a) (add 3) 31, 34, _______, _______, _______

b) (add 5) 70, 75, _______, _______, _______

c) (add 2) 24, 26, _______, _______, _______

d) (add 10) 50, 60, _______, _______, _______

e) (add 4) 31, 35, _______, _______, _______

f) (add 9) 11, 20, _______, _______, _______

g) (add 6) 10, 16, _______, _______, _______

h) (add 7) 70, 77, _______, _______, _______

2. Continue the sequence by *subtracting* the number given.

a) (subtract 2) 14, 12, _______, _______

b) (subtract 3) 15, 12, _______, _______

c) (subtract 5) 75, 70, _______, _______

d) (subtract 3) 66, 63, _______, _______

e) (subtract 4) 46, 42, _______, _______

f) (subtract 7) 49, 42, _______, _______

g) (subtract 3) 91, 88, _______, _______

h) (subtract 5) 131, 126, _______, _______

BONUS ▶

Make a rule for a pattern. Then make a pattern given by the rule.

My rule: ____

My pattern: _______, _______, _______, _______, _______

3. Which one of the following sequences was made by adding 3? Circle it.
Hint: Check all the numbers in the sequence.

A. 3, 5, 9, 12 **B.** 3, 6, 8, 12 **C.** 3, 6, 9, 12

4. Look at the sequence: 72, 64, 56, 48, 40, ...

Zannat says this sequence was made by subtracting 7 each time.

Farouk says it was made by subtracting 8.

Who is right? Explain. ____

____

____

____

____

5. What number was added each time to make the pattern?

a) 2, 5, 8, 11 add _____

b) 3, 6, 9, 12 add _____

c) 15, 17, 19, 21 add _____

d) 44, 46, 48, 50 add _____

e) 41, 46, 51, 56 add _____

f) 19, 22, 25, 28 add _____

g) 243, 245, 247, 249 add _____

h) 21, 27, 33, 39 add _____

i) 15, 18, 21, 24 add _____

j) 41, 45, 49, 53 add _____

6. What number was subtracted each time to make the pattern?

a) 18, 16, 14, 12 subtract _____

b) 35, 30, 25, 20 subtract _____

c) 100, 99, 98, 97 subtract _____

d) 41, 38, 35, 32 subtract _____

e) 17, 14, 11, 8 subtract _____

f) 99, 97, 95, 93 subtract _____

g) 180, 170, 160, 150 subtract _____

h) 100, 95, 90, 85 subtract _____

i) 27, 25, 23, 21 subtract _____

j) 90, 84, 78, 72 subtract _____

7. State the rule for the following patterns.

a) 119, 112, 105, 98, 91 *subtract* _______

b) 1, 9, 17, 25, 33, 41 *add* _______

c) 101, 105, 109, 113 _____________

d) 110, 99, 88, 77 _____________

8. Find the rule for the pattern, then fill in the blanks.

12, 17, 22, _____, _____, _____ The rule is: ______________________________

9. Look at the pattern: 5, 8, 11, 14, 17, ...

Keith says the pattern rule is "Start at 5 and subtract 3 each time."

Jane says the rule is "Add 4 each time."

Molly says the rule is "Start at 5 and add 3 each time."

a) Whose rule is correct? ______________________________

b) What mistakes did the others make? ______________________________

____

____

OA4-5 Introduction to T-tables

Abdul makes a growing pattern with blocks.

He records the number of blocks in each figure in a **T-table**.

He writes the number of blocks he adds each time he makes a new figure in a circle.

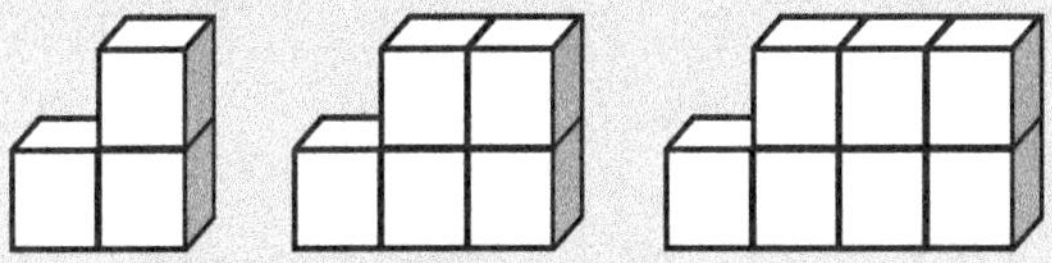

Figure	Number of Blocks
1	3
2	5
3	7

(2) (2) number of blocks *added* each time

The number of blocks in the figures are 3, 5, 7, ….

Abdul writes a **rule** for this number pattern: *Start at 3 and add 2 each time.*

1. Abdul makes another growing pattern with blocks. How many blocks does he add to make each new figure? Write your answer in the circles. Then write a rule for the pattern.

a)

Figure	Number of Blocks
1	3
2	7
3	11

Rule: *Start at 3 and* ____________
____
____

b)

Figure	Number of Blocks
1	2
2	6
3	10

Rule: ____________
____
____

c)

Figure	Number of Blocks
1	2
2	4
3	6

Rule: ____________
____
____

d)

Figure	Number of Blocks
1	1
2	6
3	11

Rule: ____________
____
____

e)

Figure	Number of Blocks
1	5
2	9
3	13

Rule: ____________
____
____

f)

Figure	Number of Blocks
1	12
2	18
3	24

Rule: ____________
____
____

g)

Figure	Number of Blocks
1	2
2	10
3	18

Rule: ____________

h)

Figure	Number of Blocks
1	3
2	6
3	9

Rule: ____________

i)

Figure	Number of Blocks
1	6
2	13
3	20

Rule: ____________

BONUS ▶ Extend the number pattern. How many blocks would be used in the 6th figure?

a)

Figure	Number of Blocks
1	2
2	7
3	12

b)

Figure	Number of Blocks
1	3
2	6
3	9

c)

Figure	Number of Blocks
1	3
2	8
3	13

2. Amy makes an increasing pattern with blocks. After making the 3rd figure, she has only 14 blocks left. Does she have enough blocks to complete the 4th figure?

a)

Figure	Number of Blocks
1	3
2	7
3	11

yes no

b)

Figure	Number of Blocks
1	7
2	10
3	13

yes no

c)

Figure	Number of Blocks
1	1
2	5
3	9

yes no

3. How many squares are needed to make the 5th figure in the pattern? Make a table to show your answer.

a)

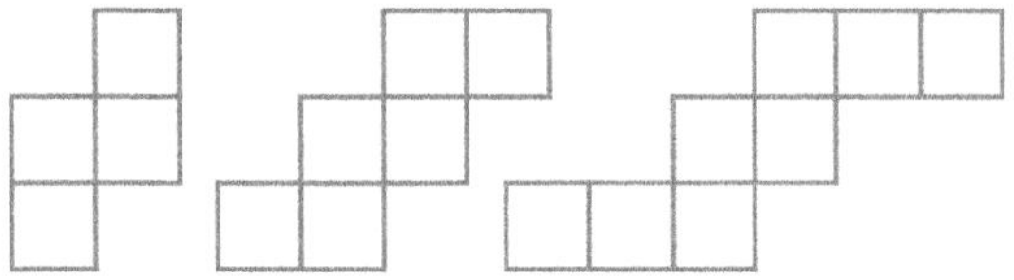

b)

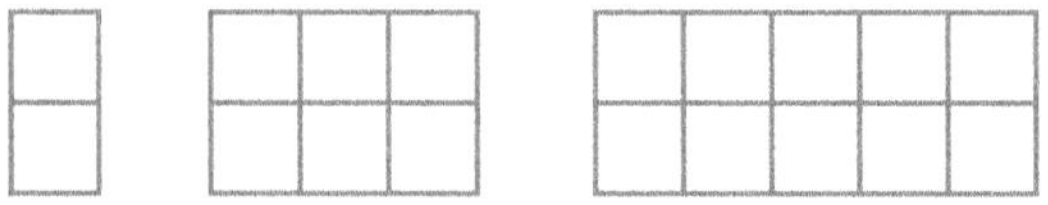

T-tables

1. Count the number of line segments in each figure. Hint: Count around the outside of the figure first, marking each line segment as you count. Example:

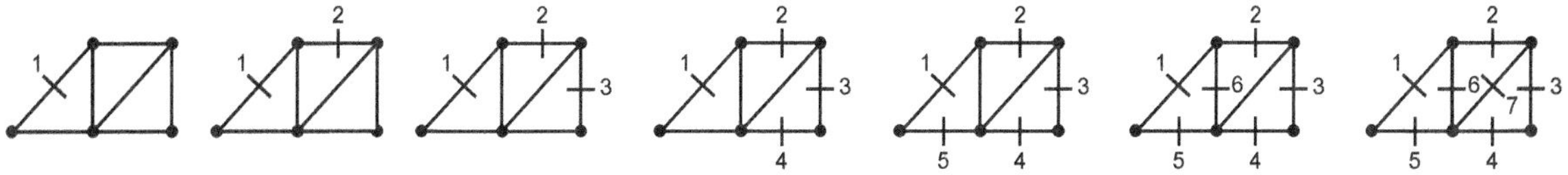

a) 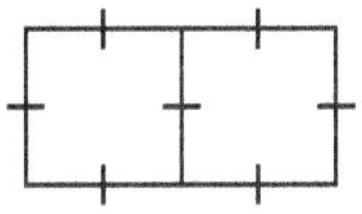 7

b) 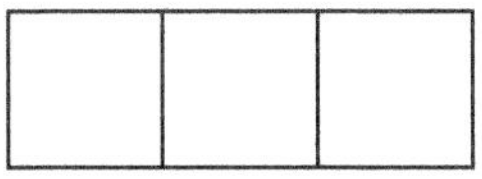 ______

c) 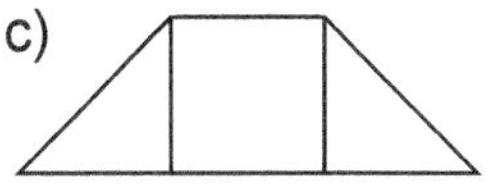 ______

d) 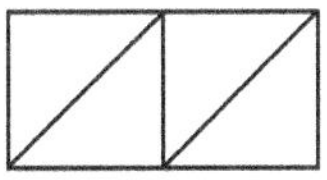 ______

e) 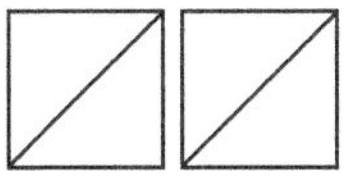 ______

f) 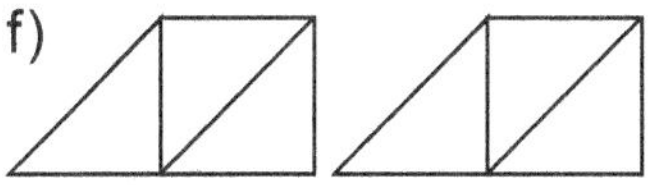 ______

2. Continue the pattern below, then complete the table.

Figure 1

Figure 2

Figure 3

Figure 4

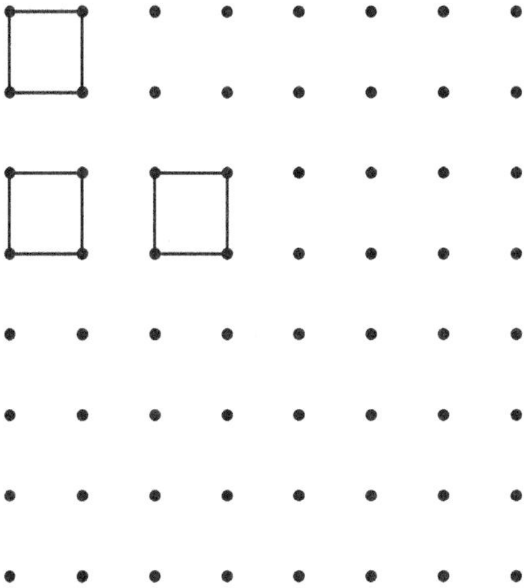

Figure	Number of Line Segments
1	4
2	8
3	
4	

How many line segments would Figure 5 have? ______

3. Continue the pattern below, then complete the table.

Figure 1

Figure 2

Figure 3

Figure 4

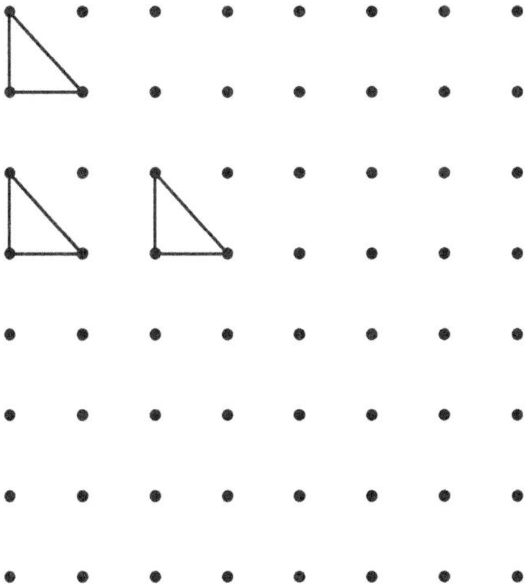

Figure	Number of Line Segments
1	
2	
3	
4	

How many line segments would Figure 5 have? ______

4. Continue the pattern below, then complete the table.

Figure 1

Figure 2

Figure 3

Figure 4

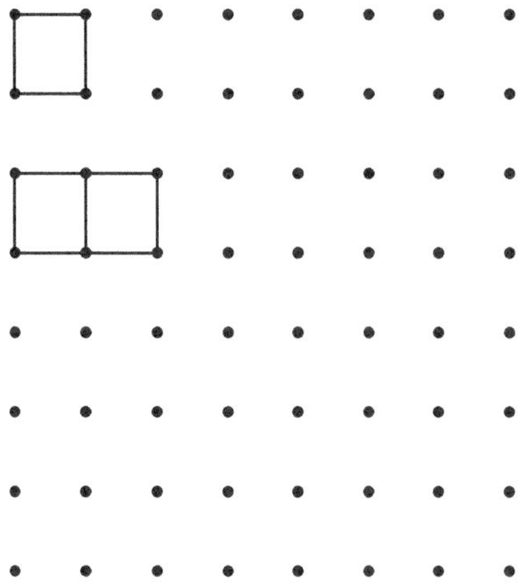

Figure	Number of Line Segments
1	
2	
3	
4	

a) How many line segments would Figure 5 have? ___________

b) How many line segments would Figure 6 have? ___________

c) How many line segments would Figure 7 have? ___________

5. Continue the pattern below, then complete the table.

Figure 1

Figure 2

Figure 3

Figure 4

Figure 5

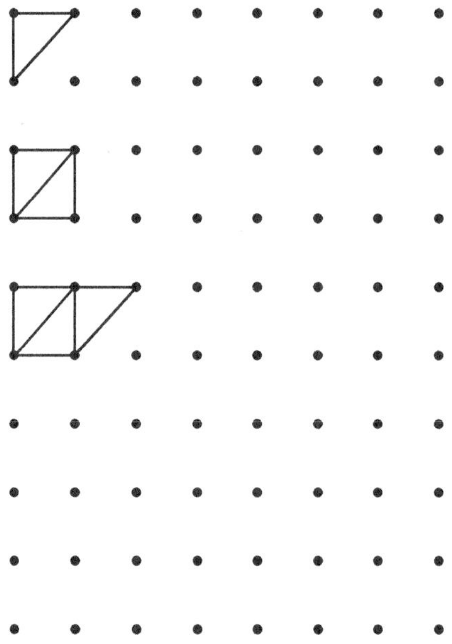

Figure	Number of Line Segments
1	
2	
3	
4	
5	

a) How many line segments would Figure 6 have? ___________

b) How many line segments would Figure 7 have? ___________

c) How many line segments would Figure 8 have? ___________

6. Complete each table. How many young would 5 animals have?

a)

Arctic Fox	Number of Cubs
1	5
2	10

b)

Wood-chuck	Number of Pups
1	4
2	8

c)

White-tailed deer	Number of Fawns
1	2
2	4

d)

Osprey	Number of Eggs
1	3
2	6

7. Complete each table. How much money would Claude earn for 4 hours of work?

a)

Hours Worked	Dollars Earned
1	$9

b)

Hours Worked	Dollars Earned
1	$10

c)

Hours Worked	Dollars Earned
1	$8

8. Peter makes a design using triangles and hexagons. He adds two triangles and a hexagon at each stage.

Stage 1:

Stage 2:

Stage 3:

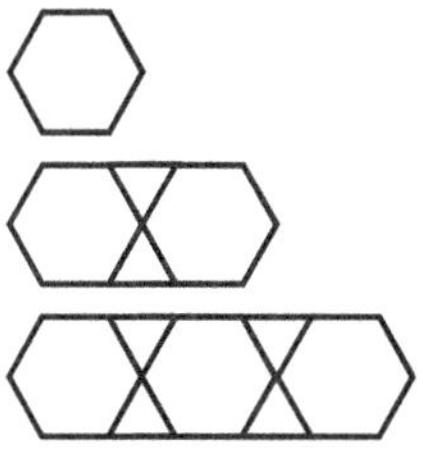

Stage	Hexagons	Triangles
1	1	0
2	2	
3		

a) Fill in the table.

b) Peter has 6 hexagons and 9 triangles. Does he have enough triangles to use all 6 hexagons? _______________

9. Hanna makes Christmas ornaments like the one shown. She has 5 trapezoids (the shaded figure). Fill in the table to show how many triangles she will need.

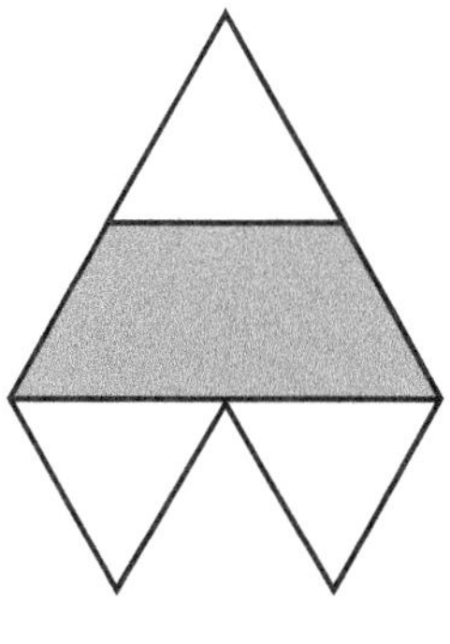

Number of Ornaments	Trapezoids	Triangles

OA4-7 Patterns Involving Time

The days of the week:
Sunday, Monday, Tuesday, Wednesday, Thursday, Friday, Saturday

The months of the year:
January, February, March, April, May, June, July, August, September, October, November, December

1. Solve the problem by filling in the T-table.

a) Harry starts work on Tuesday morning.
He repairs 4 bikes each day.

How many bikes has he repaired by

Friday evening? __________

Day	Total Number of Bikes Repaired
Tuesday	4

b) Meryl saves $20 in July.
She saves $10 each month after that.

How much has she saved by the end of

October? __________

Month	Saved
July	$20

c) During a snowstorm, 5 cm of snow falls by 6 p.m. Every hour after that, 3 cm of snow falls.

How deep is the snow at 9 p.m.?

____

Time	Depth of Snow
6 p.m.	5 cm

d) Adria's maple sapling grows 3 cm in May.
It grows 6 cm each month after that.

How tall is the sapling by the end of August?

____

Month	Height of Sapling
May	

e) Karen writes 14 pages of her book in February. She writes 8 pages every month after that.
How many pages has she written by the end of June?

f) Mario starts work on Wednesday morning.
He plants 5 trees each day.
How many trees has he planted by Friday evening?

2. Fill in the table by subtracting the same number each time.

a) Sandhu lights a candle at 6 p.m. It is 30 cm tall.

At 7 p.m., the candle is 27 cm tall.

At 8 p.m., it is 24 cm tall.

i) How many centimeters does the candle burn down every hour? __________

ii) How tall is the candle at 11 p.m.? __________

Time	Height of the Candle
6 p.m.	30 cm
7 p.m.	27 cm
8 p.m.	24 cm
9 p.m.	
10 p.m.	

(−3)

b) Lou has $35 in his savings account at the end of March. He spends $7 each month.

How much does he have in his account at the end of June? __________

Month	Savings
March	$35

c) Aponi has $38 in her savings account at the end of October. She spends $6 each month.

How much does she have at the end of January? __________

Month	Savings

d) Karen has $57 in her savings account at the end of June. She spends $6 each month.

How much does she have at the end of September? __________

Month	Savings

e) A fish tank contains 20 gallons of water at 5 p.m. Three gallons of water leak out each hour.

How much water is left in the tank at 8 p.m.? __________

Time	Amount of Water

f) The snow is 19 cm deep at 3 p.m. Two centimeters of snow melt every hour. How deep is the snow at 7 p.m.?

OA4-8 Problem Solving with Patterns

1. A marina rents canoes at $7 for the first hour and $4 for every hour after that. How much would it cost to rent a canoe for 6 hours?

2. A bookstore has a special sale: the first book you buy costs $10 and each book after that costs $5. Claude has $25.
Does he have enough to buy five books?

3. Draw pictures or make models (using blocks or counters) that match the pattern.

a)

Figure	Number of Objects
1	4
2	6
3	8

b)

Figure	Number of Objects
1	3
2	6
3	9

c)

Figure	Number of Objects
1	4
2	7
3	10

4. Edith's sapling grows 2 inches in July. It grows 3 inches each month after that.
Ron's sapling grows 3 inches in July. It grows 1 inch each month after that.
Whose sapling is taller by the end of September?

5. Chloe lights a candle at 5 p.m. It is 28 cm tall at 5 p.m. It burns down 4 cm every hour.
Dora's candle is 21 cm high when she lights it at 5 p.m. It burns down 3 cm every hour.
Whose candle is taller at 10 p.m.?

6. Crystal bikes 30 miles on the first day of a trip. She bikes 40 miles every day after that.
How far has she biked after 4 days?

BONUS ▶ Ryan is 900 miles from home on Monday morning. He drives home, traveling 200 miles every day.

a) How far from home is he on Wednesday morning?
b) On which day does he arrive home?

Day	Distance from home in the morning (miles)
Monday	900

OA4-9 Arrays

When you multiply two numbers, the result is called the **product** of the numbers.
In the **array** below, there are 3 **rows** of dots. There are 5 dots **in each row**.

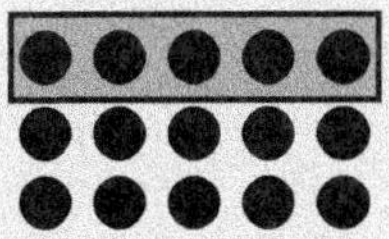

5
10
15

Carmelle counts the dots by skip counting by 5s.

Carmelle writes a multiplication equation for the array: $\mathbf{3 \times 5 = 15}$ (3 rows of 5 dots is 15 dots).

1. How many rows are there? How many dots in each row?
Write a multiplication equation for each array.

a) 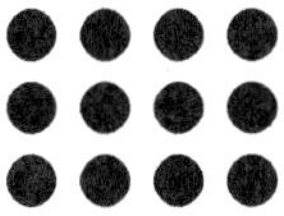

3 rows

4 dots in each row

$3 \times 4 = 12$

b) 

_____ rows

_____ dots in each row

____

c) 

_____ rows

_____ dots in each row

____

2. Write a product for each array.

a) 4×3 (rows × dots in each row) 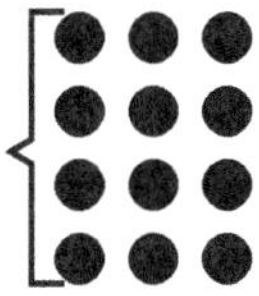

b) __________ 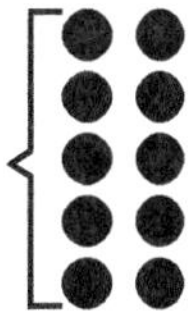

c) __________ 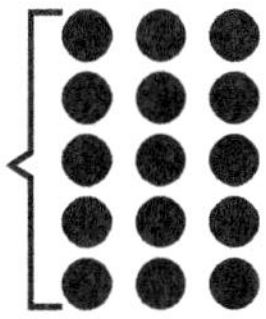

d) __________ 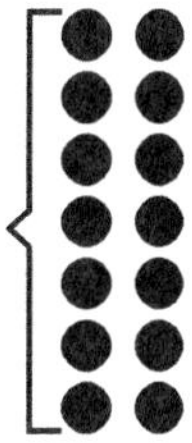

3. Draw arrays for these products.

a) 5×5 b) 3×5 c) 2×4 d) 4×3 e) 1×6 f) 2×5

4. Draw an array and write a multiplication equation to find each answer.

a) On a bus, 4 people can sit in a row. There are 6 rows of seats on the bus. How many people can ride on the bus?

b) In a garden, there are 3 rows of plants. There are 5 plants in each row. How many plants are there altogether?

c) Jenny planted 8 seeds in each row. There are 4 rows of seeds. How many seeds did Jenny plant?

We can group the dots in this array: 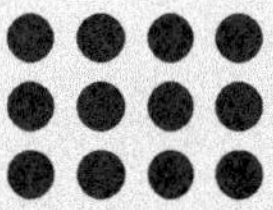 by rows: 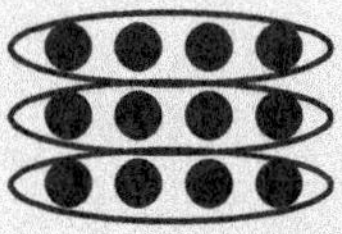 or by columns: 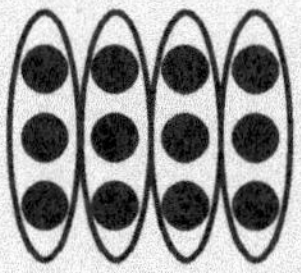

$3 \times 4 = 12$ $4 \times 3 = 12$

5. Group the dots by rows then by columns. Write two multiplication equations.

a)  

_____________ _____________

b)  

_____________ _____________

c)  

_____________ _____________

d)  

_____________ _____________

6. Fill in the blanks.

a) 2 rows of 5 dots each is the same as _____ columns of _____ dots each, so $2 \times 5 =$ _____ $\times$ _____.

b) 3 rows of 7 dots each is the same as _____ columns of _____ dots each, so $3 \times 7 =$ _____ $\times$ _____.

c) 5 rows of 8 dots each is the same as ____.

____ so $5 \times 8 =$ ______________.

7. a) The picture shows _____ rows of _____ dots each.

b) Now turn the page sideways.

After turning the page sideways, the picture shows _____ rows of _____ dots each.

c) Did turning the page change the number of dots in the picture? _____

d) Write an equation that shows your answer to c). _____ $\times$ _____ $=$ _____ $\times$ _____

8. Draw a picture to show that $2 \times 7 = 7 \times 2$.

OA4-10 Multiplication and Addition

Multiplying is a short way of adding: $4 \times 5 = \underbrace{5 + 5 + 5 + 5}_{\text{add 5 four times}}$

1. Write a sum for each product.

a) $3 \times 4 = 4 + 4 + 4$

b) $2 \times 8 =$

c) $5 \times 6 =$

d) $4 \times 2 =$

e) $3 \times 5 =$

f) $6 \times 3 =$

g) $5 \times 7 =$

h) $2 \times 1 =$

i) $1 \times 8 =$

2. Write a product for each sum.

a) $4 + 4 + 4 = 3 \times 4$

b) $5 + 5 + 5 =$

c) $4 + 4 =$

d) $2 + 2 + 2 =$

e) $9 + 9 + 9 + 9 =$

f) $1 + 1 + 1 =$

g) $6 + 6 + 6 + 6 + 6 =$

h) $8 + 8 + 8 + 8 + 8 =$

i) $3 + 3 + 3 + 3 =$

3. Write a sum and a product for each picture.

a) 3 boxes; 2 pencils in each box

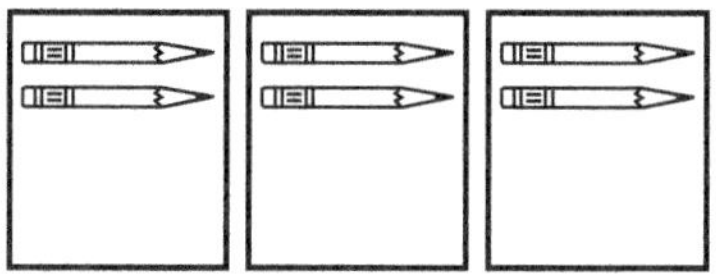

$2 + 2 + 2$

3×2

b) 3 boxes; 4 pencils in each box

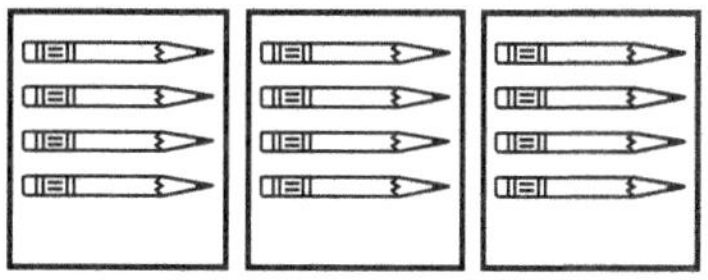

____

____

c) 4 boxes; 3 pencils in each box

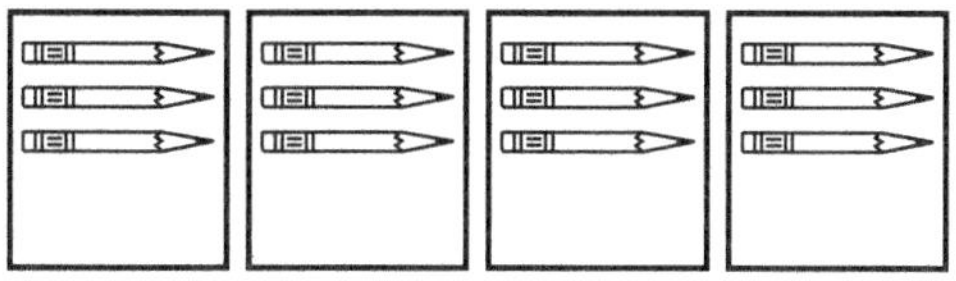

____

____

d) 2 boxes; 5 pencils in each box

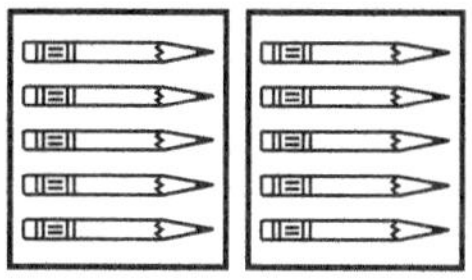

____

____

e) 5 boxes; 3 pencils in each box

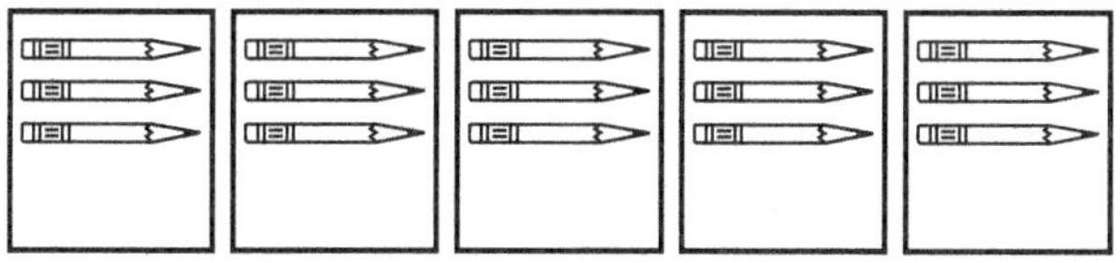

____

____

f) 4 boxes; 2 pencils in each box

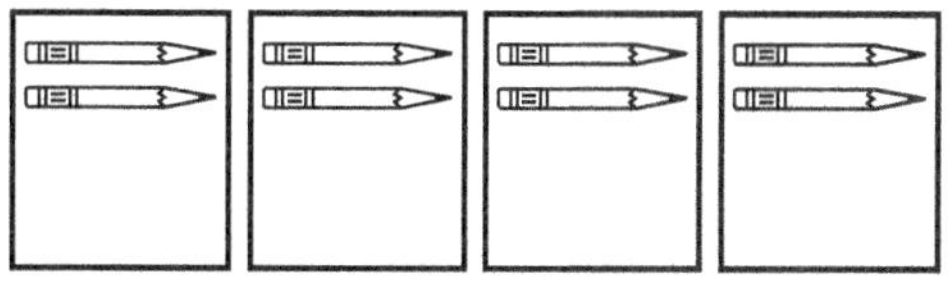

____

____

4. Add the numbers. Write your subtotals in the boxes provided.

Example: $4 + 5 + 7 =$ ______ → *add 4 + 5 (=9)* [9] $4 + 5 + 7 =$ ______ → *add 9 + 7 (=16)* [9] $4 + 5 + 7 =$ *16*

a) $2 + 3 + 5 =$ ______ b) $3 + 3 + 7 =$ ______ c) $5 + 4 + 3 =$ ______

d) $6 + 4 + 2 =$ ______ e) $8 + 3 + 4 =$ ______ f) $9 + 1 + 6 =$ ______

g) $4 + 3 + 3 + 2 =$ ______ h) $4 + 5 + 5 + 3 =$ ______ i) $6 + 7 + 3 + 5 =$ ______

5. Write a sum for each picture. Add to find out how many apples there are altogether. Check your answer by counting the apples.

a) 3 boxes; 3 apples in each box

____

b) 4 boxes; 2 apples in each box

____

c) 4 boxes; 4 apples in each box

____

d) 3 boxes; 5 apples in each box

____

6. Draw a picture, and write a sum and a product for your picture.

a) 3 vans
7 people in each van

b) 4 bags
5 books in each bag

c) 6 boxes
4 pens in each box

d) 5 boats
4 kids in each boat

7. Write a sum and a product for each situation.

a) 6 plates
8 cookies on each plate

b) 7 bags
3 gifts in each bag

c) 4 baskets
7 bananas in each basket

OA4-11 Multiplying by Skip Counting

Zainab finds the **product of 3 and 5** by skip counting on a number line.

She counts off three 5s: **5** + **5** + **5** = **15**

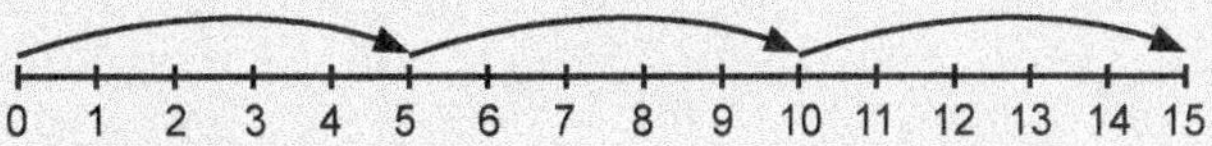

From the picture, Zainab can see that the product of 3 and 5 is 15: **3** × **5** = **15**.

1. Show how to find the products by skip counting.
Use arrows like the ones in Zainab's picture.

a) $4 \times 3 =$

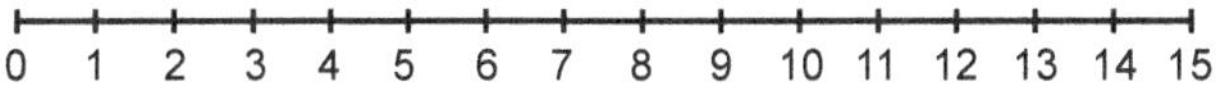

b) $7 \times 2 =$

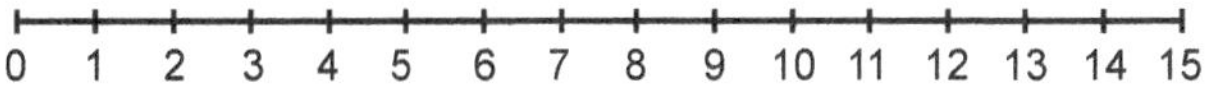

2. Use the number line to skip count by 4s, 6s, and 7s. Fill in the boxes as you count.

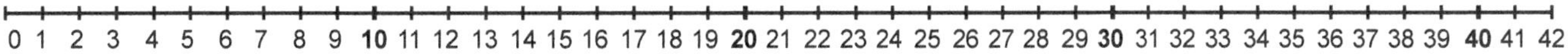

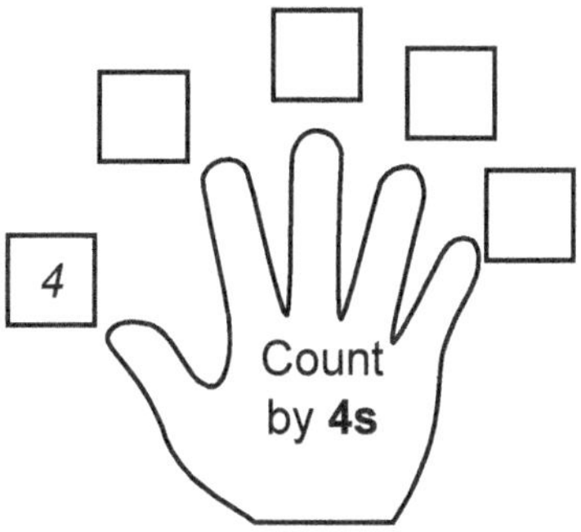

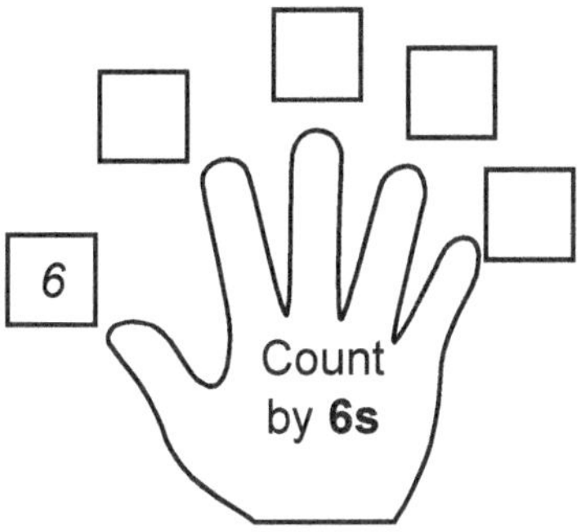

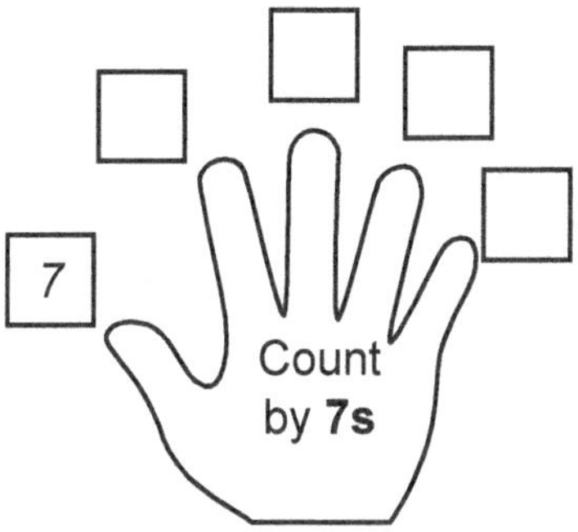

3. Find the products by skip counting on your fingers. Use the hands from Question 2 to help.

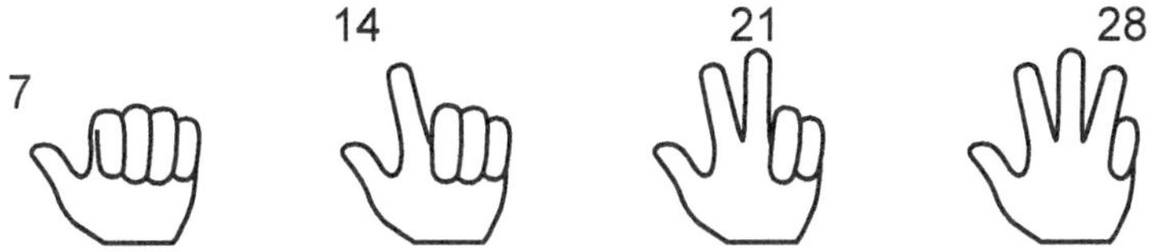

until you raise 4 fingers → **4** × **7** = **28** ← *count by 7s*

a) $4 \times 5 =$ b) $5 \times 2 =$ c) $4 \times 4 =$ d) $2 \times 6 =$ e) $7 \times 1 =$

f) $3 \times 7 =$ g) $3 \times 3 =$ h) $6 \times 1 =$ i) $2 \times 7 =$ j) $5 \times 5 =$

4. Find the number of items by skip counting. Write a multiplication equation for each picture.

a)

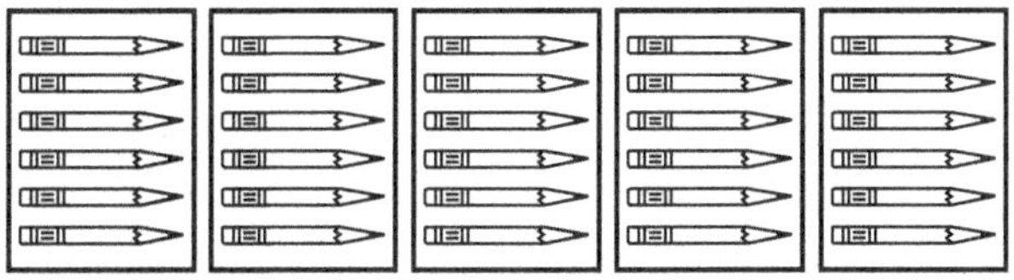

____

b)

____

OA4-12 Times as Many

1. Draw 3 times as many circles as there are squares.

a) 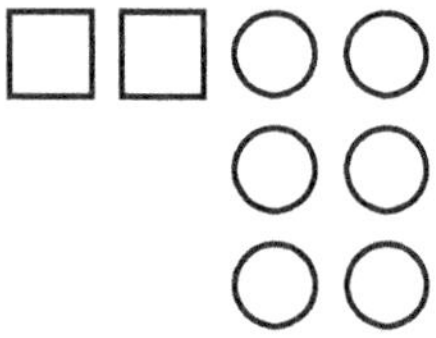

b) 

c) 

2. Write how many times as many circles as squares.

a) 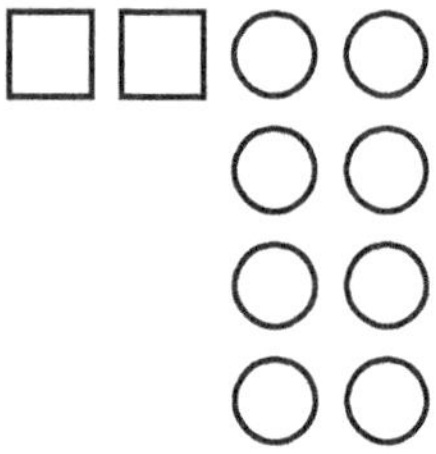

There are ______ times as many circles as squares.

b) 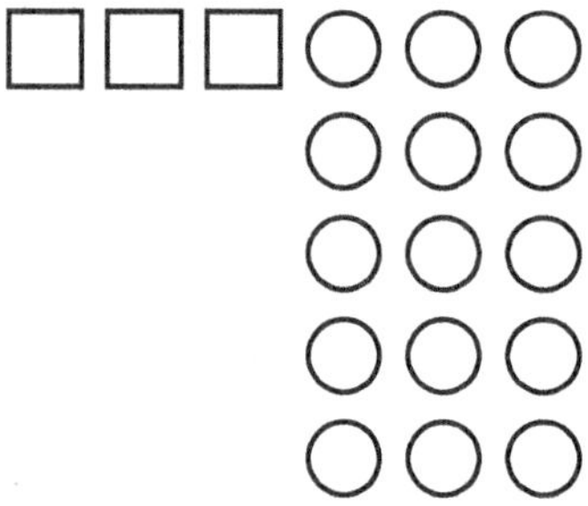

There are ______ times as many circles as squares.

c) 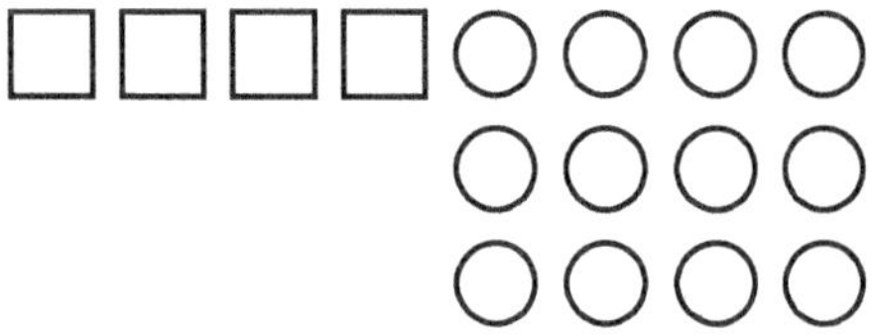

There are ______ times as many circles as squares.

d) 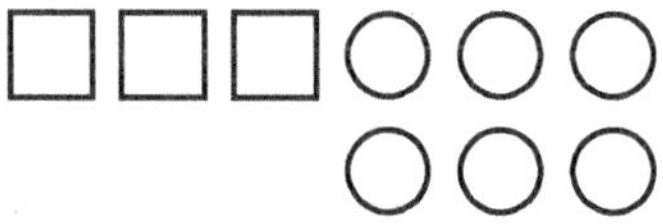

There are ______ times as many circles as squares.

3. Draw a picture and then fill in the blanks.

a) Draw twice as many circles as squares.

________ × ________ = ________

number of squares   number of of circles

b) Draw 4 times as many circles as squares.

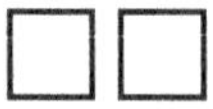

________ × ________ = ________

number of squares   number of circles

There are 2 squares and 6 circles.

There are 3 times as many circles as squares.

We can say "6 is 3 times as many as 2."

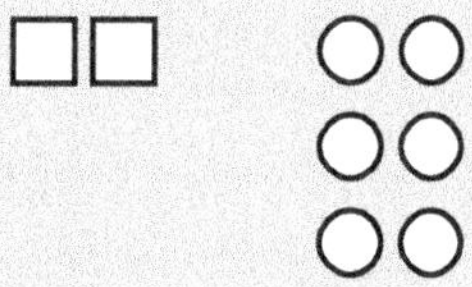

$3 \times 2 = 6$

4. a) Kyle

Rema

Rema has ______ times as many stickers as Kyle

______ is ______ times as many as ______.

b) Sam

Ravi

Ravi has ______ times as many stickers as Sam.

______ is ______ times as many as ______.

5. The magnifying glass makes each object look twice as big.

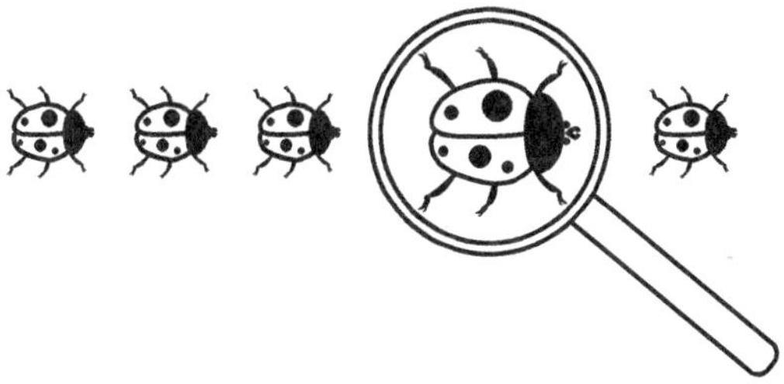

Actual length of object	Length under the magnifying glass
2 cm	
5 cm	
7 cm	

6. Use the multiplication equation to write how many times as many one number is than the other.

a) $35 = 5 \times 7$

35 is ______ times as many as 7

b) $40 = 5 \times 8$

40 is ______ times as many as 8

c) $30 = 10 \times 3$

30 is ______ times as many as 3

d) $42 = 6 \times 7$

42 is ______ times as many as 7

7. Draw a picture and write a multiplication equation.

a) There are 2 circles. There are 4 times as many triangles as circles.

b) There are 2 boys. There are 3 times as many girls as boys.

c) There are 4 blue marbles. There are twice as many red marbles as blue marbles.

8. Kyle has 6 books. Ron has three times as many books.
How many books does Ron have? Explain how you know.

NBT4-1 Place Value—Ones, Tens, Hundreds, and Thousands

1. Write the place value of the underlined digit.

REMINDER ▶

4,375

thousands hundreds tens ones

a) 3,564 *tens* b) 1,336 ____________

c) 256 ____________ d) 1,230 ____________

e) 3,859 ____________ f) 5,745 ____________ g) 238 ____________

h) 6,214 ____________ i) 87 ____________ j) 9,430 ____________

2. Write the place value of the digit 5 in each of the numbers below.
Hint: First underline the 5 in each number.

a) 5,640 ____________ b) 547 ____________ c) 451 ____________

d) 2,415 ____________ e) 1,257 ____________ f) 5,643 ____________

g) 1,563 ____________ h) 56 ____________ i) 205 ____________

You can also write numbers using a place value chart. Example:

This is the number 3,264 in a place value chart:

Thousands	Hundreds	Tens	Ones
3	2	6	4

3. Write the following numbers into the place value chart.

		Thousands	Hundreds	Tens	Ones
a)	5,231	*5*	*2*	*3*	*1*
b)	8,053				
c)	489				
d)	27				
e)	9,104				
f)	4,687				
g)	7,060				
h)	760				

NBT4-2 Place Value

The number 2,836 is a **4-digit number**.

The **digit** 2 stands for 2,000—the **value** of the digit 2 is 2,000.

The digit 8 stands for 800—the value of the digit 8 is 800.

The digit 3 stands for 30—the value of the digit 3 is 30.

The digit 6 stands for 6—the value of the digit 6 is 6.

1. Write the value of each digit.

a)

6	5	4	7

b)

8	2	3	1

c)

3	2	0	5

2. What does the digit 3 stand for in each number?

a) 237 *30*

b) 5,235

c) 6,382

d) 3,280

e) 4,305

f) 6,732

g) 3,092

h) 5,883

i) 3,852

j) 1,003

k) 1,300

l) 231

3. Fill in the blanks.

a) In the number 6,572, the digit 5 stands for ________.

b) In the number 4,236, the digit 3 stands for ________.

c) In the number 2,357, the digit 7 stands for ________.

d) In the number 8,021, the value of the digit 8 is ________.

e) In the number 6,539, the value of the digit 5 is ________.

f) In the number 3,675, the value of the digit 7 is ________.

g) In the number 1,023, the digit _____ is in the tens place.

h) In the number 1,729, the digit _____ is in the hundreds place.

i) In the number 7,253, the digit _____ is in the thousands place.

The number 684,523 is a **6-digit number**.

The digit 6 stands for 600,000—the value of the digit 6 is 600,000.

The digit 8 stands for 80,000—the value of the digit 8 is 80,000.

The digit 4 stands for 4,000—the value of the digit 4 is 4,000.

The digit 5 stands for 500—the value of the digit 5 is 500.

The digit 2 stands for 20—the value of the digit 2 is 20.

The digit 3 stands for 3—the value of the digit 3 is 3.

4. Write the value of each digit.

a)

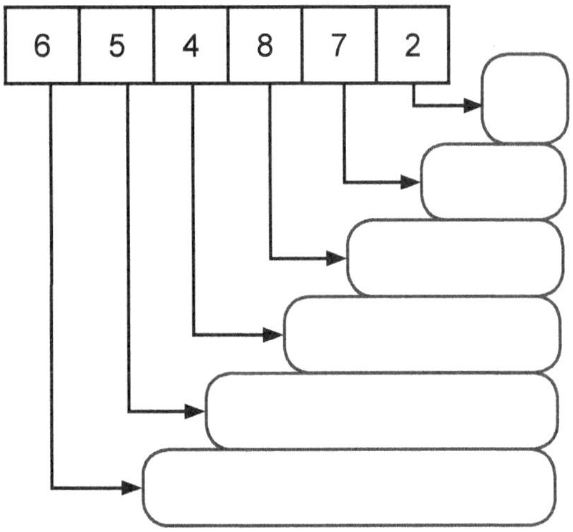

b)

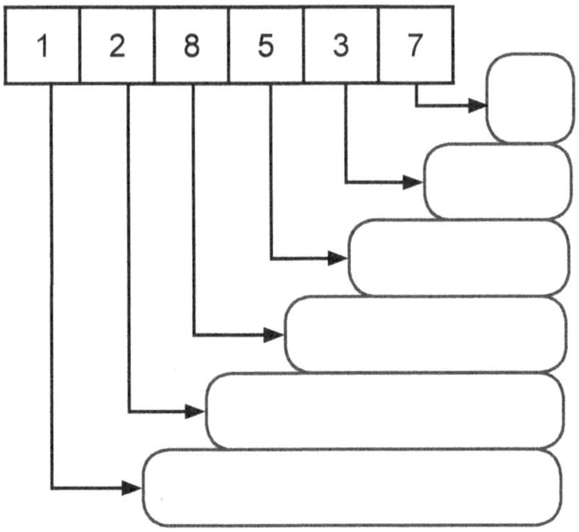

5. What does the digit 7 stand for in each number?

a) 8,476 — *70*

b) 38,725

c) 93,726

d) 730,025

e) 7,250

f) 64,297

g) 43,075

h) 382,457

6. Fill in the blanks.

a) In the number 4,523, the digit 5 stands for ____________________.

b) In the number 34,528, the digit 3 stands for ____________________.

c) In the number 420,583, the value of the digit 8 is ____________________.

d) In the number 75,320, the value of the digit 7 is ____________________.

e) In the number 723,594, the digit _____ is in the ten thousands place.

3,**1**8**1**

The first 1 ↗ ↖ The second 1

7. Write what each **1** stands for.

	Number	The first 1	The second 1
a)	4,**1**2**1**	*100*	*1*
b)	**1**,3**1**2		
c)	2,3**11**		
d)	**1**,50**1**		
e)	7,**11**4		
	BONUS ▶ **1**,832,**1**54		

8. The first number is worth how many times as much as the second number?

	First number	Second number	How many times as much
a)	3,000	30	*100*
b)	100	10	
c)	50	5	
d)	700	7	
e)	80,000	800	
	BONUS ▶ 900,000	90	

9. Find the value of each bold digit. How many times as much as the second digit is the first digit worth?

	Number	Value of first bold digit	Value of second bold digit	How many times as much
a)	**4**,1**4**2	*4,000*	*40*	*100*
b)	7,**11**5			
c)	5,**8**2**8**			
d)	**9**,**9**42			
e)	**7**3,4**7**0			
	BONUS ▶ **8**,000,**8**00			

NBT4-3 Writing Numbers

Number Words for the Ones Place					Number Words for the Tens Place				
zero	one	two	three	four	ten	twenty	thirty	forty	fifty
five	six	seven	eight	nine	sixty	seventy	eighty	ninety	

1. Write **numerals** for the number words.

a) seven _______ b) six _______

c) eight _______ d) twenty-three _______

e) thirty-two _______ f) ninety-five _______

g) two hundred seventy _________ h) four hundred seventy-nine _________

i) nine thousand, two hundred seventeen _____________

j) five thousand, three hundred ninety-one _____________

2. Write number words for the numerals.

a) 1 _____________ b) 7 _____________

c) 9 _____________ d) 6 _____________

e) 21 ___________________ f) 67 ___________________

g) 43 ___________________ h) 55 ___________________

i) 90 ___________________ j) 13 ___________________

To write a number in the hundreds:

Step 1: Cover the tens and ones digits, then write the value of the hundreds digit.
Example: 743 becomes 7 ▇ and we write "seven hundred."

Step 2: Uncover the tens and ones digits, then write their value: "forty-three."
The number 743 is written "seven hundred forty-three."

3. Write the value of the hundreds digit.

a) 342 _________________________ b) 906 _________________________

c) 891 _________________________ d) 416 _________________________

4. Finish writing the number word.

a) 207 two hundred *seven* ______________ b) 306 three hundred ______________

c) 804 eight hundred ______________ d) 590 five hundred ______________

e) 612 six hundred ______________ f) 872 eight hundred ______________

5. Write number words for the numerals.

a) 118 ______________________ b) 320 ______________________

c) 835 ______________________ d) 385 ______________________

To write a number from 1,000 to 999,999:

Step 1: Cover the hundreds, tens, and ones digits, then write the value of the uncovered digits. Example: 602,145 becomes 602, ▇ and we write "six hundred two thousand."

Step 2: Uncover the hundreds, tens, and ones digits, then write their value: "one hundred forty-five." The number 602,145 is written "six hundred two thousand, one hundred forty-five."

6. Cover the hundreds, tens, and ones digits, then write the value of the uncovered digits.

a) 300,452 *three hundred* ______________________ thousand

b) 740,203 ______________________ thousand

c) 809,512 ______________________

d) 694,352 ______________________

7. Finish writing the number word.

a) 762,340 seven hundred sixty-two thousand, ______________________

b) 843,204 eight hundred forty-three thousand, ______________________

c) 612,758 six hundred twelve thousand, ______________________

d) 2,417 __________ thousand, __________ hundred __________

e) 65,311 __________ thousand, __________ hundred __________

f) 205,416 ______________________ thousand,

__________ hundred __________

g) 98,407 ______________________ thousand,

__________ hundred __________

h) 6,432 ______________________

____

i) 880,043 ______________________

____

8. Write the numbers words for the numerals on the signs.

a)

_______________ Mile Creek

(4)

State Park

b)

House for Sale

(265)

____

____

Broadway Street

Inquire within.

c)

Score:

_______________________ points

(15)

d)

Come see the world's largest pumpkin!

____

_________________________________ kg

(681)

e)

Laptop for sale!

(650)

____ GB

f)

(36,255) ____

____ **prizes available!**

g)

Mount Whitney
(14,505 ft)

____

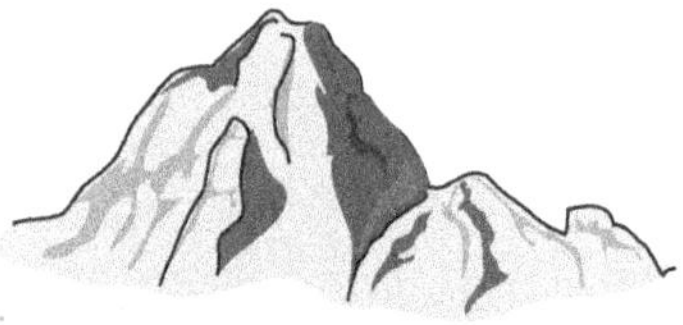

____ ft high

NBT4-4 Representation with Base Ten Materials

REMINDER ▶

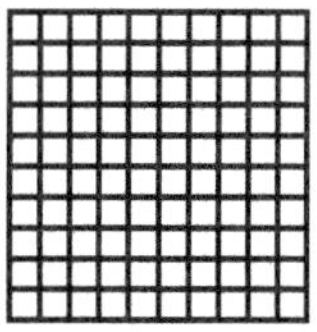 = 100  = 10  = 1

1. Write each number in expanded form (numerals and words), then as a numeral.

Example:

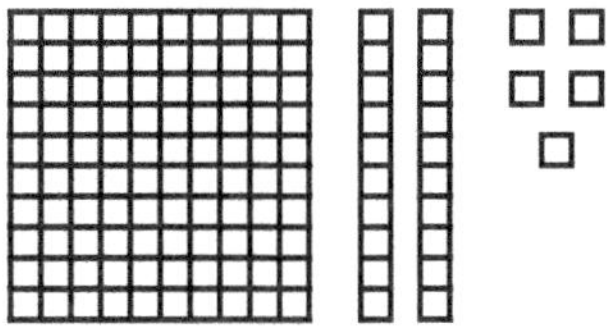

_1_ hundred + _2_ tens + _5_ ones = 125

a) 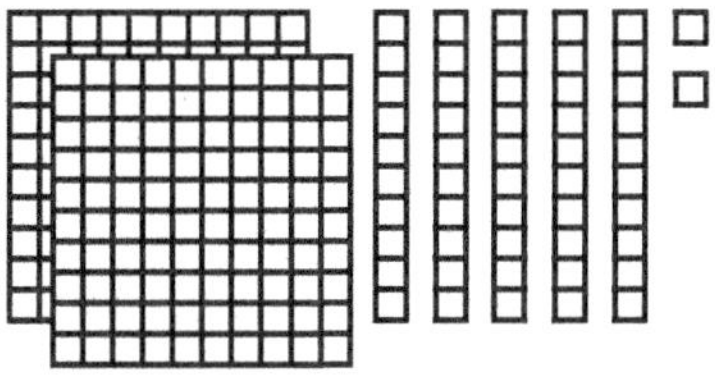

____ hundreds + ____ tens + ____ ones = ____

b) 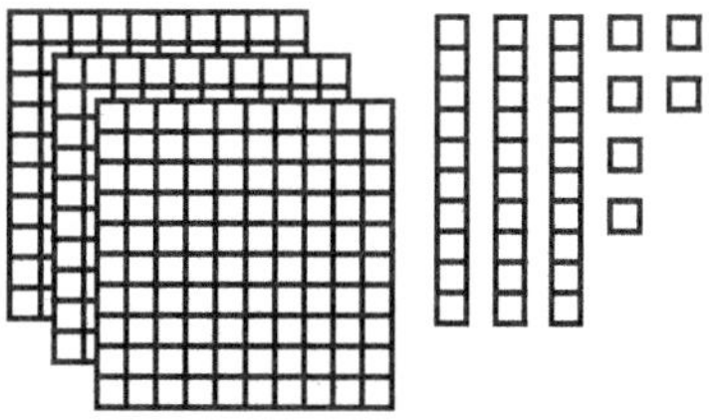

____ hundreds + ____ tens + ____ ones = ____

c) 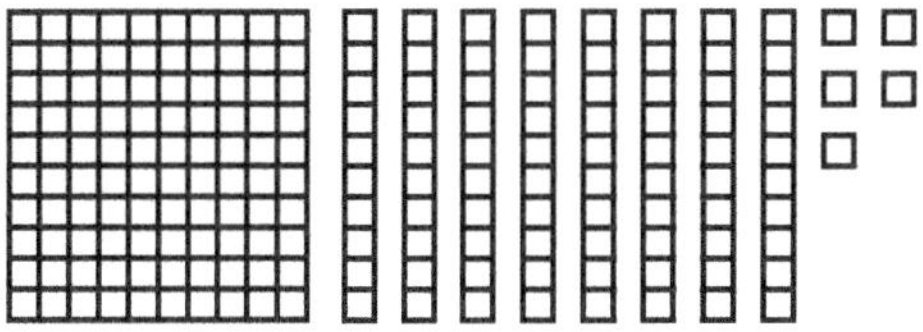

____ hundred + ____ tens + ____ ones = ____

d) 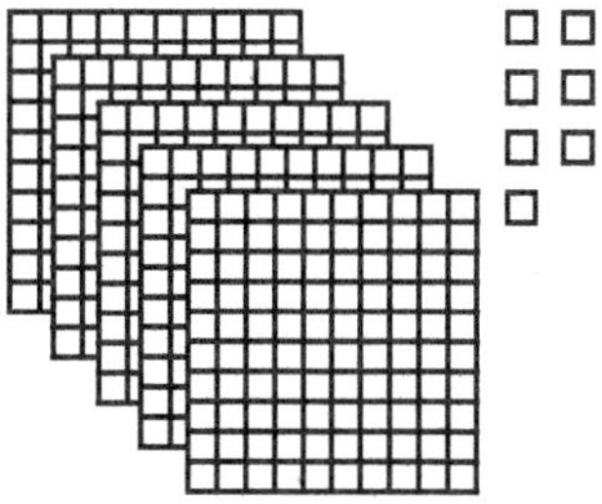

____ hundreds + ____ tens + ____ ones = ____

2. Draw the base ten model for the number.

Example: 123

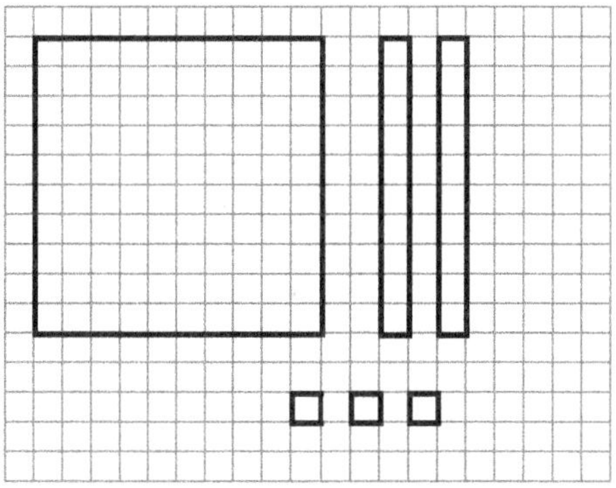

132

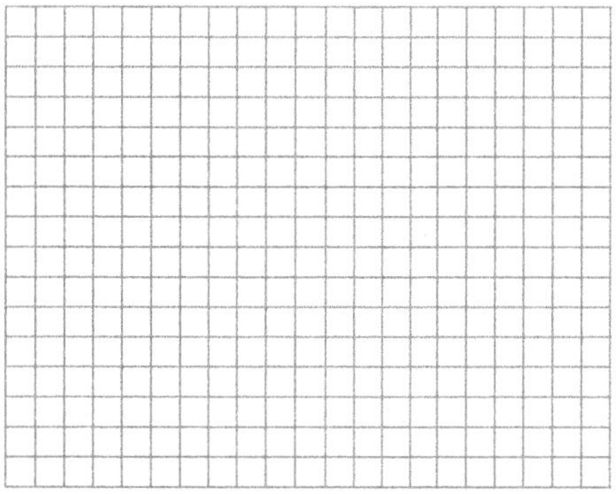

3. Draw the base ten model for the number.

a) 68 b) 350 c) 249

4. Write each number in expanded form (numerals and words), then as a numeral.

REMINDER ▶

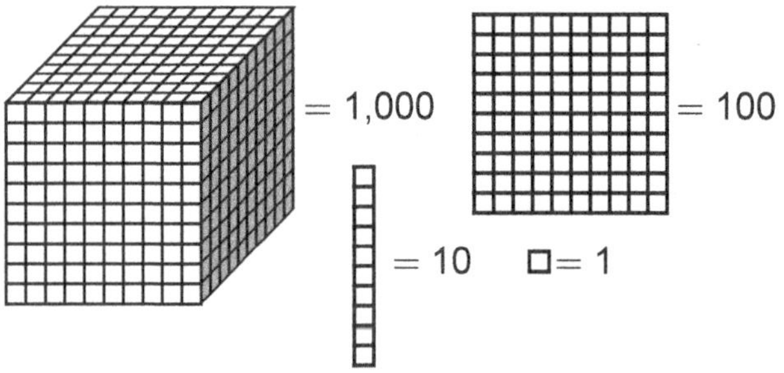

Example:

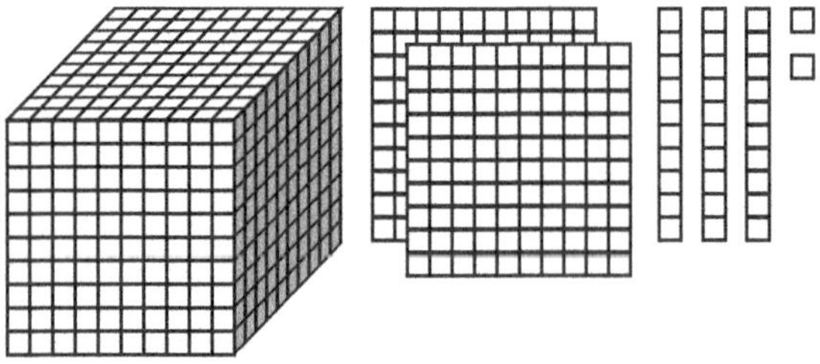

_1_ thousand + _2_ hundreds + _3_ tens + _2_ ones = 1,232

a)

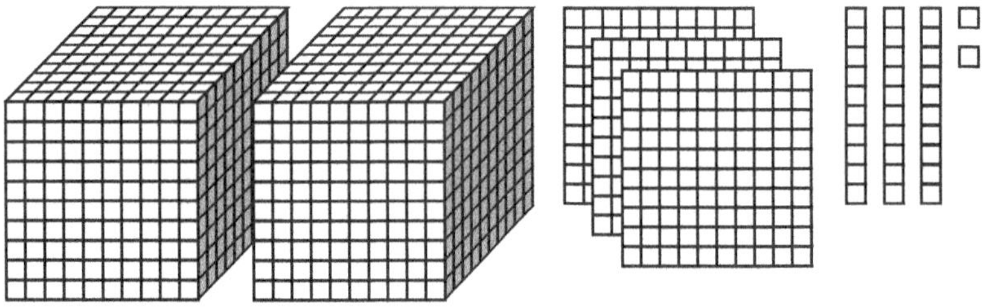

____ thousands + ____ hundreds + ____ tens + ____ ones = ____

b)

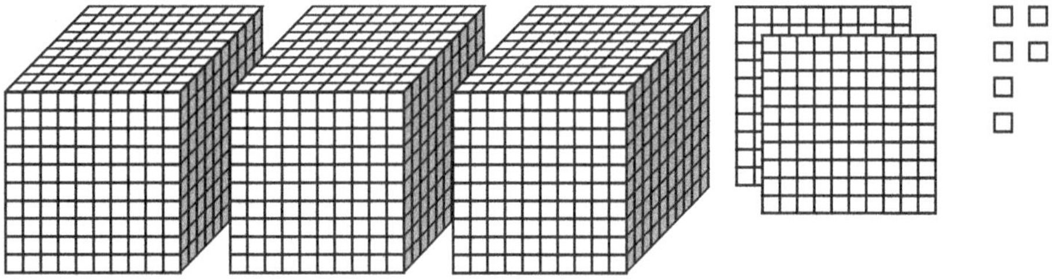

____ thousands + ____ hundreds + ____ tens + ____ ones = ____

c)

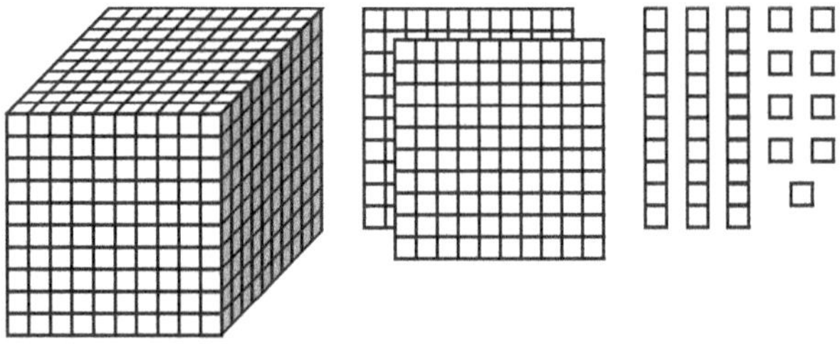

____

Representation in Expanded Form

How to draw a thousands cube:

Step 1: Draw a square. 

Step 2: Draw lines from three vertices. 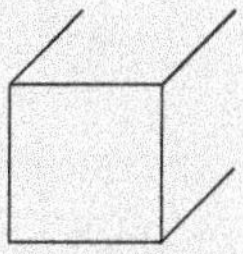

Step 3: Join the lines. 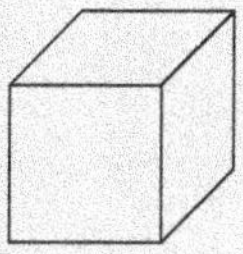

1. Represent the given numbers with base ten blocks in the place value chart. The first one has been started for you.

	Number	Thousands	Hundreds	Tens	Ones
a)	2,314	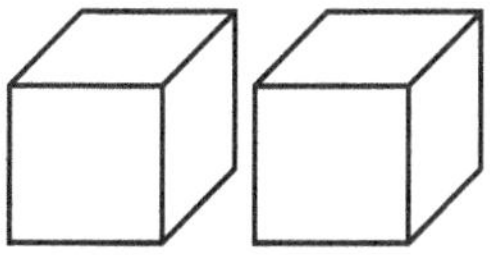	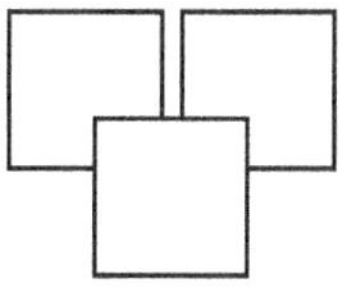		
b)	1,245				
c)	3,143				

2. Write the numbers for the given base ten blocks.

	Thousands	Hundreds	Tens	Ones	Number
a)	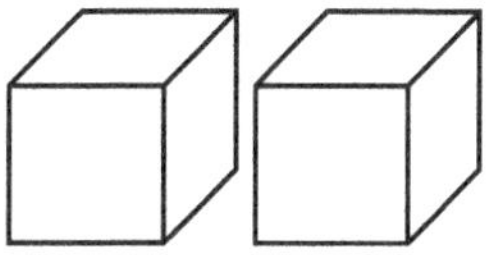	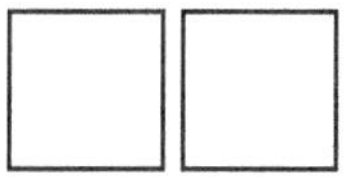			______
b)	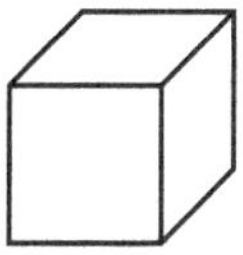	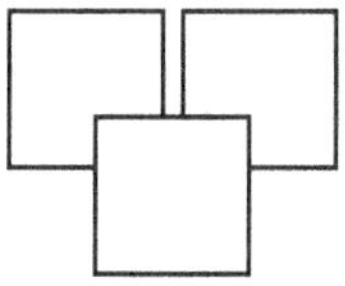	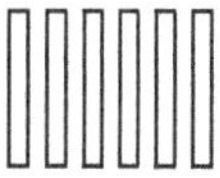		______

3. Expand the following numbers using numerals and words.

a) 2,427 = _2_ thousands + _4_ hundreds + _2_ tens + _7_ ones

b) 4,569 = ____ thousands + ____ hundreds + ____ tens + ____ ones

c) 3,875 = ____________________

d) 7,210 = ____________________

e) 623 = ____________________

4. Write each number in expanded form (using numerals).

a) 2,613 = _2,000 + 600 + 10 + 3_

b) 27 = ____________________

c) 48 = ____________________

d) 1,232 = ____________________

e) 6,103 = ____________________

f) 50,098 = ____________________

g) 300,570 = ____________________

h) 290,901 = ____________________

5. Write the number for each sum.

a) 30 + 6 = __________

b) 50 + 2 = __________

c) 60 + 5 = __________

d) 400 + 60 + 8 = __________

e) 500 + 20 + 3 = __________

f) 200 + 50 + 3 = __________

g) 5,000 + 700 + 20 + 1 = __________

h) 800,000 + 70,000 + 9,000 + 600 + 40 + 5 = __________

BONUS ▶

i) 600 + 7 = __________

j) 900 + 6 = __________

k) 800 + 70 = __________

l) 5,000 + 100 = __________

m) 5,000 + 20 = __________

n) 6,000 + 2 = __________

o) 800,000 + 100 + 3 = __________

p) 700,000 + 9,000 + 4 = __________

q) 40,000 + 100 + 5 = __________

r) 6,000 + 300 + 20 = __________

s) 80,000 + 20 = __________

t) 3,000 + 10 = __________

6. Find the missing numbers.

a) 200 + 70 + ______ = 273

b) 300 + ______ + 6 = 386

c) 6,000 + 800 + ______ + 7 = 6,827

d) 1,000 + 400 + ______ + 5 = 1,475

e) 900,000 + 80,000 + __________ + 600 + 40 + 5 = 985,645

BONUS ▶

f) 7,000 + 200 + _______ = 7,202

g) 6,000 + 300 + _______ = 6,320

h) __________ + 300 = 70,300

i) 600,000 + __________ = 600,080

j) 9,000 + _______ + _______ = 9,260

k) 10,000 + _______ + _______ = 10,703

l) 7,000 + _______ + _______ = 7,021

m) 900,000 + __________ = 980,000

7. Write each number in expanded form. Then draw a base ten model. Example:

3,213 = _3,000_ + _200_ + _10_ + _3_

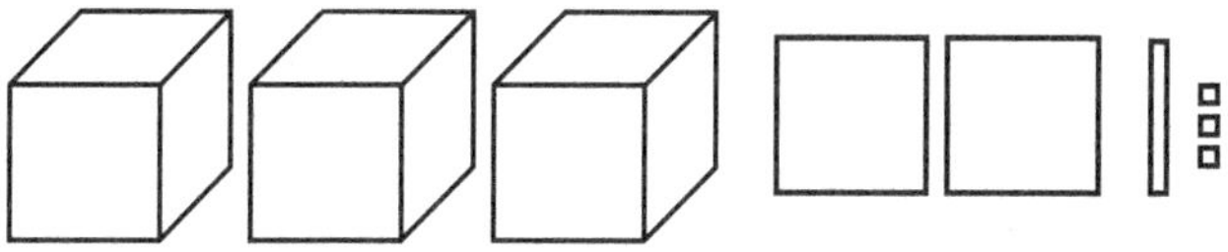

a) 2,317 = ____________ + ____________ + ____________ + ____________

b) 1,446 = ____________ + ____________ + ____________ + ____________

BONUS ▶

Feliz has ...

- 1,000 stamps from Canada
- 200 stamps from Portugal
- 30 stamps from Spain
- 9 stamps from Egypt

How many stamps does he have in total? _______

NBT4-6 Comparing and Ordering Numbers

1. Write the number using numerals (in the box) and words (on the line below). Then circle the greater number in each pair.

a) i) 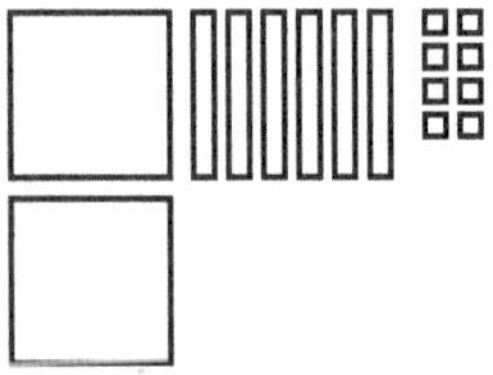 268

ii) 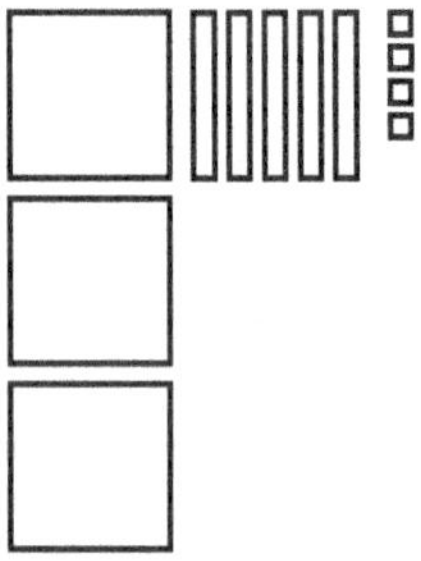

b) i) 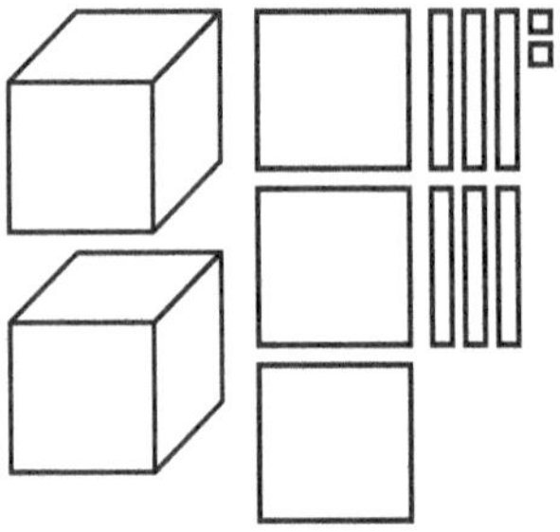

ii) 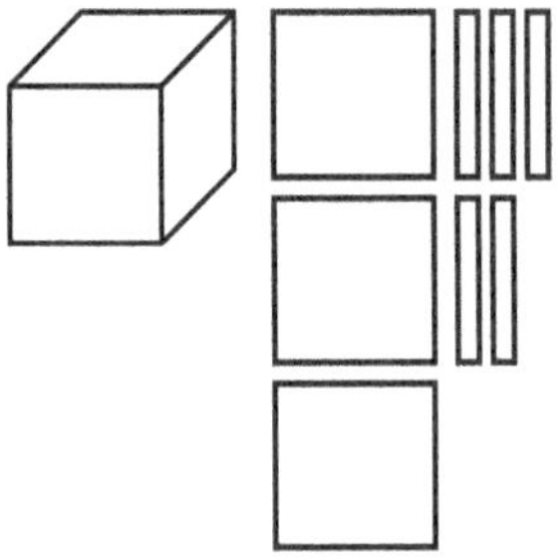

c) Explain how you knew which number in part b) was greater.

2. Write the number in each box. Then circle the larger number in each pair.

a) i) 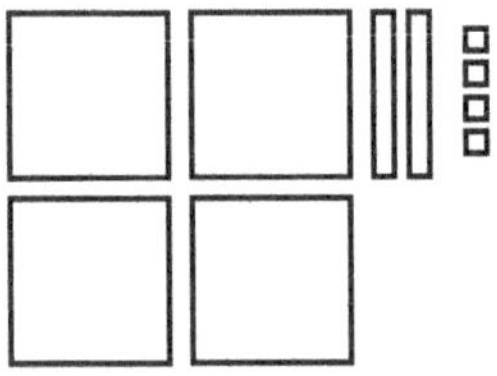

ii) 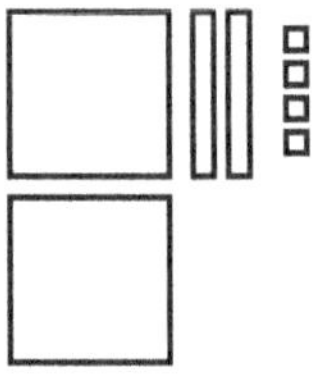

b) i) 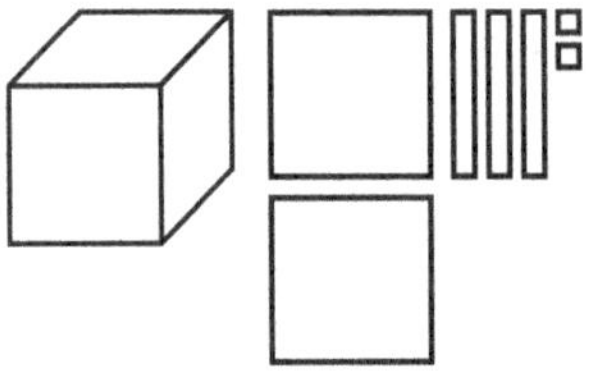

ii) 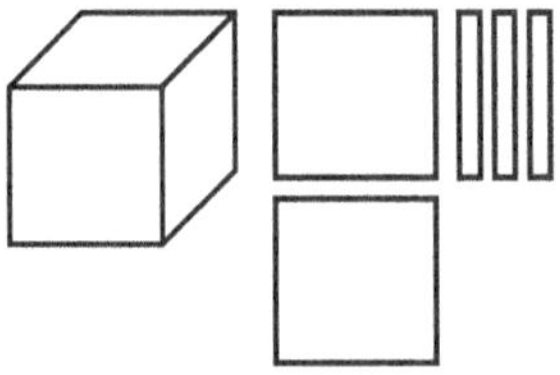

3. Draw base ten models for the following pairs of numbers. Circle the larger number.

a) four hundred sixteen 460

b) one thousand, three hundred 1,007

4. Write the **value** of each digit. Then complete the sentence.

a)

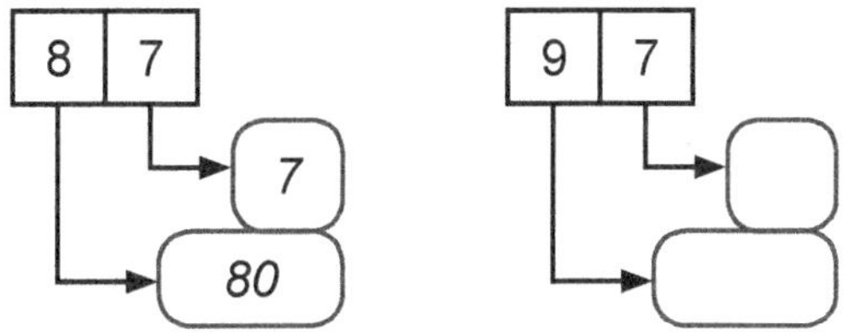

________ is greater than ________

b)

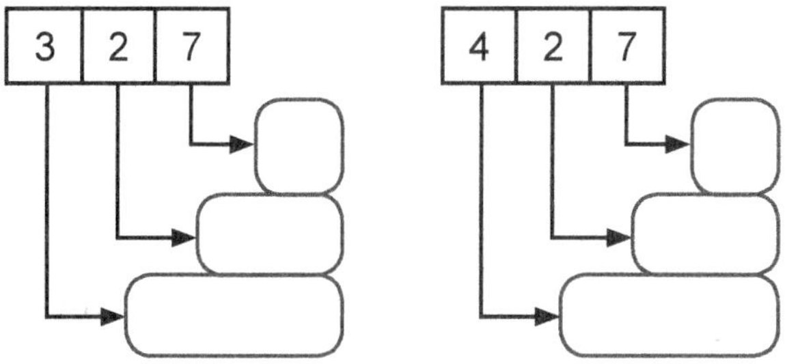

________ is greater than ________

c)

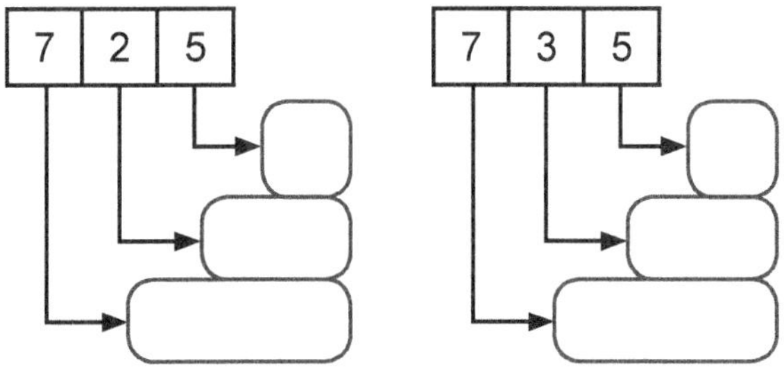

________ is greater than ________

d)

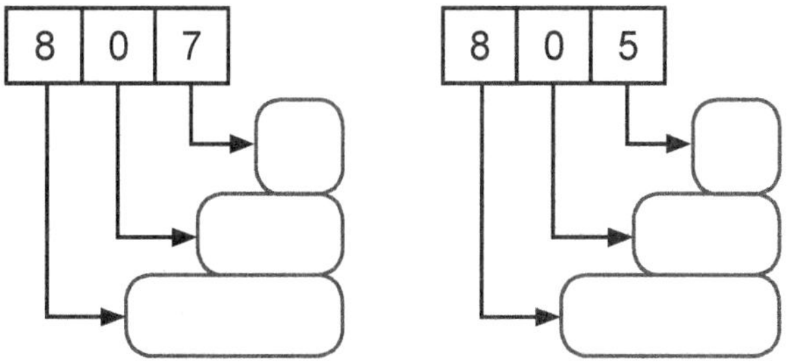

________ is greater than ________

5. Circle the digits that are different in each pair of numbers. Then write the greater number in the box.

a) 2,475
2,465
2,475

b) 1,360
1,260

c) 4,852
4,858

d) 6,325
7,325

e) 384
584

f) 2,906
2,904

g) 875
865

h) 238
231

i) 83,752
83,762

j) 273,605
272,605

k) 614,852
614,858

l) 383,250
483,250

m) 812 349
813,349

n) 569,274
579,274

o) 323
324

p) 195,385
196,385

6. Read the numbers from left to right. Circle the first pair of digits you find that are different. Then write the greater number in the box.

a)	b)	c)	d)
1,583	6,293	5,769	9,432
1,597	6,542	6,034	9,431
☐	☐	☐	☐

e)	f)	g)	h)
642,856	384,207	576,986	621,492
642,874	389,583	603,470	621,483
☐	☐	☐	☐

7. Read the numbers from left to right. Underline the first pair of digits you find that are different. Then circle the greater number.

a) 2,342 2,351
b) 5,201 5,275
c) 6,327 6,102
d) 7,851 7,923
e) 75,542 75,540
f) 92,346 87,237
g) 35,028 35,019
h) 657,283 752,549
i) 211,308 214,567

8. Circle the greater number.

a) 2,175 3,603
b) 4,221 5,012
c) 6,726 6,591
d) 3,728 3,729
e) 8,175 8,123
f) 5,923 6,000
g) 387 389
h) 418 481
i) 2,980 298
j) 38,712 38,912
k) 643,219 647,208
l) 27,413 265,412
m) 648,193 658,094
n) 805,742 508,742
o) 123,456 98,765

9. Write $<$ (less than) or $>$ (greater than) in the box to make each statement true.

a) 3,275 ☐ 4,325
b) 2,132 ☐ 2,131
c) 5,214 ☐ 5,216
d) 528 ☐ 3,257
e) 7,171 ☐ 7,105
f) 287 ☐ 25
g) one thousand, one hundred six ☐ 2,107
h) three hundred fifty thousand, four hundred three ☐ 305,430

NBT4-7 Differences of 1, 10, 100, 1,000, 10,000, and 100,000

1. Write "10 more" or "10 less" in the blanks.

a) 90 is ______________ than 80
b) 30 is ______________ than 40
c) 10 is ______________ than 20
d) 100 is ______________ than 90

2. Write "100 more" or "100 less" in the blanks.

a) 600 is ______________ than 500
b) 700 is ______________ than 800
c) 700 is ______________ than 600
d) 800 is ______________ than 900

3. Write "1,000 more" or "1,000 less" in the blanks.

a) 7,000 is ______________ than 6,000
b) 17,000 is ______________ than 18,000

4. Write the value of the digits. Then say how much more or less the first number is than the second.

a)

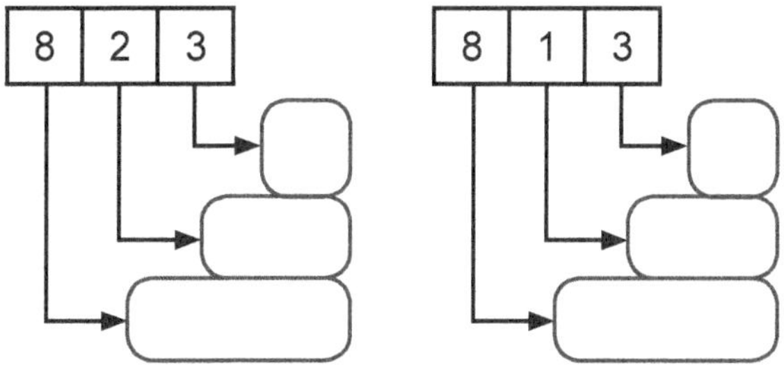

823 is ______________ than 813

b)

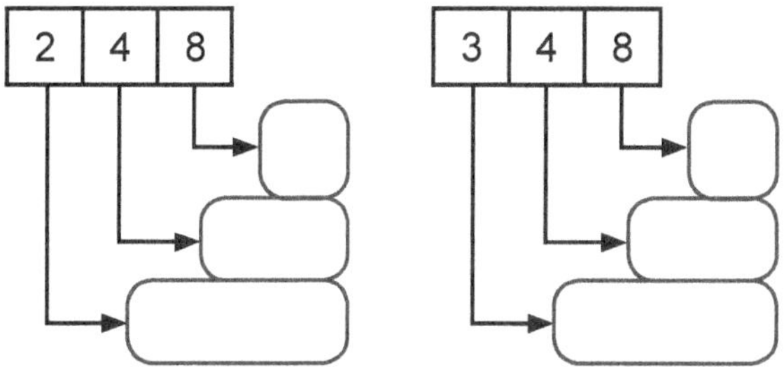

248 is ______________ than 348

5. Circle the digits that are different in each pair of numbers. Then fill in the blanks.

a) 2,652
2,752
2,652 is ___*100*___
___*less*___ than 2,752

b) 271,382
271,482
271,382 is ______________
______________ than 271,482

c) 346,830
347,830
346,830 is ______________
______________ than 347,830

d) 435,621
425,621
435,621 is ______________
______________ than 425,621

e) 38,405
38,415
38,405 is ______________
______________ than 38,415

f) 605,872
705,872
605,872 is ______________
______________ than 705,872

NBT4-8 Counting by 10s, 100s, and 1,000s

1. Count by 10s to continue the pattern.

a) 30, 40, 50, _______, _______, _______

b) 10, 20, 30, _______, _______, _______

c) 50, 60, 70, _______, _______, _______

d) 23, 33, 43, _______, _______, _______

e) 27, 37, 47, _______, _______, _______

f) 15, 25, 35, _______, _______, _______

g) 49, 59, 69, _______, _______, _______

h) 1, 11, 21, _______, _______, _______

i) 100, 110, 120, _______, _______, _______

j) 160, 170, 180, _______, _______, _______

2. Count by 100s to continue the pattern.

a) 100, 200, 300, _______, _______, _______

b) 600, 700, 800, _______, _______, _______

c) 300, 400, 500, _______, _______, _______

d) 1,000, 1,100, 1,200, _______, _______, _______

3. A bag holds 100 marbles. How many marbles fit in …

a) 2 bags? _________

b) 5 bags? _________

4. Count by 100s to complete the pattern.

a) 101, 201, 301, _______, _______, _______

b) 110, 210, 310, _______, _______, _______

c) 227, 327, 427, _______, _______, _______

d) 6,399, 6,499, 6,599, _______, _______

e) 2,045, 2,145, 2,245, _______, _______

f) 832,525, 832,625, 832,725, _______, _______

5. Count by 1,000s to continue the pattern.

a) 1,000, 2,000, _______, _______, _______

b) 38,000, 39,000, __________, __________

6. A bag holds 1,000 nails. How many nails fit in …

a) 3 bags? _______

b) 5 bags? _______

7. Count down by 100s.

a) 700, 600, 500, _______, _______, _______

b) 321,000, 320,900, 320,800, _______, _______

c) 82,200, 82,100, __________, __________

d) 605,100, 605,000, __________, __________

8. Count down by 1,000s.

a) 9,000, 8,000, 7,000, _______, _______

b) 32,000, 31,000, __________, __________

NBT4-9 Comparing Numbers (Advanced)

1. Mark each number on the number line. Then circle the greatest number.

A. 5,800 **B.** 5,700 **C.** 5,200

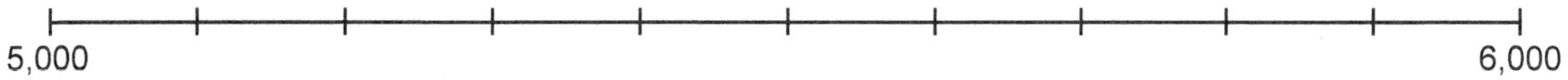

2. Fill in the boxes with any digits that will make the number statements true.

a) □ □ 5 < 3 □ 2

b) □ 2 □ □ > 5 □ □ 9

3. St. Louis is 456 miles away from Detroit.

Chicago is 237 miles away from Detroit.

Which city is farther from Detroit? ______________________________

4. If you place non-zero digits in the boxes below, which number must be greater? Explain.

□ 4 7 or □ □ 2 3

5. List all the two-digit numbers you can make with the digits given (use each digit only once). Then circle the greatest number.

a) 6, 7, and 8 b) 2, 9, and 4 c) 5, 2, and 0

6. Create the greatest possible four-digit number using the digits given. Use each digit only once.

a) 4, 3, 2, 6 ________________ b) 7, 8, 9, 4 ________________ c) 0, 4, 1, 2 ______________

7. Create the greatest possible number using these digits. Use each digit only once.

a) 3, 4, 1, 2, 8 ______________ b) 2, 8, 9, 1, 5 ______________ c) 3, 6, 1, 5, 4 ______________

8. Use the digits to create the greatest number, the least number, and a number in between.

	Digits	Greatest Number	Number in Between	Least Number
a)	8 5 7 2 1			
b)	2 1 5 3 9			
c)	3 0 1 5 3			

9. Arrange the numbers in order, starting with the least number.

a) 683,759 693,238 693,231

______, ______, ______

b) 473,259 42,380 47,832

______, ______, ______

c) 385,290 928,381 532,135

______, ______, ______

d) 2,575 38,258 195

______, ______, ______

10. What is the greatest number less than 10,000 whose digits are all the same? ______

11. Identify the greater number by writing > or <.

a) 63,752 ☐ 63,750

b) 927,385 ☐ 928,303

c) 572,312 ☐ 59,238

d) 230,075 ☐ 230,123

12. a) Which city has a population greater than 670,000?

______

b) Write the populations in order from least to greatest.

______

City	Population
Detroit	871,121
Baltimore	631,366
Boston	617,594

13. What is the greatest possible number you can create that has …

a) 3 digits? ______

b) 4 digits? ______

c) 5 digits? ______

14. Using the digits 0, 1, 2, 3, 4, create an even number greater than 42,000 and less than 43,000.

15. Using the digits 4, 5, 6, 7, 8, create an odd number greater than 64,000 and less than 68,000.

16. Fill in the box with the digit that will make the statement true.

a) 54,☐21 is between 54,348 and 54,519.

b) 76,☐99 is between 76,201 and 76,316.

NBT4-10 Counting Coins

1. Write the name and value of each coin.

a) 

Name ______________

Value ______________

b) 

Name ______________

Value ______________

c) 

Name ______________

Value ______________

d) 

Name ______________

Value ______________

2. a) How many pennies do you need to make a nickel? ______________

b) How many pennies do you need to make a dime? ______________

c) How many nickels do you need to make a dime? ______________

d) How many nickels do you need to make a quarter? ______________

e) How many pennies do you need to make a quarter? ______________

f) You have one nickel. How many dimes do you need to add to make a quarter? ______________

3. Count on by 5s from the given number.

a) 80, _____, _____, _____ b) 40, _____, _____, _____ c) 60, _____, _____, _____

d) 70, _____, _____, _____ e) 105, _____, _____, _____ f) 120, _____, _____, _____

4. Count on by nickels from the given amount.

a) 55¢, *60¢*, _____, _____ b) 75¢, _____, _____, _____ c) 85¢, _____, _____, _____

5. Count on by 10s from the given number.

a) 30, _____, _____, _____ b) 60, _____, _____, _____ c) 80, _____, _____, _____

d) 70, _____, _____, _____ e) 100, _____, _____, _____ f) 120, _____, _____, _____

6. Count on by dimes from the given amount.

a) 55¢, _____, _____, _____ b) 70¢, _____, _____, _____ c) 85¢, _____, _____, _____

7. Count on by 5s, then by 1s.

a) 5, ___, ___, ___ | ___, ___, ___
Count by 5s | Continue counting by 1s

b) ___, ___, ___, ___, ___ | ___, ___, ___
Count by 5s | Continue counting by 1s

8. Count on by the first coin value given, then by the second coin value.

a) 10, ___, ___ | ___, ___, ___
Count by 10s | Continue counting by 5s

b) ___, ___ | ___, ___, ___, ___
Count by 10s | Continue counting by 5s

c) ___, ___, ___ | ___, ___
Count by 25s | Continue counting by 10s

d) ___, ___, ___ | ___, ___
Count by 25s | Continue counting by 5s

9. Count on by the first number given, then by the following numbers given.

a) 25, 50, 75 | 80, 85 | 86
Count by 25s | by 5s | by 1s

b) ___, ___ | ___, ___ | ___, ___
Count by 25s | by 10s | by 5s

c) ___, ___ | ___ | ___, ___, ___
Count by 25s | by 10s | by 5s

d) ___, ___, ___ | ___, ___ | ___, ___
Count by 25s | by 10s | by 1s

10. Count on by the first coin value given, then by the others as the coin type changes.

a) 10, 20, 30, 35, 40, 41

b) ___, ___, ___, ___, ___, ___

BONUS ▶

___, ___, ___, ___, ___, ___, ___, ___, ___, ___, ___

11. Complete each pattern.

a) _10_, _20_, _30_ | _35_, _40_ | _41_

Count by 10s | by 5s | by 1s

b) ____, ____ | ____, ____ | ____, ____, ____

Count by 25s | by 10s | by 1s

c) ____, ____ | ____, ____ | ____, ____

Count by 25s | by 5s | by 1s

d) ____, ____, ____ | ____, ____ | ____, ____

Count by 25s | by 10s | by 5s

BONUS ▶

____, ____ | ____, ____, ____ | ____, ____ | ____, ____

Count by 25s | by 10s | by 5s | by 1s

12. Write the total amount of money, in cents, for the number of coins given in the charts. Count by the greater coin values first.

a)

Nickels	Pennies
7	4

Total amount = ________

b)

Quarters	Dimes
4	2

Total amount = ________

c)

Quarters	Nickels	Pennies
3	1	2

Total amount = ________

d)

Quarters	Dimes	Nickels	Pennies
2	1	2	6

Total amount = ________

13. What is the total amount in cents? Count by the greater coin values first.

a) 

Total amount = ________

b) 

Total amount = ________

c) 

Total amount = ________

d) 

Total amount = ________

BONUS ▶

Total amount = ________

NBT4-11 Which Coins Are Missing?

1. Fill in the missing amounts, counting by 5s.

a) 14, ____, 24, 29 b) 30, ____, ____, 45 c) 67, ____, ____, 82

d) 18, ____, ____, 33 e) 71, ____, ____, 86 f) 45, ____, ____, 60

2. Fill in the missing amounts, counting by 10s.

a) 63, ____, 83 b) 24, ____, ____, 54 c) 39, ____, ____, 69

3. Write the coin value needed to make the total. Choose from the options given.

a) 

= 16¢

10¢ or 1¢

b)  = 20¢

10¢ or 5¢

c)  = 21¢

10¢ or 1¢

d)  = 75¢

25¢ or 10¢

e)  = 40¢

10¢ or 5¢

f)  = 40¢

25¢ or 5¢

4. Draw the additional *nickels* needed to make the total.

a) 

= 20¢

b)  = 12¢

c)  = 31¢

d)  = 26¢

e)  = 45¢

f)  = 30¢

5. Draw the additional *dimes* needed to make the total.

a)  = 50¢

b)  = 62¢

c)  = 35¢

d)  = 46¢

e)  = 85¢

f)  = 50¢

6. Draw the additional coins needed to make each total.

a)  + How many dimes? = 80¢

b)  + How many nickels? = 40¢

c)  + How many dimes? = 40¢

d)  + How many quarters? = 100¢

BONUS ▶

Draw two additional coins to make each total.

a) 21¢ 

b) 35¢ 

c) 50¢ 

d) 17¢ 

e) 31¢ 

f) 65¢ 

7. How much money does each child have?

a) Rina has two quarters and a dime. She has ________¢.

b) Leon has three quarters, two dimes, and six pennies. He has ________.

c) Marissa has six nickels and a quarter. She has ________.

d) Angela has seven nickels, a dime, and two pennies. She has ________.

8. Draw a picture to show the extra coins each child will need. Try to use the fewest coins.

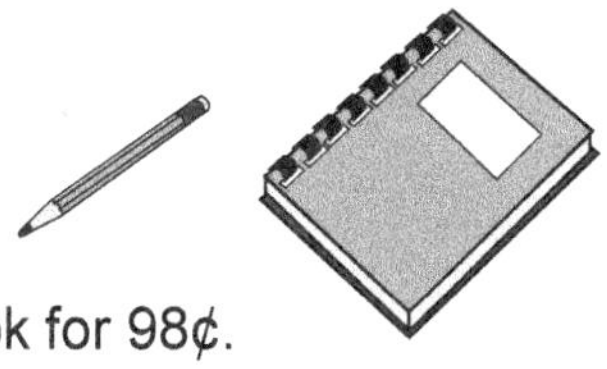

a) Tashi has 25¢. He wants to buy a pencil for 45¢.

b) Zoltan has 3 quarters, a dime, and a nickel. He wants to buy a notebook for 98¢.

c) Miguel has 2 quarters and 3 dimes. He wants to buy a book for 99¢.

9. Show how to make 80¢ using only …

a) dimes and quarters

b) nickels and quarters

10. Make up a problem like one of the problems in Question 8 and solve it.

NBT4-12 Least Number of Coins

1. Use the least number of coins to make the totals. First, find out how many dimes you need.

a) 12¢ (5¢) (5¢) (1¢) (1¢) *incorrect*

(10¢) (1¢) (1¢) *correct*

b) 16¢

c) 22¢

d) 8¢

e) 15¢

f) 20¢

g) 17¢

h) 24¢

i) 11¢

j) 23¢

k) 19¢

BONUS ▶ 26¢

2. Fill in the amounts: a) 2 quarters = ______¢ b) 3 quarters = ______¢ c) 4 quarters = ______¢

3. What is the greatest amount you could pay in quarters without going over the total amount? Draw the quarters to show your answer.

	Total Amount	Greatest amount you could pay in quarters
a)	35¢	
c)	78¢	
e)	59¢	
g)	49¢	
i)	82¢	
k)	29¢	

	Total Amount	Greatest amount you could pay in quarters
b)	53¢	
d)	83¢	
f)	64¢	
h)	31¢	
j)	95¢	
l)	72¢	

4. Find the greatest amount you could pay in quarters and the amount remaining. Then represent the amount remaining using the least number of coins.

	Total Amount	Amount paid in quarters	Amount remaining	Amount remaining in coins
a)	83¢	*75¢*	*83¢ 75¢ = 8¢*	(5¢) (1¢) (1¢) (1¢)
b)	56¢			
c)	33¢			
d)	85¢			
e)	97¢			

5. Use the least number of coins to make the totals. Start by finding the greatest amount you can make in quarters, as in Question 4.

a) 30¢ (10¢) (10¢) (10¢) *incorrect*

(25¢) (5¢) *correct*

b) 76¢

c) 40¢

d) 53¢

6. Show how you could make 55¢ using the least number of coins. Use play money to help you.

7. Trade coins to make each amount with the least number of coins. Draw a picture to show your final answer.

a) 

b) 

c) 

d) 

e) 

f) 

8. Show how you could trade each amount for the least number of coins.

a) 5 dimes

b) 4 dimes and 3 nickels

c) 2 quarters and 3 dimes

NBT4-13 Making Change Using Mental Math

1. Calculate the change owing for each purchase.

a) Price of a pencil = 42¢
Amount paid = 50¢
Change = ________

b) Price of an eraser = 34¢
Amount paid = 50¢
Change = ________

c) Price of a sharpener = 81¢
Amount paid = 90¢
Change = ________

d) Price of a ruler = 56¢
Amount paid = 60¢
Change = ________

e) Price of a marker = 78¢
Amount paid = 80¢
Change = ________

f) Price of a notebook = 63¢
Amount paid = 70¢
Change = ________

2. Count up by 10s to find the change owing from a dollar (100¢).

Price	Change
90¢	*10¢*
70¢	
50¢	

Price	Change
40¢	
10¢	
30¢	

Price	Change
20¢	
60¢	
80¢	

3. Find the change owing for each purchase. Count up by 10s.

a) Price of a lollipop = 50¢
Amount paid = $1.00
Change = ________

b) Price of an eraser = 60¢
Amount paid = $1.00
Change = ________

c) Price of an apple = 30¢
Amount paid = $1.00
Change = ________

d) Price of a banana = 90¢
Amount paid = $1.00
Change = ________

e) Price of a patty = 80¢
Amount paid = $1.00
Change = ________

f) Price of a pencil = 20¢
Amount paid = $1.00
Change = ________

g) Price of a gumball = 10¢
Amount paid = $1.00
Change = ________

h) Price of a juice = 40¢
Amount paid = $1.00
Change = ________

i) Price of a Popsicle = 70¢
Amount paid = $1.00
Change = ________

4. Find the smallest 2-digit multiple of 10 that is *greater* than the number given.

a) 72 [*80*] b) 54 [ ] c) 47 [ ] d) 26 [ ] e) 58 [ ] f) 7 [ ]

You need to pay 17¢. You pay a dollar (100¢). How much change will you get?

Step 1: Find the smallest multiple of 10 greater than 17¢.

(17¢) → [20¢] → (100¢)

Step 2: Find the differences: 20   17 and 100   20

(17¢) —3→ [20¢] —80→ (100¢)

Step 3: Add the differences: 3¢ + 80¢. **Change = 83¢**

5. Make change from a dollar for each amount.

a) (68¢) → [ ] → (100¢)

Change = ___________

b) (72¢) → [ ] → (100¢)

Change = ___________

c) (53¢) → [ ] → (100¢)

Change = ___________

d) (23¢) → [ ] → (100¢)

Change = ___________

e) (48¢) → [ ] → (100¢)

Change = ___________

f) (84¢) → [ ] → (100¢)

Change = ___________

6. Find change from a dollar (100¢). Do the work in your head.

a) 58¢ ________ b) 64¢ ________ c) 27¢ ________ d) 36¢ ________ e) 52¢ ________

f) 29¢ ________ g) 97¢ ________ h) 14¢ ________ i) 89¢ ________ j) 91¢ ________

BONUS ▶ Find the change in your head.

a) Price: 37¢ Amount paid: 50¢

Change: __________

b) Price: 58¢ Amount paid: 75¢

Change: __________

NBT4-14 Regrouping

Carl has 5 tens blocks and 17 ones blocks. He regroups 10 ones blocks as 1 tens block.

5 tens + 17 ones = 6 tens + 7 ones

1. Regroup 10 ones as 1 ten.

a) 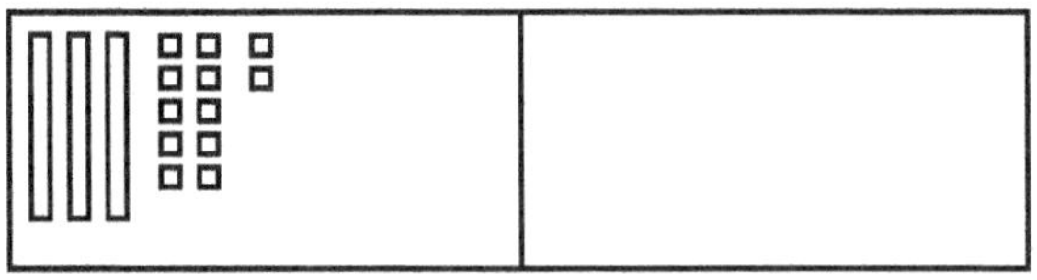

____ tens + ____ ones = ____ tens + ____ ones

b) 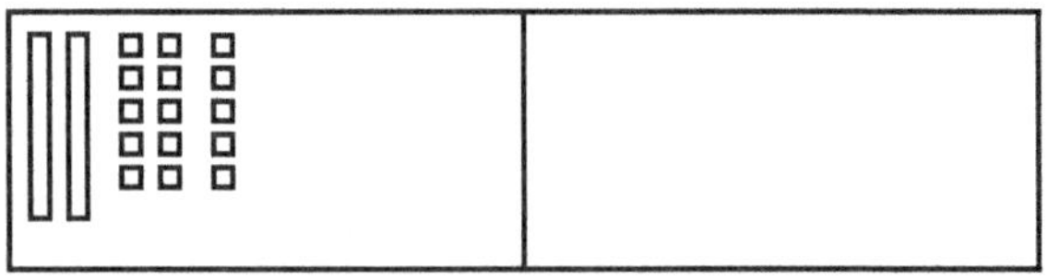

____ tens + ____ ones = ____ tens + ____ ones

c) 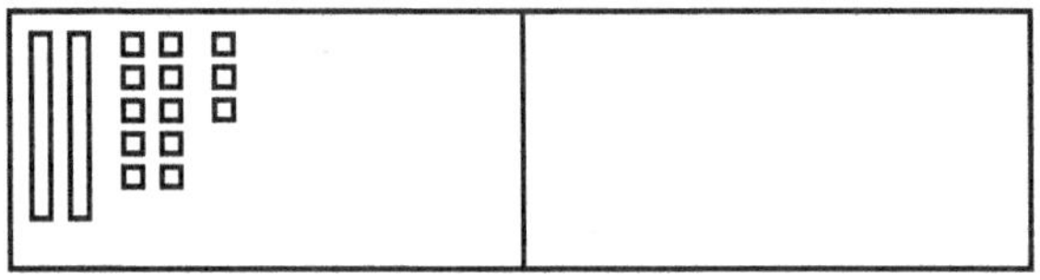

____ tens + ____ ones = ____ tens + ____ ones

d) 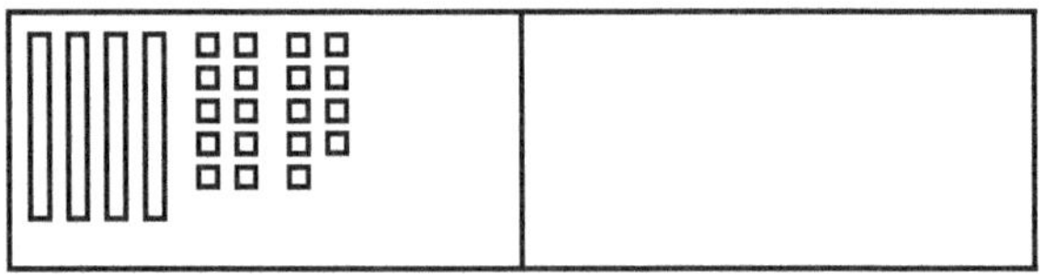

____ tens + ____ ones = ____ tens + ____ ones

2. How many ones can you regroup as tens? Complete the tables.

a)

Tens	Ones
6	(2)5
6 + (2) = 8	*5*

= *85*

b)

Tens	Ones
8	32

= ____

c)

Tens	Ones
5	31

= ____

d)

Tens	Ones
7	17

= ____

e)

Tens	Ones
6	29

= ____

f)

Tens	Ones
1	52

= ____

3. Regroup ones as tens.

a) 23 ones = ____ tens + ____ ones

b) 56 ones = ____ tens + ____ ones

c) 86 ones = ____ tens + ____ ones

d) 58 ones = ____ tens + ____ ones

e) 18 ones = ____ ten + ____ ones

f) 72 ones = ____ tens + ____ ones

g) 80 ones = ____ tens + ____ ones

h) 7 ones = ____ tens + ____ ones

i) 98 ones = ____ tens + ____ ones

Mehmet has 2 hundreds blocks, 15 tens blocks, and 6 ones blocks. He regroups 10 tens blocks as 1 hundreds block.

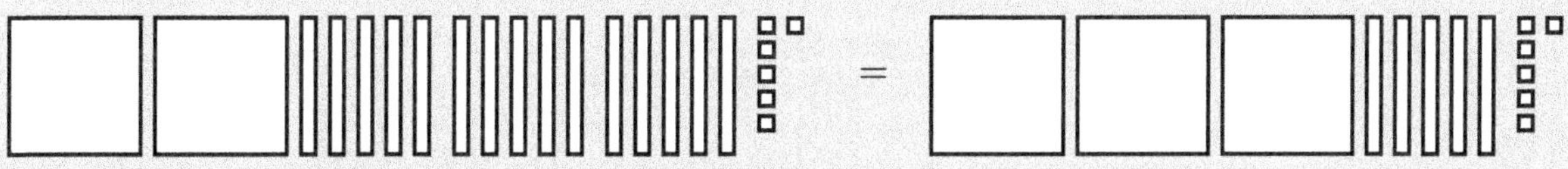

2 hundreds + 15 tens + 6 ones = 3 hundreds + 5 tens + 6 ones

4. Complete the tables by regrouping 10 tens as 1 hundred.

a)

Hundreds	**Tens**
5	11
5 + 1 = 6	*1*

b)

Hundreds	**Tens**
2	15

c)

Hundreds	**Tens**
6	17

d)

Hundreds	**Tens**
6	12

e)

Hundreds	**Tens**
2	17

f)

Hundreds	**Tens**
5	10

5. Choose a table from Question 4 and model your answer using blocks.

6. Regroup as many tens as hundreds as you can.
Remember: 10 tens = 1 hundred, 20 tens = 2 hundreds, 30 tens = 3 hundreds, and so on.

a) 3 hundreds + 13 tens + 4 ones = ____ hundreds + ____ tens + ____ ones

b) 5 hundreds + 21 tens + 1 one = ____ hundreds + ____ ten + ____ one

c) 3 hundreds + 10 tens + 5 ones = ______________________________

d) 1 hundred + 34 tens + 7 ones = ______________________________

7. Regroup tens as hundreds or ones as tens.

a) 4 hundreds + 2 tens + 19 ones = *4 hundreds + 3 tens + 9 ones*

b) 7 hundreds + 25 tens + 2 ones = ______________________________

c) 2 hundreds + 43 tens + 6 ones = ______________________________

d) 7 hundreds + 1 ten + 61 ones = ______________________________

e) 0 hundreds + 26 tens + 3 ones = ______________________________

Maya has 1 thousands block, 11 hundreds blocks, 1 tens block, and 2 ones blocks.
She regroups 10 hundreds blocks as 1 thousands block.

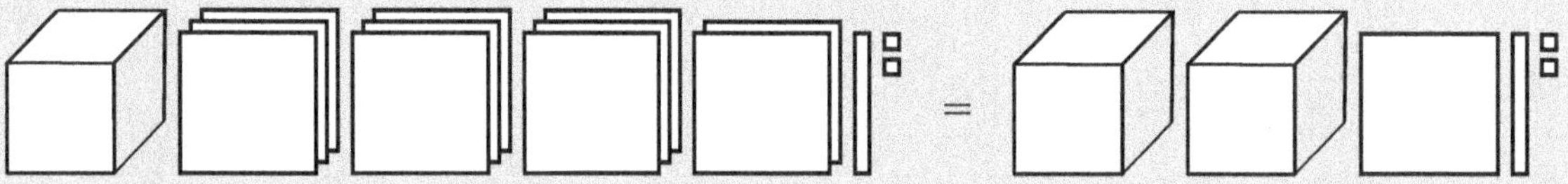

1 thousand + 11 hundreds + 1 ten + 2 ones = 2 thousands + 1 hundred + 1 ten + 2 ones

8. Complete the tables by regrouping 10 hundreds as 1 thousand.

a)

Thousands	Hundreds
3	12
3 + 1 = 4	*2*

b)

Thousands	Hundreds
4	13

c)

Thousands	Hundreds
7	14

9. Choose a table from Question 8 and model your answer using blocks.

10. Regroup hundreds as thousands, tens as hundreds, or ones as tens.

a) 5 thousands + 12 hundreds + 3 tens + 1 one

= ___*6*___ thousands + ___*2*___ hundreds + ___*3*___ tens + ___*1*___ one

b) 3 thousands + 15 hundreds + 1 ten + 6 ones

= ______ thousands + ______ hundreds + ______ ten + ______ ones

c) 3 thousands + 26 hundreds + 5 tens + 1 one

= ______ thousands + ______ hundreds + ______ tens + ______ one

d) 6 thousands + 6 hundreds + 23 tens + 5 ones

= ____

e) 6 thousands + 14 hundreds + 7 tens + 25 ones

= ____

11. Roger wants to build a model of the number three thousand, two hundred twelve.

He has 3 thousands blocks, 1 hundreds block, and 24 ones blocks.

Can he build the model?

Use diagrams and numbers to justify your answer.

Adding 2-Digit Numbers

1. Add the numbers by drawing a simple picture and by adding the digits.

a) 15 + 43

	With base ten materials		With numerals	
	Tens	Ones	Tens	Ones
15			1	5
43			4	3
sum		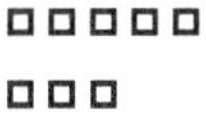	5	8

15 + 43 = ________

b) 25 + 22

	With base ten materials		With numerals	
	Tens	Ones	Tens	Ones
25				
22				
sum				

25 + 22 = ________

c) 31 + 27

	With base ten materials		With numerals	
	Tens	Ones	Tens	Ones
31				
27				
sum				

31 + 27 = ________

d) 13 + 24

	With base ten materials		With numerals	
	Tens	Ones	Tens	Ones
13				
24				
sum				

13 + 24 = ________

2. Add the numbers by adding the digits.

a) $\begin{array}{r} 3\ 4 \\ +\ 4\ 3 \\ \hline \end{array}$ b) $\begin{array}{r} 7\ 7 \\ +\ 1\ 2 \\ \hline \end{array}$ c) $\begin{array}{r} 5\ 4 \\ +\ 3\ 5 \\ \hline \end{array}$ d) $\begin{array}{r} 1\ 0 \\ +\ 4\ 9 \\ \hline \end{array}$ e) $\begin{array}{r} 1\ 6 \\ +\ 2\ 3 \\ \hline \end{array}$

f) $\begin{array}{r} 1\ 6 \\ +\ 2\ 1 \\ \hline \end{array}$ g) $\begin{array}{r} 5\ 2 \\ +\ 2\ 4 \\ \hline \end{array}$ h) $\begin{array}{r} 8\ 1 \\ +\ 1\ 1 \\ \hline \end{array}$ i) $\begin{array}{r} 4\ 3 \\ +\ 3\ 1 \\ \hline \end{array}$ j) $\begin{array}{r} 7\ 5 \\ +\ 1\ 4 \\ \hline \end{array}$

NBT4-16 Adding with Regrouping

1. Add the numbers by drawing a picture and by adding the digits.
   Use base ten materials to show how to combine the numbers and how to regroup.

a) 16 + 25

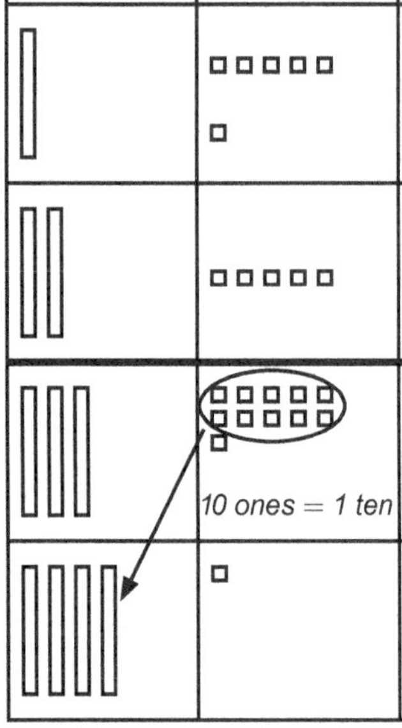

	With base ten materials		With numerals	
	Tens	Ones	Tens	Ones
16			1	6
25			2	5
sum			3	11
			4	1

16 + 25 = *41*

b) 25 + 37

	With base ten materials		With numerals	
	Tens	Ones	Tens	Ones
25				
37				
sum				

25 + 37 = ________

c) 29 + 36

	With base ten materials		With numerals	
	Tens	Ones	Tens	Ones
29				
36				
sum				

29 + 36 = ________

d) 18 + 35

	With base ten materials		With numerals	
	Tens	Ones	Tens	Ones
18				
35				
sum				

18 + 35 = ________

2. Add the numbers by regrouping.

Step 1: Regroup 10 ones as 1 ten.

tens go here

a)

	1	
	1	5
+	1	8
		3

ones go here

b)

	6	4
+	1	6

c)

	7	5
+	1	9

d)

	6	6
+	1	7

e)

	1	5
+	3	8

f)

	1	3
+	1	9

g)

	2	4
+	3	8

h)

	5	4
+	1	8

i)

	2	7
+	6	9

j)

	4	6
+	4	8

Step 2: Add the numbers in the tens column.

k)

	1	
	1	2
+	1	8
	3	*0*

l)

	1	
	1	3
+	1	7
		0

m)

	1	
	1	5
+	2	8
		3

n)

	1	
	2	6
+	2	6
		2

o)

	1	
	3	8
+	2	7
		5

3. Add the numbers by regrouping.

a)

	1	
	3	6
+	1	8
	5	*4*

b)

	3	7
+	1	8

c)

	5	9
+	1	8

d)

	3	7
+	4	3

e)

	5	7
+	2	6

f)

	6	3
+	2	9

g)

	5	8
+	4	7

h)

	1	8
+	7	7

i)

	5	9
+	1	3

j)

	7	5
+	1	6

Sometimes the sum of two 2-digit numbers is a 3-digit number.

Example:

1		
	7	5
+	8	2
1	5	7

7 tens + 8 tens = 15 tens = 1 hundred + 5 tens, so we need to regroup 10 tens as 1 hundred.

4. Add by regrouping 10 tens as 1 hundred.

a)

1		
	7	5
+	8	2
1	5	7

b)

	8	4
+	6	3

c)

	7	2
+	6	5

d)

	9	1
+	9	6

e)

	8	5
+	7	3

5. Add by regrouping 10 ones as 1 ten and 10 tens as 1 hundred.

a)

1	1	
	7	5
+	6	7
1	4	2

b)

	8	6
+	3	9

c)

	5	8
+	4	7

d)

	7	6
+	7	8

e)

	3	5
+	6	5

	1	
	8	6
+	7	9
1	6	5

You need to regroup 6 + 9 = 15 as 1 ten and 5 ones, but you can write 1 + 8 + 7 tens = 16 tens directly.

6. Add by regrouping when you need to.

a)

	8	5
+	3	4

b)

	7	4
+	2	8

c)

	7	9
+	8	8

d)

	6	4
+	3	9

e)

	7	5
+	2	5

7. Add by regrouping. Use grid paper.

a) 37 + 48 b) 29 + 83 c) 66 + 39 d) 75 + 48 e) 91 + 87

Adding 3-Digit Numbers

Dalha adds 152 + 273 using base ten materials.

152 = 1 hundred + 5 tens + 2 ones

+ **273** = 2 hundreds + 7 tens + 3 ones

= 3 hundreds + 12 tens + 5 ones

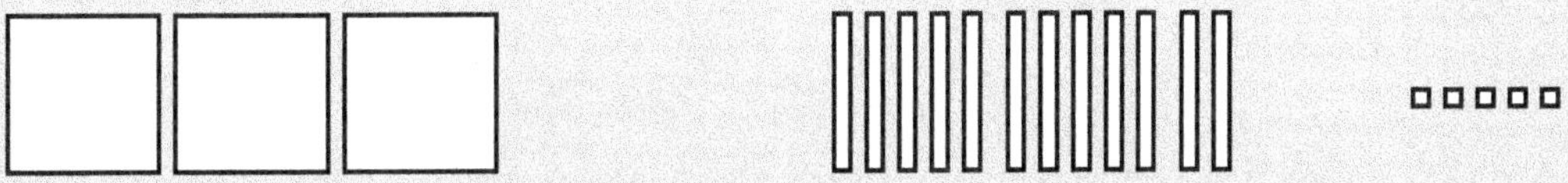

To get the final answer, Dalha regroups 10 tens as 1 hundred.

= 4 hundreds + 2 tens + 5 ones

1. Add the numbers using base ten materials or a picture. Record your work below.

a) 353 ______ hundreds + ______ tens + ______ ones

+ 164 + ______ hundred + ______ tens + ______ ones

= ______ hundreds + ______ tens + ______ ones

after regrouping = ______ hundreds + ______ ten + ______ ones

b) 462 ______ hundreds + ______ tens + ______ ones

+ 375 + ______ hundreds + ______ tens + ______ ones

= ______ hundreds + ______ tens + ______ ones

after regrouping = ______ hundreds + ______ tens + ______ ones

2. Add. You will need to regroup.

a) [*1*]
  5 2 6
+ 2 9 3
  8 1 9

b) [ ]
  6 4 5
+ 1 8 3

c) [ ]
  3 7 4
+ 4 6 2

d)
  4 8 2
+ 4 7 7

e)
  2 8 4
+ 5 9 5

3. Add, regrouping where necessary.

	a)	b)	c)	d)	e)
	3 2 8	7 4 7	9 1 5	3 4 6	2 1 8
+	1 4	5 1 6	4 5	2 0 5	3 4 8

	f)	g)	h)	i)	j)
	5 6 4	7 4 8	7 2 6	5 6 4	4 4 4
+	5 5 3	4 2 4	6 4 8	6 7 2	2 0 9

4. Line the numbers up correctly in the grid, then add.

a) 218 + 265 b) 272 + 213 c) 643 + 718 d) 937 + 25

	2	1	8
+	2	6	5

e) 146 + 273 f) 816 + 925 g) 369 + 119 h) 847 + 910

5. Add. You will need to regroup twice.

a)

	1	1	
	3	8	7
+	2	4	3
	6	3	0

b)

	8	2	2
+	9	7	8

c)

	1	3	2
+		7	9

d)

	5	8	6
+		3	9

BONUS ▶

Use the pattern in your answers to a), b), and c) to find the sums in d) and e) without adding.

	a)	b)	c)	d)	e)
	9	9 9	9 9 9	9, 9 9 9	9 9, 9 9 9
+	9	9 9	9 9 9	9, 9 9 9	9 9, 9 9 9

6. Add the numbers. Use grid paper.

a) 22 + 36 + 21 b) 324 + 112 + 422 c) 248 + 167 + 539

Adding Larger Numbers

Amber adds 1,852 + 2,321 using base ten materials.

1,852 = 1 thousand + 8 hundreds + 5 tens + 2 ones

+ 2,321 = 2 thousands + 3 hundreds + 2 tens + 1 one

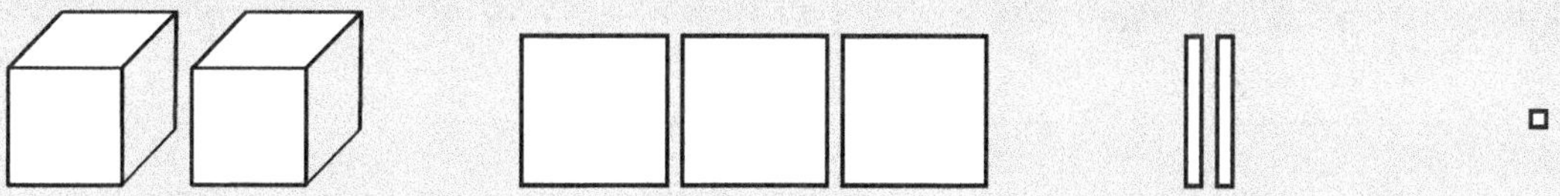

= 3 thousands + 11 hundreds + 7 tens + 3 ones

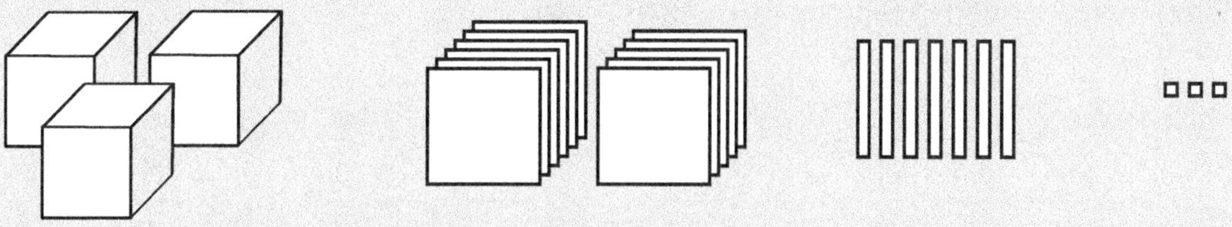

To get the final answer, Amber regroups 10 hundreds as 1 thousand.

= 4 thousands + 1 hundred + 7 tens + 3 ones

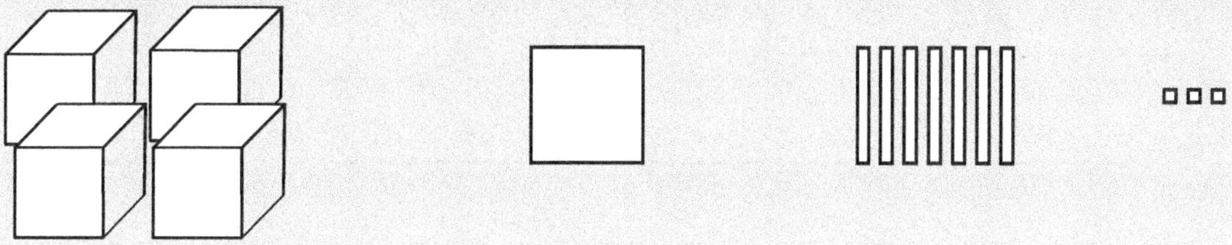

1. Add the numbers and record your work below. Use base ten materials or draw a picture to show the addition.

a) 2,543   _______ thousands + _______ hundreds + _______ tens + _______ ones

+ 3,621   + _______ thousands + _______ hundreds + _______ tens + _______ one

= _______ thousands + _______ hundreds + _______ tens + _______ ones

after regrouping = _______ thousands + _______ hundred + _______ tens + _______ ones

b) 3,824   _______ thousands + _______ hundreds + _______ tens + _______ ones

+ 1,654   + _______ thousand + _______ hundreds + _______ tens + _______ ones

= _______ thousands + _______ hundreds + _______ tens + _______ ones

after regrouping = _______ thousands + _______ hundreds + _______ tens + _______ ones

2. Add. (You will need to regroup.)

a)	b)	c)	d)	e)
1				
5,265	6,454	3,747	1,821	1,824
+ 2,912	+ 1,833	+ 2,621	+ 2,772	+ 5,773
8,177				

3. Add. You will need to regroup 10 tens as 1 hundred.

a)	b)	c)	d)	e)
3,483	2,569	5,486	8,364	1,294
+ 1,334	+ 1,260	+ 1,131	+ 1,472	+ 5,093

4. Add. You will need to regroup 10 ones as 1 ten.

a)	b)	c)	d)	e)
2,436	8,127	7,588	5,425	6,254
+ 1,125	+ 1,743	+ 2,108	+ 2,347	+ 2,639

5. Add by regrouping where necessary.

a)	b)	c)	d)	e)
2,354	9,683	5,871	8,525	9,879
+ 2,831	+ 1,742	+ 4,833	+ 1,533	+ 2,723

f)	g)	h)	i)	j)
7,546	7,624	6,690	9,975	3,945
+ 4,822	+ 1,601	+ 3,712	+ 3,751	+ 3,451

k)	l)	m)	n)	o)
4,534	6,754	3,214	2,509	5,372
+ 2,542	+ 1,360	+ 4,852	+ 621	+ 521

p)	q)	r)	s)	t)
6,827	9,856	4,321	6,231	8,032
+ 85	+ 742	+ 5,932	+ 7,489	+ 518

6. Add, regrouping where necessary.

a) $\begin{array}{r} 35{,}846 \\ +\ 21{,}135 \\ \hline \end{array}$ b) $\begin{array}{r} 43{,}564 \\ +\ 82{,}813 \\ \hline \end{array}$ c) $\begin{array}{r} 56{,}534 \\ +\ 3{,}294 \\ \hline \end{array}$ d) $\begin{array}{r} 98{,}854 \\ +\ 1{,}063 \\ \hline \end{array}$

e) $\begin{array}{r} 256{,}752 \\ +\ 372{,}334 \\ \hline \end{array}$ f) $\begin{array}{r} 693{,}473 \\ +\ 855{,}243 \\ \hline \end{array}$ g) $\begin{array}{r} 356{,}753 \\ +\ 9{,}233 \\ \hline \end{array}$ h) $\begin{array}{r} 478{,}230 \\ +\ 3{,}488 \\ \hline \end{array}$

7. Add by lining the digits up correctly in the grid. In some questions you may have to regroup twice.

a) 2,468 + 7,431 b) 8,596 + 1,235 c) 6,650 + 2,198 d) 8,359 + 48

e) 73,246 + 18,382 f) 145,683 + 329,234

8. Add, regrouping where necessary.

a) 5,326 + 1,234 + 6,762 b) 3,658 + 6,343 + 4,534 c) 389 + 3,247 + 712 + 52

BONUS ▶

A **palindrome** is a number (or word) that reads the same forward and backward.

For example: 363, 51,815 and 2,375,732 are all palindromes.

You can create a palindrome from any number. Example:

Step 1: Start with 124. Reverse the digits. 124 → 421

Step 2: Add the two numbers. 124 + 421 = 545

Step 3: If the sum in Step 2 is not a palindrome, repeat Steps 1 and 2 with the new number. Most numbers will eventually become palindromes if you keep repeating these steps.

Create palindromes from the following numbers.

a) 216 b) 154 c) 651 d) 23,153 e) 371 f) 258 g) 1,385

NBT4-19 Subtraction

To subtract 48 − 32, Bradley makes a model of 48.

Then he crosses out 3 tens and 2 ones because 32 = 3 tens + 2 ones.

48	48 − 32	=	16

1. Subtract by crossing out tens and ones blocks. Draw your final answer in the right-hand box.

a)	39 − 18	= *21*	b)	25 − 11	=
	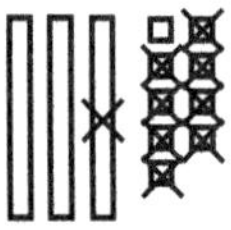	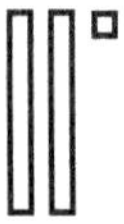			

c)	43 − 21	=	d)	45 − 32	=

2. Write how many tens and ones in each number. Then subtract the tens and ones to find the final answer.

a)
45 = _4_ tens + _5_ ones
− 32 = _3_ tens + _2_ ones
= _1_ ten + _3_ ones
= _13_

b)
57 = ___ tens + ___ ones
− 34 = ___ tens + ___ ones
= ___ tens + ___ ones
= ______

c)
84 = ___ tens + ___ ones
− 63 = ___ tens + ___ ones
= ___ tens + ___ one
= ______

d)
89 = ___ tens + ___ ones
− 56 = ___ tens + ___ ones
= ___ tens + ___ ones
= ______

e)
77 = ___ tens + ___ ones
− 44 = ___ tens + ___ ones
= ___ tens + ___ ones
= ______

f)
67 = ___ tens + ___ ones
− 45 = ___ tens + ___ ones
= ___ tens + ___ ones
= ______

3. Subtract by writing the number of tens and ones in each number.

a)
$$\begin{array}{rl} & 36 = 30 + 6 \\ - & 24 = 20 + 4 \\ \hline & \quad = 10 + 2 \\ & \quad = 12 \end{array}$$

b)
$$\begin{array}{rl} & 84 = \\ - & 52 = \\ \hline & \quad = \\ & \quad = \end{array}$$

c)
$$\begin{array}{rl} & 98 = \\ - & 37 = \\ \hline & \quad = \\ & \quad = \end{array}$$

d)
$$\begin{array}{rl} & 73 = \\ - & 12 = \\ \hline \end{array}$$

e)
$$\begin{array}{rl} & 26 = \\ - & 24 = \\ \hline \end{array}$$

f)
$$\begin{array}{rl} & 88 = \\ - & 33 = \\ \hline \end{array}$$

4. Subtract the numbers by subtracting the digits.

a) $\begin{array}{r} 54 \\ -\ 23 \\ \hline \end{array}$ b) $\begin{array}{r} 86 \\ -\ 73 \\ \hline \end{array}$ c) $\begin{array}{r} 36 \\ -\ 15 \\ \hline \end{array}$ d) $\begin{array}{r} 64 \\ -\ 32 \\ \hline \end{array}$ e) $\begin{array}{r} 95 \\ -\ 42 \\ \hline \end{array}$ f) $\begin{array}{r} 89 \\ -\ 40 \\ \hline \end{array}$

5. a) Draw a picture of 543 using hundreds, tens, and ones blocks. Show how you would subtract 543 − 421.

b) Now subtract 543 − 421 by lining up the digits and subtracting. Do you get the same answer?

6. Subtract.

a) $\begin{array}{r} 7,532 \\ -\ 4,121 \\ \hline \end{array}$ b) $\begin{array}{r} 65,356 \\ -\ 44,245 \\ \hline \end{array}$ c) $\begin{array}{r} 955,763 \\ -\ 523,011 \\ \hline \end{array}$

NBT4-20 Subtraction with Regrouping

Farkan subtracts 46 – 18 using base ten materials.

Step 1:
Farkan represents 46 with base ten materials.

Tens	Ones
4	6

Here is how Farkan uses numerals to show his work:

```
  46
  18
 ----
```

Step 2:
8 (the ones digit of 18) is greater than 6 (the ones digit of 46) so Farkan regroups 1 tens block as 10 ones blocks.

Tens	Ones
3	16

Here is how Farkan shows the regrouping:

```
  3 16
  4̸ 6̸
  1  8
 ------
```

Step 3:
Farkan subtracts 18 (he takes away 1 tens block and 8 ones blocks).

Tens	Ones
2	8

And now Farkan can subtract 16 – 8 ones and 3 – 1 tens:

```
  3 16
  4̸ 6̸
  1  8
 ------
  2  8
```

1. In these questions, Farkan doesn't have enough ones to subtract. Help him by regrouping 1 tens block as 10 ones. Show how he would change his subtraction statement.

a) **63 – 26**

Tens	Ones	Tens	Ones
6	3	5	13

```
     6  3   →      5  13
                   6̸  3̸
  –  2  6       –  2  6
```

b) **64 – 39**

Tens	Ones	Tens	Ones
6	4		

```
     6  4   →      6  4
  –  3  9       –  3  9
```

c) **42 – 19**

Tens	Ones	Tens	Ones
4	2		

```
     4  2   →      4  2
  –  1  9       –  1  9
```

d) **35 – 27**

Tens	Ones	Tens	Ones
3	5		

```
     3  5   →      3  5
  –  2  7       –  2  7
```

2. Subtract by regrouping.

a)

	3	*13*
	~~4~~	~~3~~
–	2	7
	1	*6*

b)

	5	6
–	1	8

c)

	6	4
–	3	9

d)

	7	0
–	2	8

e)

	5	5
–	3	7

f)

	8	0
–	5	7

g)

	3	8
–	1	9

h)

	2	2
–		6

i)

	4	4
–		9

j)

	9	0
–	7	5

3. For the questions where you need to regroup, write "regroup" in the blank. If you don't need to regroup, write "OK." Then find the answer.

a) *4 14*
~~54~~
– 19
35
regroup — *4 is less than 9*

b) 77 – 56 *OK*

c) 85 – 53 ______

d) 95 – 18 ______

e) 66 – 54 ______

f) 84 – 17 ______

g) 82 – 29 ______

h) 26 – 15 ______

i) 45 – 9 ______

j) 12 – 8 ______

k) 30 – 19 ______

l) 52 – 9 ______

m) 47 – 19 ______

n) 23 – 8 ______

o) 60 – 49 ______

p) 80 – 41 ______

q) 93 – 24 ______

r) 79 – 42 ______

4. Subtract by regrouping 1 hundred as 10 tens. The first one has been started for you.

a)

	2	11	
	~~3~~	~~1~~	5
−	1	6	2

b)

	5	3	8
−	2	9	5

c)

	3	1	7
−	1	8	6

d)

	9	4	2
−	5	7	0

5. For the questions below, you will have to regroup *twice.* Example:

Step 1	**Step 2**	**Step 3**	**Step 4**	**Step 5**
		14	14	14
4 14	4 14	7 ~~4~~ 14	7 ~~4~~ 14	7 ~~4~~ 14
8 ~~5~~ ~~4~~	8 ~~5~~ ~~4~~	~~8~~ ~~5~~ ~~4~~	~~8~~ ~~5~~ ~~4~~	~~8~~ ~~5~~ ~~4~~
− 3 6 7	− 3 6 7	− 3 6 7	− 3 6 7	− 3 6 7
	7	7	8 7	4 8 7

a)

	6	3	4
−	1	5	6

b)

	5	8	5
−		9	6

c)

	5	3	2
−	2	3	5

d)

	8	5	4
−	3	7	7

To subtract 3,245 − 1,923, Sara regroups 1 thousands block as 10 hundreds blocks.

thousands	hundreds	tens	ones
3	2	4	5

thousands	hundreds	tens	ones
2	12	4	5

thousands	hundreds	tens	ones
1	3	2	2

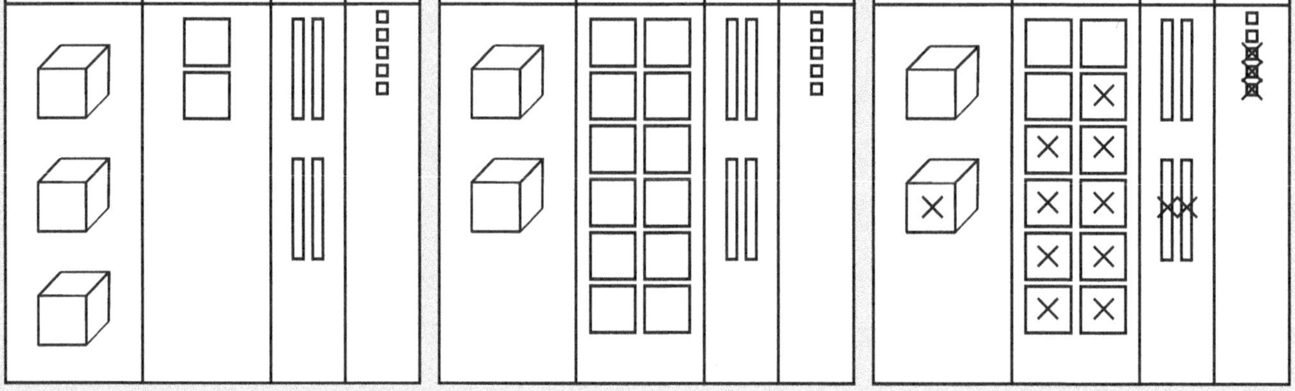

6. Subtract by regrouping 1 thousand as 10 hundreds.

a)

	7	13		
	~~8~~	~~3~~	6	4
−	4	8	3	1
	3	*5*	*3*	*3*

b)

	5	6	9	3
−	2	7	1	1

c)

	5	7	5	8
−	2	9	4	2

NBT4-21 Subtraction with Regrouping (Advanced)

To subtract from 100, you need to regroup from the hundreds before you can regroup from the tens.

	1	0	0
−		5	7

→

	0	10	
	~~1~~	~~0~~	0
−		5	7

→

		9	
		~~10~~	10
	~~1~~	~~0~~	~~0~~
−		5	7

→

		9	
		~~10~~	10
	~~1~~	~~0~~	~~0~~
−		5	7
		4	3

1. a) Subtract by regrouping.

i)

	1	0	0
−		3	8

ii)

	1	0	0
−		8	6

iii)

	1	0	0
−		7	2

iv)

	1	0	0
−		2	3

b) Subtract from 99 without regrouping.

i)

	9	9
−	3	8
	6	*1*

ii)

	9	9
−	8	6

iii)

	9	9
−	7	2

iv)

	9	9
−	2	3

c) How do your answers to part a) and part b) compare? Why is this the case?

To subtract from 100 or 1,000, first subtract from 99 or 999.

$$\begin{array}{r} 99 \\ -\ 27 \\ \hline 72 \end{array} \xrightarrow{\text{add 1}} \begin{array}{r} 100 \\ -\ 27 \\ \hline 73 \end{array} \qquad \begin{array}{r} 999 \\ -\ 346 \\ \hline 653 \end{array} \xrightarrow{\text{add 1}} \begin{array}{r} 1000 \\ -\ 346 \\ \hline 654 \end{array}$$

2. Subtract by using 99 or 999.

a) 100 − 28

	9	9
−	2	8

so 100 − 28 = ______

b) 1,000 − 247

	9	9	9
−	2	4	7

so 1,000 − 247 = ______

c) 1,000 − 762

d) 1,000 − 84

BONUS ▶ 1,000,000 − 841,290

Parts and Totals

1. The bars in each picture represent quantities of red and green apples. Fill in the blanks.

a) 5 red apples
3 green apples

5 red

3 green

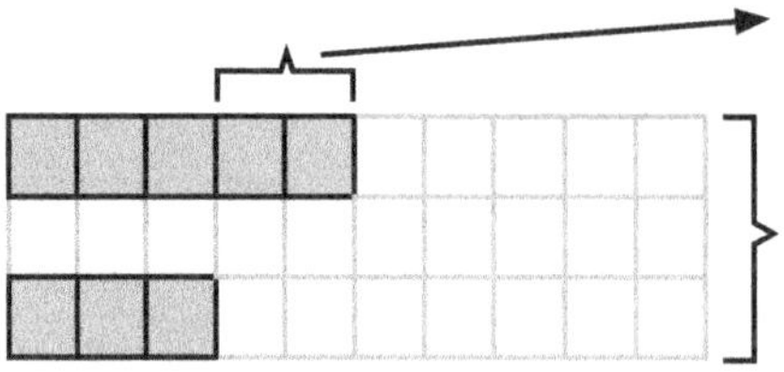

difference: *2 apples*

total: *8 apples*

b) 4 green apples
2 more red apples than green apples

______

______

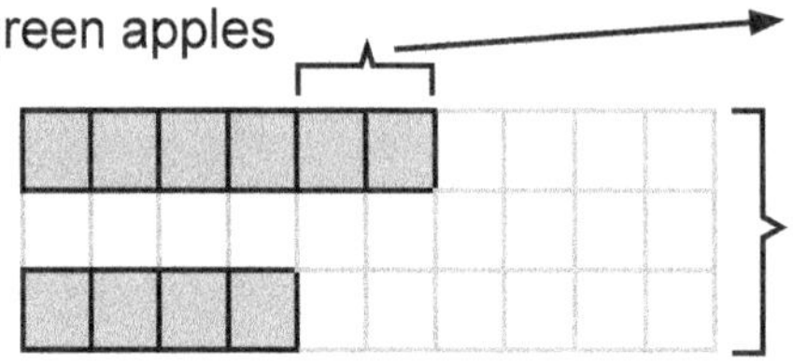

difference: ______

total: ______

c) 7 green apples
3 more green apples than red apple

______

______

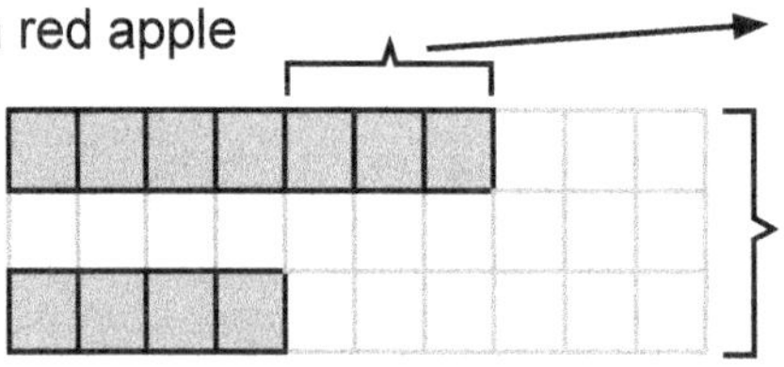

difference: ______

total: ______

d) 10 apples in total
3 green apples

______

______

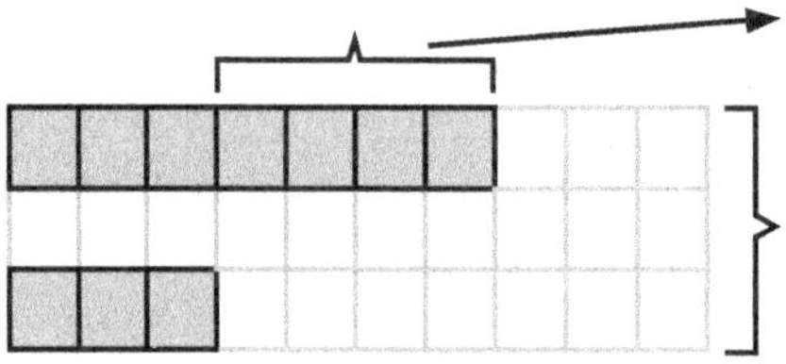

difference: ______

total: ______

2. Complete the table.

	Red Apples	Green Apples	Total Number of Apples	How many more of one color of apple?
a)	2	5	7	3 more green apples than red
b)	3		8	
c)		2	9	
d)	4			1 more red apple than green

3. Draw a picture (as in Question 1) and make a table (as in Question 2) for the quantities.

a) 4 red apples
4 more green apples than red apples

b) 12 apples in total
7 green apples

BONUS ▶ 10 apples in total
2 more red apples than green apples

4 green marbles	}	**Parts 1 and 2**
5 red marbles		
9 marbles altogether		**Total**

4. Draw a picture on grid paper (as in Question 1) to complete each row.
Circle the number in the table that answers each question.

		Part 1	**Part 2**	**Total**	**Difference Between Parts**
a)	Helen has 7 green marbles and 9 red marbles. How many marbles does she have?	*7*	*9*	*(16)*	*2*
b)	Helen has 12 green marbles and 4 red marbles. How many more green marbles than red marbles does she have?				
c)	A sandwich costs 3 dollars, and a drink costs 1 dollar. How much do the sandwich and the drink cost together?				
d)	A sandwich costs 5 dollars, and a drink costs 2 dollars. How much less than a sandwich does the drink cost?				
e)	Peter biked 9 miles. Lavi biked 6 miles. How many miles did they bike altogether?				
f)	Bilal jogged 8 miles. Hong jogged 12 miles. How much farther did Hong jog than Bilal?				

5. For each part of Question 4, was the answer the total, a part, or the difference?

a) *total*　　　　b) ____________

c) ____________　　　　d) ____________

e) ____________　　　　f) ____________

6. Draw a picture on grid paper (as in Question 1) for each problem.

a) Ron has 13 red stickers and 6 blue stickers. How many stickers does he have?

b) Claire has 6 pets. Two are dogs and the rest are cats. How many cats does she have?

c) Peter walked 7 miles. Lavi walked 3 miles. How much farther did Peter walk?

NBT4-23 Parts and Totals (Advanced)

1. Fill in the table. Then circle the number that is the answer to the question.

		Green Grapes	Purple Grapes	Total Number of Grapes	Difference Between Types of Grapes
a)	There are 8 green grapes. There are 5 more green grapes than purple grapes. How many purple grapes are there?	*8*	(*3*)	*11*	*5 more green than purple*
b)	There are 7 green grapes. There are 12 grapes altogether. How many purple grapes are there?				
c)	There are 16 green grapes and 49 purple grapes. How many grapes are there altogether?				
d)	There are 7 more green grapes than purple grapes. There are 5 purple grapes. How many grapes are there altogether?				
e)	There are 17 green grapes. There are 32 grapes altogether. How many more green grapes than purple grapes are there?				
f)	There are 26 green grapes. There are 9 fewer purple grapes than green grapes. How many grapes are there altogether?				
g)	There are 5 more green grapes than purple grapes. There are 7 green grapes. How many grapes are there altogether?				

2. a) There are 7 dogs at the shelter. There are 3 more cats than dogs at the shelter. How many cats and dogs are at the shelter?

b) There are apples and pears on the table. There are 8 apples and 3 fewer pears. How many apples and pears are on the table?

c) Darya invited 17 friends to a birthday party. Seven of them are boys. How many more girls than boys did Darya invite to the party?

NBT4-24 Fact Families

1. Write in words what each **equation** says.

a) $3 + 5 = 8$ Start with ______, add ______ more, end up with ______.

b) $7 - 4 = 3$ Start with ______, take away ______, end up with ______.

c) $8 - 2 = 6$ ____.

d) $5 + 4 = 9$ ____.

Jane and Bob each find how many circles altogether.

Jane starts with the big circles and writes $2 + 6 = 8$.

Bob starts with the small circles and writes $6 + 2 = 8$.

2. What does the first number represent?

a)

$\mathbf{4} + 2 = 6$

the small circles

b)

$\mathbf{3} + 5 = 8$

____

c)

$\mathbf{5} + 1 = 6$

____

d)

$\mathbf{2} + 3 = 5$

____

3. Write two addition equations for each picture.

a)

Start with the big circles. *$2 + 5 = 7$*

Start with the small circles. *$5 + 2 = 7$*

b)

Start with the big circles. ______________

Start with the small circles. ______________

c)

Start with the big circles. ______________

Start with the small circles. ______________

d)
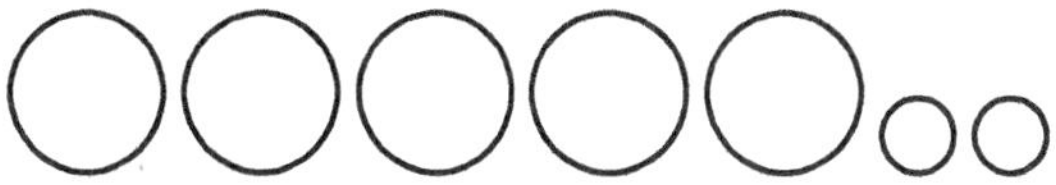

Start with the big circles. ______________

Start with the small circles. ______________

Jane and Bob each start with the same picture.

Jane takes away the big circles and writes $5 - 2 = 3$.

Bob takes away the small circles and writes $5 - 3 = 2$.

4. Write two subtraction equations for each picture.

a) 

Take away the big circles. $7 - 3 = 4$

Take away the small circles. $7 - 4 = 3$

b) 

Take away the big circles. ______

Take away the small circles. ______

c) 

Take away the big circles. ______

Take away the small circles. ______

d) 

Take away the big circles. ______

Take away the small circles. ______

You can write two addition equations and two subtraction equations for the picture.

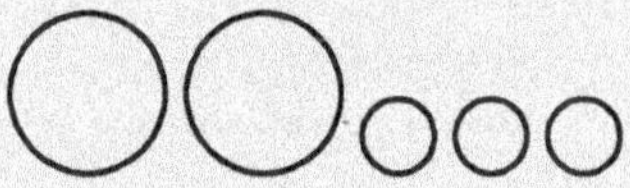

$2 + 3 = 5$ $\quad$ $5 - 2 = 3$

$3 + 2 = 5$ $\quad$ $5 - 3 = 2$

The four equations make up a **fact family.**

5. Write the fact family for the picture.

a) 

______

______

b) 

______

______

6. Complete the fact family for each equation.

a) $3 + 6 = 9$

$6 + 3 = 9$

$9 - 6 = 3$

$9 - 3 = 6$

b) $8 - 1 = 7$

______

______

______

c) $4 - 3 = 1$

______

______

______

7. Write the fact family for $3 + 3 = 6$. How is it different from the fact families in Question 6?

8. Fill in the table.

	Green Grapes	Purple Grapes	Total Number of Grapes	Fact Family for Total	How many more of one type of grape?
a)	7	2	9	$7 + 2 = 9$ $2 + 7 = 9$ $9 - 2 = 7$ $9 - 7 = 2$	5 more green than purple
b)	6		10		
c)	2	9			
d)		5			4 more green than purple

9. Write the correct sign (+ or −) in the box.

a) number of green grapes ☐ number of purple grapes = how many more green than purple grapes

b) number of green grapes ☐ number of purple grapes = how many grapes altogether

c) number of grapes altogether ☐ number of green grapes = number of purple grapes

d) number of green grapes ☐ how many more purple than green grapes = how many purple grapes

e) number of purple grapes ☐ number of green grapes = how many more purple than green grapes

NBT4-25 Sums and Differences

1. A glass can hold 255 kidney beans.
How many beans can two glasses hold?

2. Alice's class raised $312 for charity. Sophie's class raised $287.

a) Whose class raised more money?
How did you find the answer?

b) How much money did the two classes raise altogether?

3. At a summer camp, 324 children are enrolled in baseball. There are 128 *more* children enrolled in swimming than in baseball.

a) How many children are enrolled in swimming?

b) How many children are enrolled in swimming or baseball altogether?

4. A coast redwood tree in California is 376 feet tall. The top of a treehouse in Crossville, Tennessee, is 97 feet above the ground.

How far above the top of the treehouse is the top of the tree?

5. Emma flies 2,457 miles on one day and 1,357 miles the next day.

How many miles did she fly in the two days?

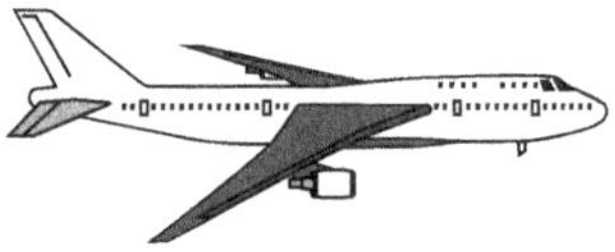

6. What is the greatest 3-digit number you can add to 275 without having to regroup any place values?

275

7. The length of Falling Spring Cave in Missouri is 5,305 feet. The length of Fulford Cave in Colorado is 5,279 feet.

How much longer is Falling Spring Cave than Fulford Cave?

8. The border between the United States and Canada is about 5,525 miles long. The total length of the Great Wall of China, including its branches, is about 5,500 miles.

How much longer than the Great Wall of China is the Canada/US border?

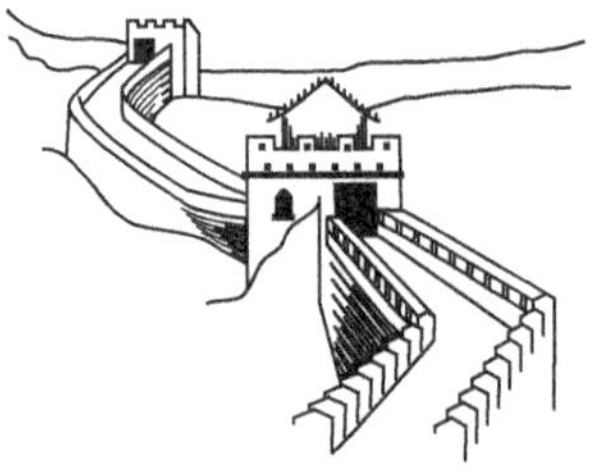

9. 2,375 tickets to a concert were sold one day, and 3,528 tickets were sold the next day.

How many tickets were sold altogether on those two days?

NBT4-26 Larger Numbers (Review)

1. Write the place value of the underlined digit.

a) $1\underline{2},643$ *thousands*

b) $\underline{2}3,121$

c) $60,\underline{1}72$

d) $\underline{9},375$

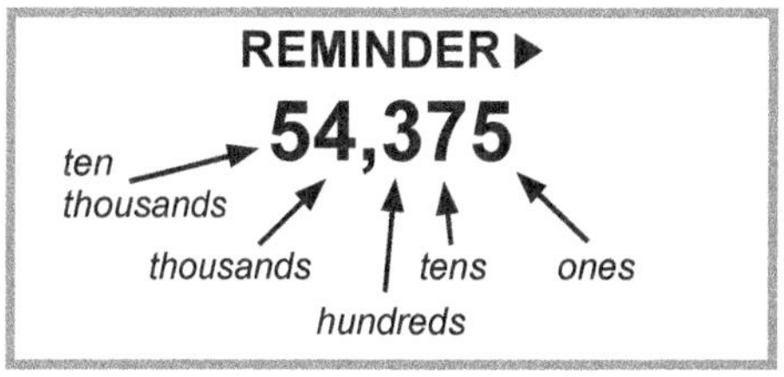

2. Write the numeral for the number words.

a) twenty-two thousand, five hundred forty-four ________________

b) one thousand, four hundred twenty ________________

c) sixty-three thousand, nine hundred thirty-six ________________

d) five hundred four thousand, ninety ________________

3. Write the number words for the numerals.

a) 61,145 = ________________________________

b) 84,929 = ________________________________

4. Write the number in expanded form (using numerals).

a) 17,359 = ________________________________

b) 72,664 = ________________________________

c) 50,137 = ________________________________

5. Circle the greater number.

a) 142,727 or 25,848

b) 632,165 or 632,166

c) 498,400 or 497,500

6. Add or subtract.

a) $\begin{array}{r} 14263 \\ +\ 72334 \\ \hline \end{array}$

b) $\begin{array}{r} 77651 \\ +\ 12348 \\ \hline \end{array}$

c) $\begin{array}{r} 81642 \\ +\ 9321 \\ \hline \end{array}$

d) $\begin{array}{r} 72347 \\ -\ 31112 \\ \hline \end{array}$

e) $\begin{array}{r} 57836 \\ -\ 17412 \\ \hline \end{array}$

f) $\begin{array}{r} 10000 \\ -\ 7162 \\ \hline \end{array}$

NBT4-27 Concepts in Number Sense

1. In a class of 62 children, 17 are boys. How many girls are in the class? Show your work. How can you check your answer using addition?

2. This table shows the lengths of the Great Lakes.

a) Write the lengths in order from shortest to longest.

b) How much longer than Lake Huron is Lake Michigan?

c) How much longer than the shortest lake is the longest lake?

Lake	Length
Lake Ontario	120 miles
Lake Superior	217 miles
Lake Michigan	191 miles
Lake Huron	128 miles
Lake Erie	150 miles

3. Use the numbers 1, 2, 3, 4, 5, 6 to make the greatest sum possible and the greatest difference possible.

$$\begin{array}{rccc} & \square & \square & \square \\ + & \square & \square & \square \\ \hline \square & \square & \square & \square \end{array} \qquad \begin{array}{rccc} & \square & \square & \square \\ - & \square & \square & \square \\ \hline & \square & \square & \square \end{array}$$

4. Find the error in Ezra's sum.

$$\begin{array}{rcc} & 2 & \\ & 4 & 5 \\ + & 2 & 7 \\ \hline & 8 & 1 \end{array}$$

5. Leonardo da Vinci, the great Italian inventor and artist, lived from 1452 to 1519.

a) How old was he when he died?

b) Leonardo painted his masterpiece the *Mona Lisa* in 1503. How old was he then?

6. Write the number that is ...

a) ten less than 1,000

b) ten more than 1,000

c) 100 less than 1,000

d) 100 more than 1,000

7. Pens cost 49¢. Erasers cost 45¢. Ben has 95¢. Does he have enough money to buy a pen and an eraser? Justify your answer.

8. Josh wants to add the numbers below. He starts by adding the ones digits. Explain why Josh wrote the number 1 above the 3 in 35.

Explain why Josh wrote the number 1 here →

$$\begin{array}{rcc} & 1 & \\ & 3 & 5 \\ + & 4 & 7 \\ \hline & & 2 \end{array}$$

9. The table gives the area of some of the largest islands in North America.

a) How much greater than the area of the smallest island is the area of the largest island?

b) How much greater is the area of Ellesmere Island than Newfoundland?

Island	Area in square miles
Baffin Island	195,928
Ellesmere Island	75,769
Newfoundland	42,031
Cuba	40,543

10. Use each of the digits 4, 5, 6, 7, 8 once to create …

a) the greatest odd number possible.

b) a number between 56,700 and 57,000.

c) an even number whose tens digit and hundreds digit add to 12.

d) a number as close to 70,000 as possible (explain how you know your answer is correct).

11. There are 321,212 species of plants and 1,234,400 species of animals.

How many more species of animals are there than plants?

12. Use the numbers 1, 2, 3, 4 once in each problem.

a)
```
   □ □
+  2 □
------
   □ 6
```

b)
```
   □ □
−  □ □
------
   1 1
```

c)
```
   □ □
+  □ □
------
   5 5
```

d)
```
  □ □ □
−     □
--------
  1 2 8
```

e)
```
   4 □
+  □ □
------
   6 □
```

f)
```
   □ □
−  □ □
------
     7
```

13. Here are some important events in the history of science.

- In 1543, Copernicus published a book claiming the Sun is the center of our solar system.
- In 1610, Galileo Galilei used his newly invented telescope to discover the moons of Jupiter.
- In 1667, Isaac Newton announced his law of gravity.

a) How long ago did Copernicus publish his book?

b) How many years passed between each event?

OA4-13 Rounding on a Number Line

1. Draw an arrow to show whether the circled number is closer to 0 or 10.

a) **0** 1 2 (3) 4 5 6 7 8 9 **10**

b) **0** 1 2 3 4 5 6 (7) 8 9 **10**

c) **0** 1 2 3 (4) 5 6 7 8 9 **10**

d) **0** 1 2 3 4 5 6 7 8 (9) **10**

2. a) Which one-digit numbers are closer to 0? ______________________

b) Which one-digit numbers are closer to 10? ______________________

c) Why is 5 a special case? ______________________

3. Draw an arrow to show if you would round to 10 or 20 or 30.

a) **10** 11 12 (13) 14 15 16 17 18 19 **20** 21 22 23 24 25 26 27 28 29 **30**

b) **10** 11 12 13 14 15 16 17 18 19 **20** 21 (22) 23 24 25 26 27 28 29 **30**

c) **10** 11 12 13 14 15 16 17 18 19 **20** 21 22 23 24 25 26 (27) 28 29 **30**

4. Draw an arrow to show which multiple of 10 the number in the circle is closest to.

a) **250** 251 252 253 254 255 256 257 (258) 259 **260**

b) **330** (331) 332 333 334 335 336 337 338 339 **340**

5. Circle the correct answer. Use the number lines in Questions 3 and 4 to help.

a) 27 is closer to: 20 or 30

b) 24 is closer to: 20 or 30

c) 19 is closer to: 10 or 20

d) 13 is closer to: 10 or 20

e) 26 is closer to: 20 or 30

f) 12 is closer to: 10 or 20

g) 251 is closer to: 250 or 260

h) 258 is closer to: 250 or 260

i) 333 is closer to: 330 or 340

j) 339 is closer to: 330 or 340

6. Draw an arrow to the nearest ten, then round each number to the nearest ten.

a) 10 11 12 (13) 14 15 16 (17) 18 19 20 21 22 23 24 25 26 27 28 (29) 30

Round to: _____ _____ _____

b) 40 41 42 43 (44) 45 46 47 48 49 50 51 52 (53) 54 55 56 57 (58) 59 60

Round to: _____ _____ _____

c) 60 61 62 63 64 65 66 67 (68) 69 70 (71) 72 73 74 75 76 (77) 78 79 80

Round to: _____ _____ _____

d) 250 251 252 (253) 254 255 256 257 258 259 260 261 262 263 (264) 265 (266) 267 268 269 270

Round to: _____ _____ _____

e) 330 331 332 (333) 334 335 336 337 338 339 340 341 342 343 (344) 345 (346) 347 348 349 350

Round to: _____ _____ _____

7. Circle the correct answer. Then round the number to the nearest ten.

a) 27 is closer to 20 or (30).
Round to ___30___.

b) 16 is closer to 10 or 20.
Round to ________.

c) 39 is closer to 30 or 40.
Round to ________.

d) 31 is closer to 30 or 40.
Round to ________.

e) 62 is closer to 60 or 70.
Round to ________.

f) 251 is closer to 250 or 260.
Round to ________.

g) 348 is closer to 340 or 350.
Round to ______.

h) 258 is closer to 250 or 260.
Round to ________.

i) 341 is closer to 340 or 350.
Round to _______.

j) 256 is closer to 250 or 260.
Round to ________.

Rounding on a Number Line (Hundreds and Thousands)

1. Draw an arrow to show whether the circled number is closer to 0 or 100.

a) 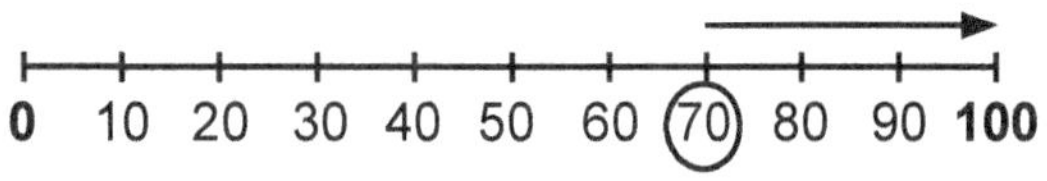

b) 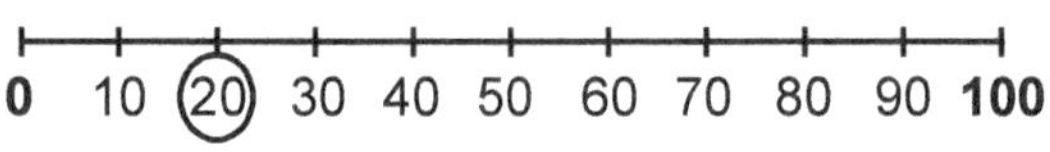

c) 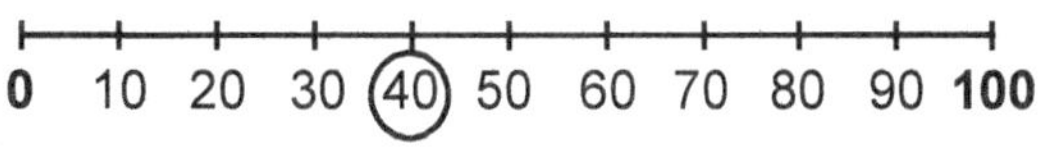

d) 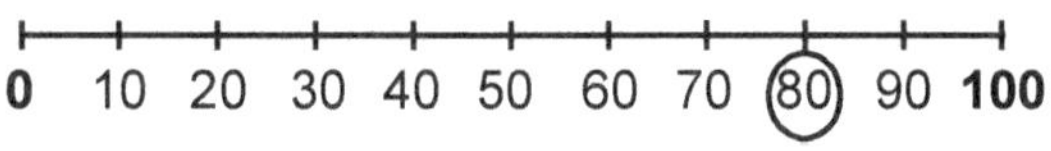

2. Is 50 closer to 0 or to 100? Why is 50 a special case?

____

3. Would you round to 0 or 100?

a) Round 80 to: 0 or 100

b) Round 40 to: 0 or 100

c) Round 10 to: 0 or 100

d) Round 60 to: 0 or 100

4. Draw an arrow to show which hundred you would round to.

a) 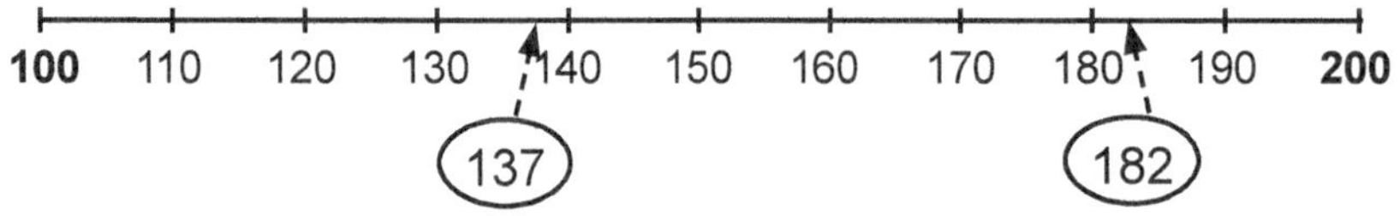

Round to: _____ _____

b) 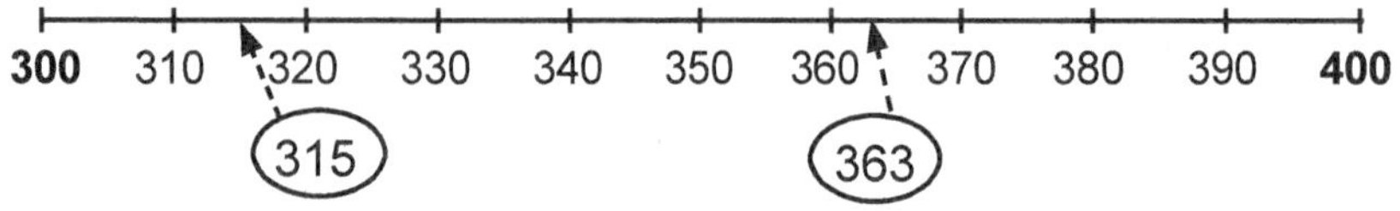

Round to: _____ _____

5. Circle the correct answer.

a) 153 is closer to: 100 or 200

b) 189 is closer to: 100 or 200

c) 117 is closer to: 100 or 200

d) 135 is closer to: 100 or 200

e) 370 is closer to: 300 or 400

f) 332 is closer to: 300 or 400

BONUS ▶

Show the approximate position of each number on the line. What hundred would you round to?

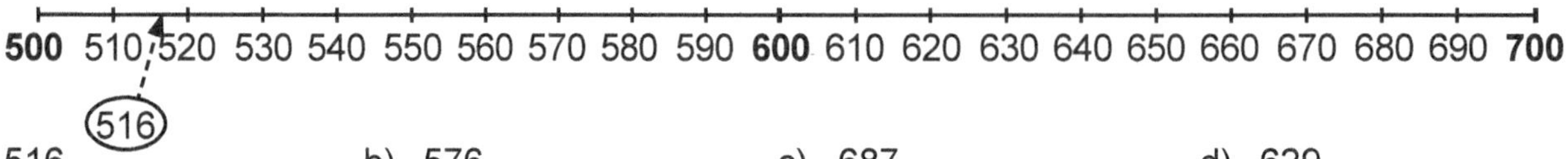

a) 516 Round to: ________

b) 576 Round to: ________

c) 687 Round to: ________

d) 629 Round to: ________

6. Draw an arrow to show whether the circled number is closer to 0 or 1,000.

a) b) c) d)

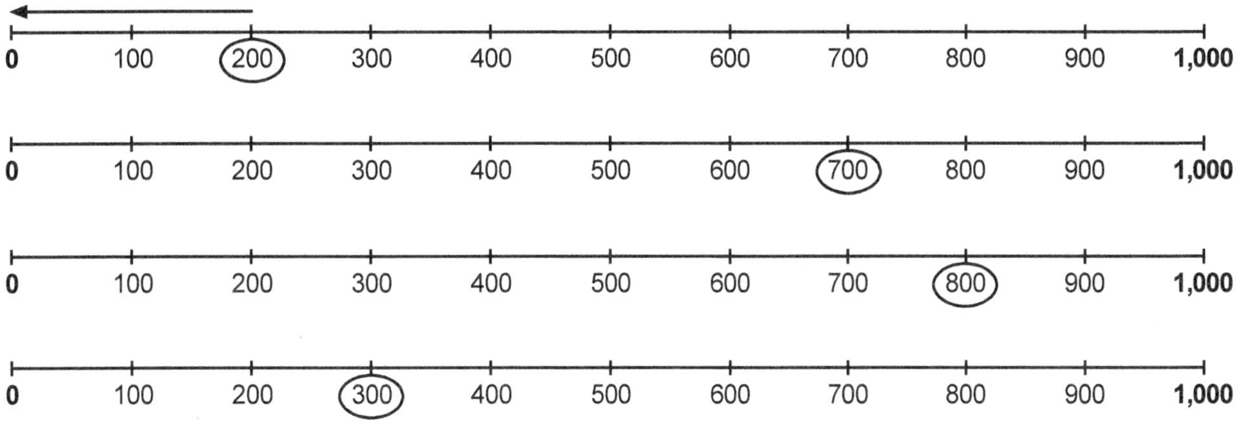

7. Is 500 closer to 0 or 1,000? Why is 500 a special case?

____

8. Circle the correct answer.

a) 100 is closer to: 0 or 1,000

b) 900 is closer to: 0 or 1,000

c) 600 is closer to: 0 or 1,000

d) 400 is closer to: 0 or 1,000

9. Draw an arrow to show which thousand you would round to.

a)

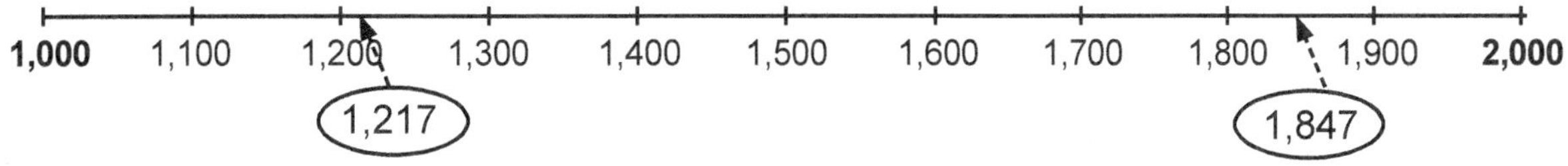

Round to: __________ __________

b)

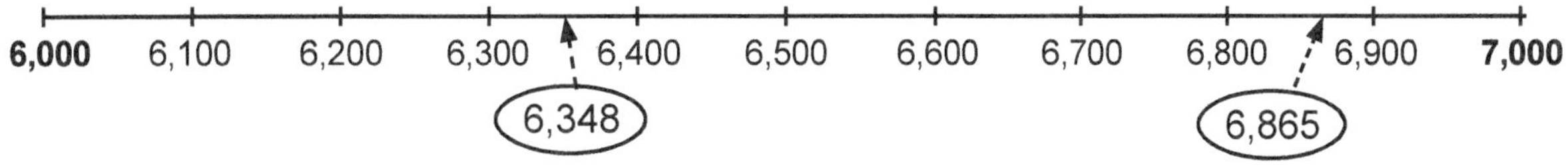

Round to: __________ __________

10. Circle the correct answer.

a) 1,953 is closer to: 1,000 or 2,000

b) 3,487 is closer to: 3,000 or 4,000

c) 6,293 is closer to: 6,000 or 7,000

d) 8,612 is closer to: 8,000 or 9,000

e) 5,521 is closer to: 5,000 or 6,000

f) 3,190 is closer to: 3,000 or 4,000

11. Write a rule for rounding a four-digit number to the nearest thousand.

OA4-15 Rounding

To round to the nearest ten, look at the ones digit.

0, 1, 2, 3, or 4—you round down
5, 6, 7, 8, or 9—you round up

1. Round to the nearest ten.

a) 16 ☐	b) 23 ☐	c) 72 ☐
d) 66 ☐	e) 81 ☐	f) 93 ☐
g) 14 ☐	h) 59 ☐	i) 65 ☐

2. Round to the nearest ten. Underline the tens digit first. Then put your pencil on the digit to the right (the ones digit). This digit tells you whether to round up or down.

a) 1<u>4</u>5 ↓ *150*	b) 172 ☐	c) 320 ☐
d) 255 ☐	e) 784 ☐	f) 667 ☐
g) 441 ☐	h) 939 ☐	i) 316 ☐
j) 520 ☐	k) 985 ☐	l) 534 ☐
m) 758 ☐	n) 845 ☐	o) 293 ☐

To round to the nearest hundred, look at the tens digit.

0, 1, 2, 3, or 4—you round down
5, 6, 7, 8, or 9—you round up

Example: 345. The 4 tells you to round down, so round 345 to 300.

3. Round to the nearest hundred. Underline the hundreds digit first. Then put your pencil on the digit to the right (the tens digit).

a) <u>3</u>40 ↓ *300*	b) 880 ☐	c) 650 ☐
d) 170 ☐	e) 240 ☐	f) 620 ☐
g) 710 ☐	h) 580 ☐	i) 980 ☐
j) 930 ☐	k) 750 ☐	l) 290 ☐
m) 851 ☐	n) 158 ☐	o) 338 ☐
p) 411 ☐	q) 658 ☐	r) 149 ☐
s) 291 ☐	t) 372 ☐	u) 868 ☐
v) 207 ☐	w) 525 ☐	x) 459 ☐

To round 2,531 to the nearest hundred, underline the hundreds digit: 2,<u>5</u>31

Then look at the tens digit. The 3 tells you to round down: 2,500

4. Round to the nearest hundred. Underline the hundreds digit first.
Then put your pencil on the digit to the right (the tens digit).

a) 2,<u>1</u>56 *2,200*   b) 4,389 ____   c) 3,229 ____

d) 1,905 ____   e) 5,251 ____   f) 9,127 ____

g) 6,472 ____   h) 8,783 ____   i) 7,255 ____

j) 1,098 ____   k) 3,886 ____   l) 4,624 ____

m) 8,077 ____   n) 6,382 ____   o) 9,561 ____

p) 2,612 ____   q) 5,924 ____

BONUS ▶

r) 2,963 ____   s) 997 ____   t) 3,982 ____

To round to the nearest thousand, look at the hundreds digit.

0, 1, 2, 3, or 4—you round down
5, 6, 7, 8, or 9—you round up

Example: 7,826. The 8 tells you to round up, so round 7,826 to 8,000.

5. Round to the nearest thousand. Underline the thousands digit first.
Then put your pencil on the digit to the right (the hundreds digit).

a) <u>2</u>,757 *3,000*   b) 9,052 ____   c) 6,831 ____

d) 3,480 ____   e) 5,543 ____   f) 4,740 ____

g) 8,193 ____   h) 2,607 ____   i) 6,107 ____

j) 9,125 ____   k) 5,114 ____   l) 7,649 ____

m) 1,336 ____   n) 9,538 ____   o) 4,226 ____

p) 7,311 ____   q) 28,644 ____   r) 32,750 ____

s) 79,928 ____   t) 91,347 ____   u) 67,812 ____

OA4-16 Rounding on a Grid

1. Underline the digit you want to round to. Then say whether you would round up or down.

a) hundreds

3	8	5	2

round up (circled)
round down

b) hundreds

2	3	4	5

round up
round down

c) hundreds

6	5	4	3

round up
round down

d) tens

7	3	4	2

round up
round down

e) tens

2	1	3	5

round up
round down

f) thousands

2	0	7	5

round up
round down

g) thousands

4	6	5	2	3

round up
round down

h) ten thousands

8	3	0	6	4

round up
round down

i) ten thousands

1	2	5	5	9

round up
round down

To round to the underlined digit:

Step 1: Decide whether to round up or down.

2	3	7	8

round up

2	3	4	5

round down

Step 2: To round up, add 1 to the digit. To round down, keep the digit the same.

2	3	7	8
	4		

2	3	4	5
	3		

Step 3: The digits to the right of the rounded digits become 0. The digits to the left remain the same.

2	3	7	8
2	4	0	0

2	3	4	5
2	3	0	0

2. Round each number to the given digit.

a) thousands

3	2	0	1

round up (ru)
round down (rd)

b) thousands

6	8	7	5

ru
rd

c) hundreds

4	3	1	7

ru
rd

d) hundreds

3	9	2	1

ru
rd

e) tens

8	6	8	1

ru
rd

f) tens

5	2	3	7

ru
rd

g) hundreds

5	0	0	7	ru
				rd

h) tens

2	8	5	7	ru
				rd

i) tens

6	3	1	2	ru
				rd

j) thousands

8	4	2	1	3	ru
					rd

k) ten thousands

7	2	1	0	3	ru
					rd

l) hundreds

9	3	5	6	8	ru
					rd

m) hundreds

1	4	2	3	7	5	ru
						rd

n) tens

2	7	5	1	3	ru
					rd

o) ten thousands

4	6	1	2	7	3	ru
						rd

If you need to round the digit 9 up, you will have to regroup.

Example: Round 3,995 to the nearest hundred.

3	$\underline{9}$	8	5
	10		

900 rounds up to 1,000

3	$\underline{9}$	8	5
4	0		

Regroup the 10 hundreds as 1 thousand and add it to the 3 thousands.

3	$\underline{9}$	8	5
4	0	0	0

Complete the rounding.

3. Round each number to the underlined place value. You will need to regroup.

a) $2,1\underline{9}5$ ______ b) $3,\underline{9}82$ ______ c) $13,2\underline{9}6$ ______ d) $46,\underline{9}81$ ______

e) $3\underline{9}5,321$ ______ f) $72\underline{9},893$ ______ g) $74,3\underline{9}9$ ______ h) $604,\underline{9}93$ ______

4. Round each number to the underlined place value (regroup if necessary).

a) $3,1\underline{9}2$ ______ b) $3\underline{9},621$ ______ c) $13,2\underline{9}1$ ______ d) $\underline{9},723$ ______

e) $\underline{9},423$ ______ f) $34\underline{9},423$ ______ g) $47\underline{9},723$ ______ h) $3\underline{9}5,321$ ______

5. Round each number to the nearest ten thousand.

a) 492,306 b) 495,306 c) 809,312 d) 849,312

OA4-17 Estimating Sums and Differences

Mathematicians use the sign $\approx$ to mean **approximately equal to**.

1. Estimate by rounding to the nearest *ten*.

a) 52 → *50* + 34 → + *30* = *80*

b) 19 + 65 → ___ + ___ = ___

c) 47 + 11 → ___ + ___ = ___

d) 95 − 62 → ___ − ___ = ___

e) 32 + 11 $\approx$ *30 + 10* = *40*

f) 74 + 32 $\approx$ ______ = ______

g) 37 + 25 $\approx$ ______ = ______

h) 84 + 28 $\approx$ ______ = ______

i) 25 + 37 $\approx$ ______ = ______

j) 28 − 12 $\approx$ ______ = ______

k) 36 + 21 $\approx$ ______ = ______

l) 85 − 17 $\approx$ ______ = ______

2. Estimate by rounding to the nearest *hundred*.

a) 170 → *200* + 350 → + *400* = *600*

b) 190 + 650 → ___ + ___ = ___

c) 470 − 110 → ___ − ___ = ___

d) 950 − 620 → ___ − ___ = ___

e) 540 + 210 $\approx$ ______ = ______

f) 550 + 330 $\approx$ ______ = ______

g) 210 + 770 $\approx$ ______ = ______

h) 750 + 220 $\approx$ ______ = ______

i) 380 + 420

j) 871 − 543

k) 483 + 283

l) 689 − 214

3. Estimate by rounding to the nearest *thousand*.

a) 1,275 → *1,000* + 3,940 → + *4,000* = *5,000*

b) 4,729 + 3,132 → ___ + ___ = ___

c) 2,570 + 634 → ___ + ___ = ___

d) 39,172 − 24,529 → ___ − ___ = ___

4. Round each number to the nearest *hundred*. Then find the sum or difference.

a) 3,272 + 1,235

b) 3,581 − 1,826

c) 4,821 − 3,670

5. Mumtaz collected 75 books for charity and Elizabeth collected 18 books.
About how many did they collect altogether?

6. Class 4A collected 287 books and class 4B collected 476 books for charity.

a) About how many books did 4A and 4B collect altogether?

b) Is your estimate higher or lower than the actual answer? How do you know?

7. A store has the following items for sale:

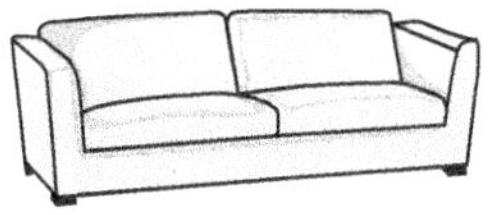

Sofa $472 Armchair $227 Table $189 Desk $382 Lamp $112

What could you buy if you had $800 to spend? Estimate to find out.
Then add the actual prices to check your estimate.

8. Daniel estimates $432 + 512$ as $400 + 500 = 900$.

a) Calculate the actual sum.

b) Is Daniel's estimate higher or lower than the actual sum?
Why does this make sense?

9. Maya adds numbers. Use estimation to decide whether her answers are reasonable.

a) $378 + 463 = 1,021$ b) $3,516 + 4,209 = 7,725$ c) $2,435 + 3,351 = 4,786$

10. Round the number to each place value given (regroup if necessary).

		Tens	**Hundreds**	**Thousands**
a)	3,485			
b)	8,502			
	BONUS ▶ 9,697			

BONUS ▶ Write every number that satisfies all three statements.

When rounded to the nearest ten, it is 6,500.
When rounded to the nearest hundred, it is 6,500.
When rounded to the nearest thousand, it is 6,000.

BONUS ▶ The estimated difference between two numbers is 400.
What might the original numbers be?

NBT4-28 Multiplying by Adding On

Marisol knows how to find 3×6 by adding three 6s ($6 + 6 + 6 = 18$). Her teacher asks her how she can find 4×6 *quickly* (without adding four 6s).

Marisol knows that 4×6 is one more 6 than 3×6. She shows this in two ways:

With a picture

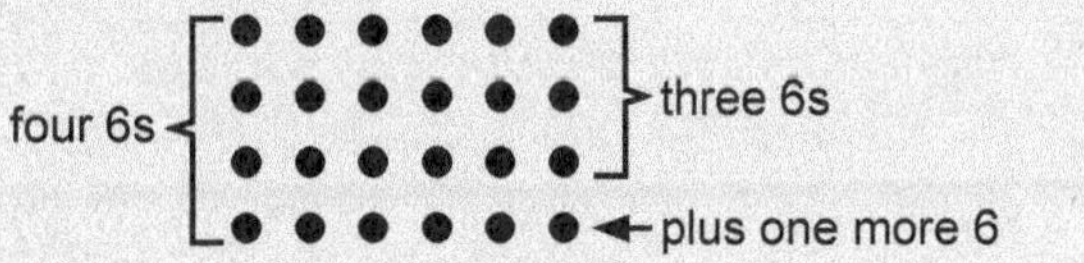

By adding

$4 \times 6 = 6 + 6 + 6 + 6$

three 6s plus one more 6

Marisol knows that $\mathbf{4} \times \mathbf{6} = \mathbf{3} \times \mathbf{6} + \mathbf{6}$.

She knows $3 \times 6 = 18$, so $4 \times 6 = 18 + 6 = 24$.

1. Write a product for each array.

a)

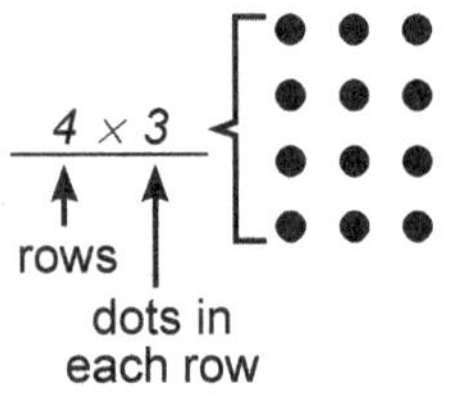

b)

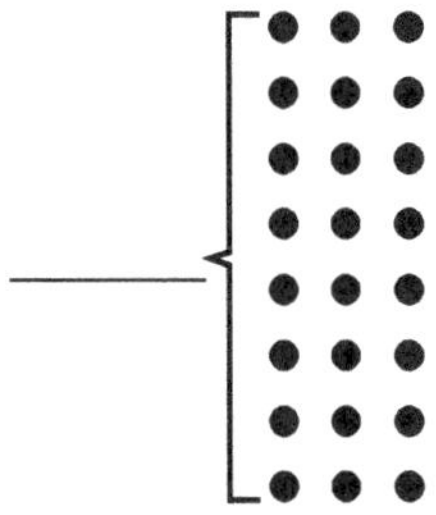

c)

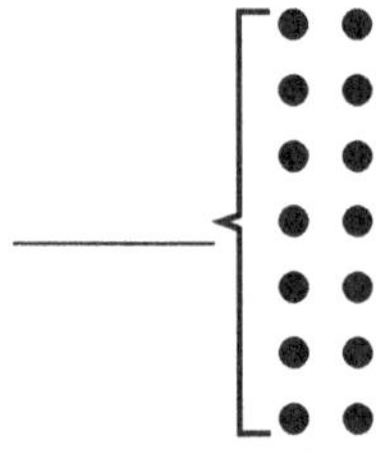

d)

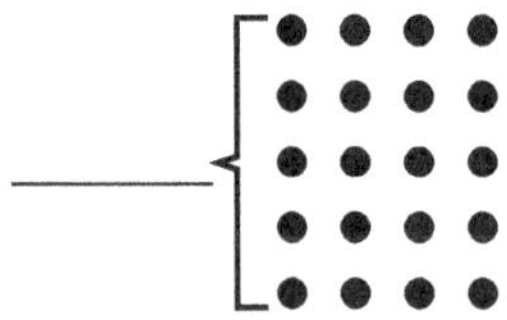

2. Fill in the missing products and number.

a)

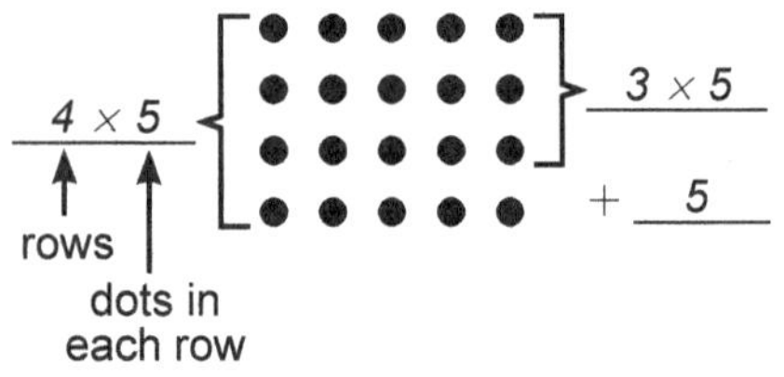

b)

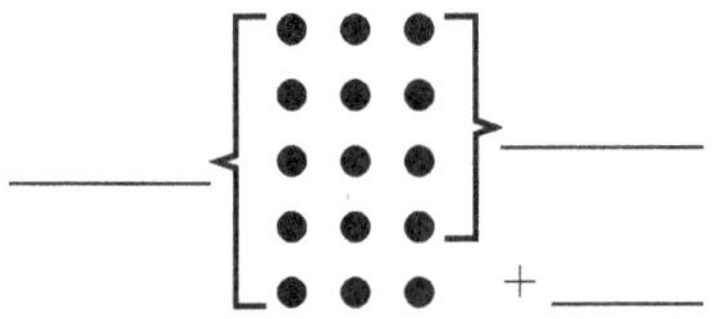

c)

d)

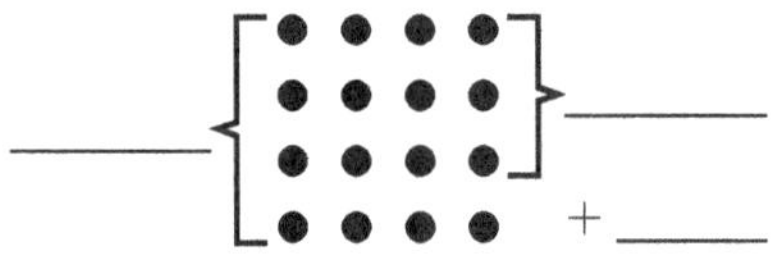

e)

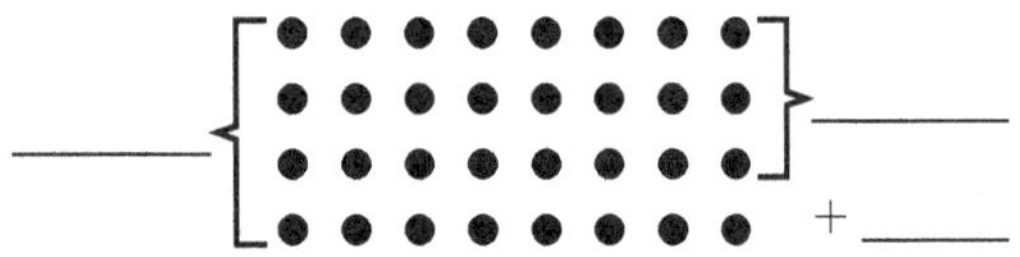

f)

3. Fill in the missing products and number. Then write an equation.

a) 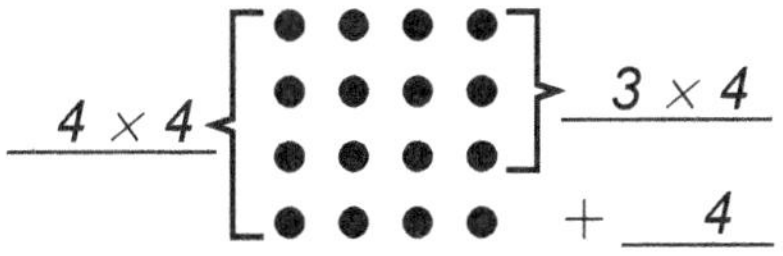

$4 \times 4 = (3 \times 4) + 4$

b) 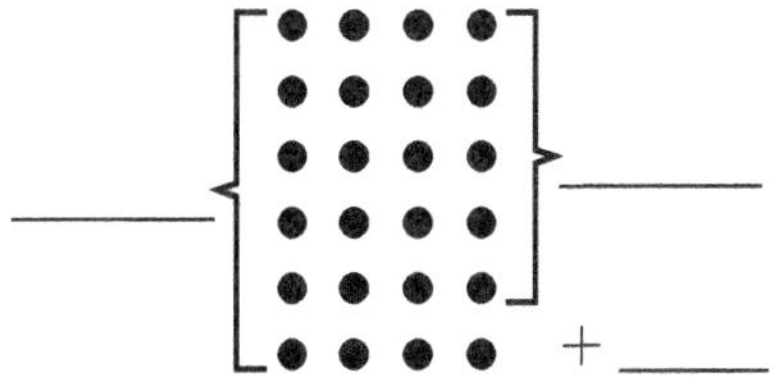

c) 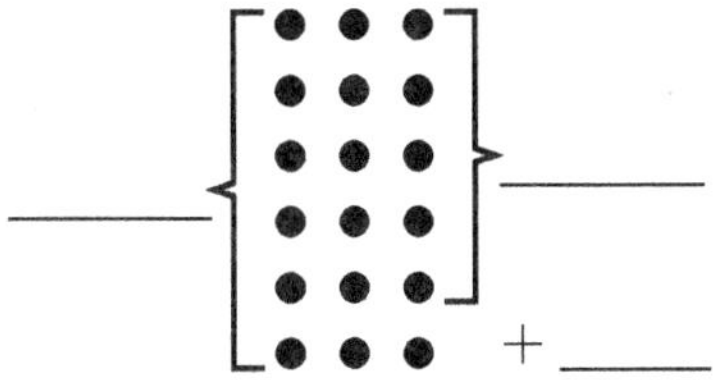

d) 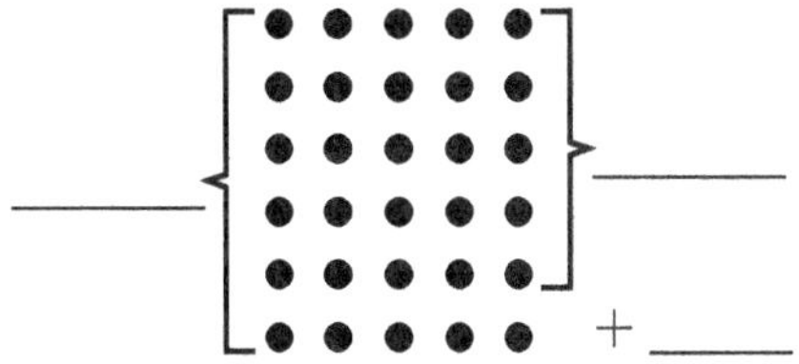

You can always turn a product into a smaller product and a sum.

$5 \times 3 = (\mathbf{4} \times 3) + \mathbf{3}$ — take 1 away from 5; add an extra 3

$9 \times 4 = (\mathbf{8} \times 4) + \mathbf{4}$ — take 1 away from 9; add an extra 4

4. Turn each product into a smaller product and a sum.

a) $4 \times 2 = (3 \times$ __2__ $) +$ __2__
b) $5 \times 7 = (4 \times$ ____ $) +$ ____
c) $8 \times 3 = (7 \times$ ____ $) +$ ____
d) $3 \times 6 = (2 \times$ ____ $) +$ ____
e) $7 \times 4 = ($____ $\times$ ____ $) +$ ____
f) $9 \times 6 = ($____ $\times$ ____ $) +$ ____
g) $5 \times 5 =$ ____________
h) $8 \times 7 =$ ____________
i) $7 \times 6 =$ ____________
j) $6 \times 4 =$ ____________

5. Find each answer by turning the product into a smaller product and a sum.

a) $5 \times 3 = (4 \times 3) + 3$
$= 12 + 3$
$= 15$

b) $6 \times 3 =$ ____________
$=$ ____________
$=$ ____________

c) $6 \times 4 =$ ____________
$=$ ____________
$=$ ____________

d) $4 \times 4 =$ ____________
$=$ ____________
$=$ ____________

e) 6×6
f) 3×7
g) 7×5
h) 6×8

NBT4-29 Multiplying Tens, Hundreds, and Thousands

To multiply 3 × 20, Christie makes 3 groups of 2 tens blocks (20 = 2 tens).

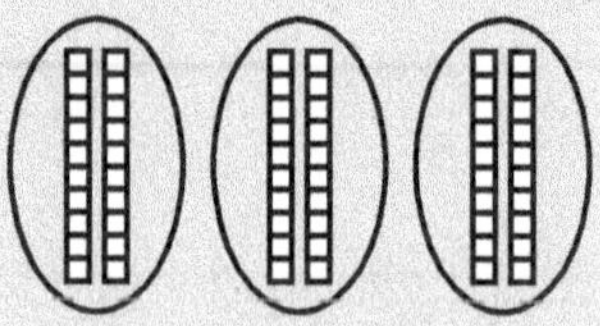

3 × 20 = 3 × 2 tens = 6 tens = 60

To multiply 3 × 200, Christie makes 3 groups of 2 hundreds blocks (200 = 2 hundreds).

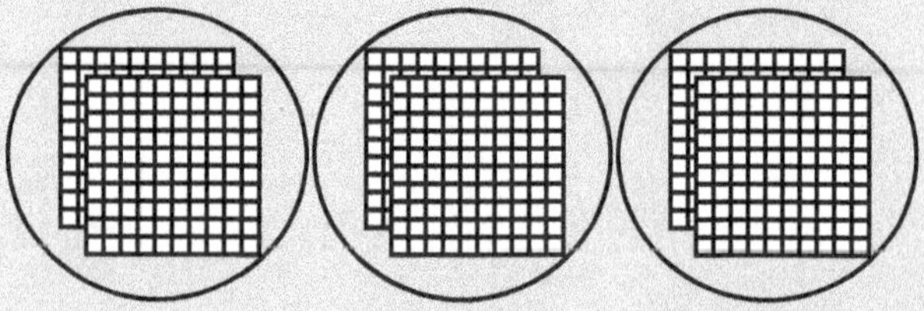

3 × 200 = 3 × 2 hundreds = 6 hundreds = 600

Christie notices a pattern: 3 × 2 = 6 3 × 20 = 60 3 × 200 = 600

1. Draw a model for each multiplication statement, then calculate the answer. The first one is started for you.

a) 4 × 20

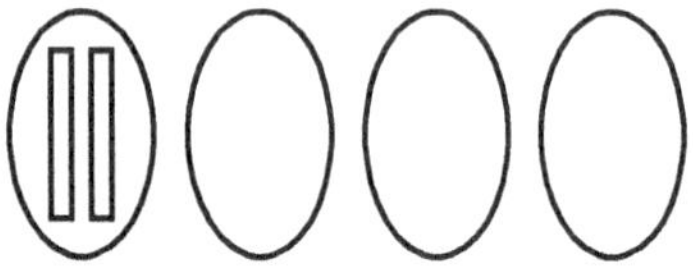

4 × 20 = 4 × _____ tens = _____ tens = _____

b) 2 × 30

2 × 30 = 2 × _____ tens = _____ tens = _____

2. Regroup to find the answer.

a) 3 × 70 = 3 × __7__ tens = __21__ tens = __210__

b) 3 × 50 = 3 × _____ tens = _____ tens = _____

c) 5 × 50 = 5 × _____ tens = _____ tens = _____

d) 4 × 60 = 4 × _____ tens = _____ tens = _____

3. Complete the pattern by multiplying.

a)	b)	c)	d)
2 × 2 = _____	5 × 1 = _____	2 × 4 = _____	3 × 3 = _____
2 × 20 = _____	5 × 10 = _____	2 × 40 = _____	3 × 30 = _____
2 × 200 = _____	5 × 100 = _____	2 × 400 = _____	3 × 300 = _____

4. Multiply.

a) 4 × 30 = _____ b) 5 × 30 = _____ c) 4 × 40 = _____ d) 2 × 50 = _____

e) 3 × 100 = _____ f) 4 × 500 = _____ g) 3 × 60 = _____ h) 6 × 400 = _____

i) 2 × 700 = _____ j) 6 × 70 = _____ k) 8 × 40 = _____ l) 2 × 900 = _____

5. Draw a base ten model to show 4 × 2,000. Use a cube to represent a thousand.

6. You know that 3 × 2 = 6. How can you use this fact to multiply 3 × 2,000?

REMINDER ▶

$10 \times$ □ $=$ 

10×1 one $= 1$ ten

$10 \times$ 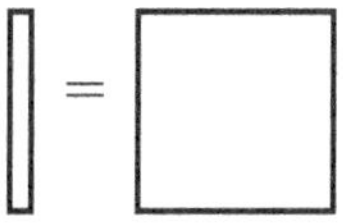

10×1 ten $= 1$ hundred

$10 \times$ 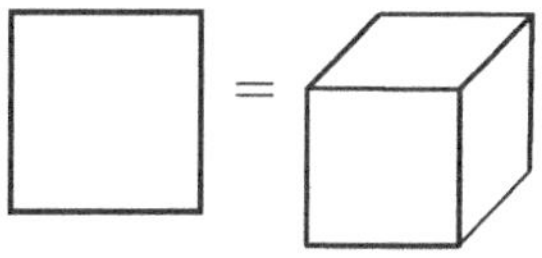

10×1 hundred $= 1$ thousand

7. Draw a model for each multiplication statement, then calculate the answer.

a) $10 \times 30 = 10 \times$ 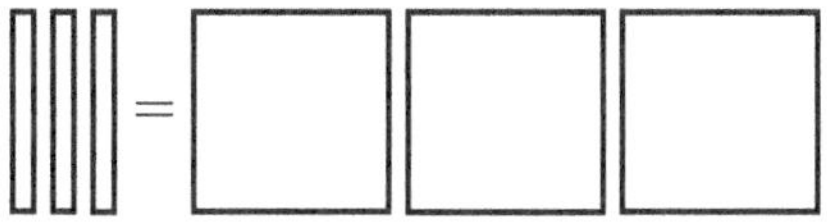 $=$ *300*

b) $10 \times 200 = 10 \times$ 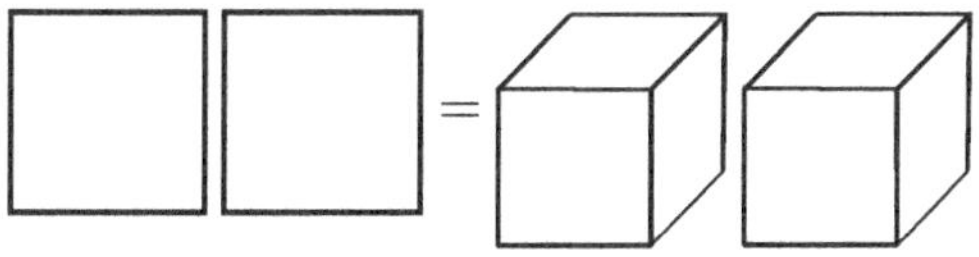 $=$ ________

c) $10 \times 40 = 10 \times$  $=$ $=$ ________

d) $10 \times 5 = 10 \times$ □□□□□ $=$ $=$ ________

e) $10 \times 20 = 10 \times$ $=$ $=$ ________

f) $10 \times 4 = 10 \times$ $=$ $=$ ________

8. Multiply.

a) $10 \times 6 =$ ________ b) $10 \times 70 =$ ________ c) $10 \times 800 =$ ________

d) $10 \times 90 =$ ________ e) $10 \times 5 =$ ________ f) $10 \times 400 =$ ________

g) $10 \times 500 =$ ________ **BONUS ▶** $10 \times 200{,}000{,}000 =$ ________________

To multiply 20 × 60, Solmaz multiplies 2 × (10 × 60).
The picture shows why this works.

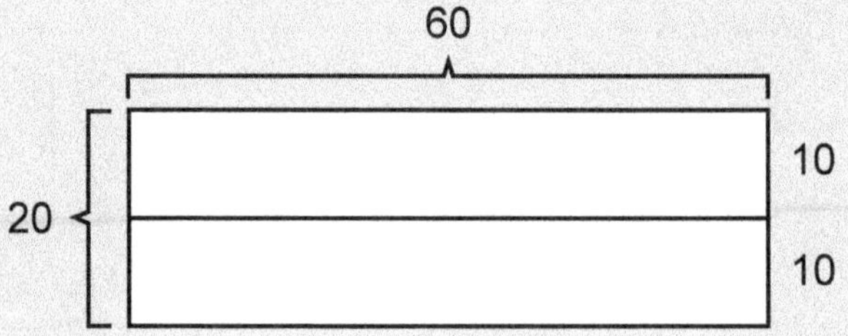

Two 10 × 60 rectangles make one 20 × 60 rectangle.

9. Multiply.

a) 20 × 60 = 2 × (10 × 60)
= 2 × _600_
= _1,200_

b) 30 × 500 = 3 × (10 × 500)
= 3 × ______
= ______

c) 40 × 800 = 4 × (10 × 800)
= 4 × ______
= ______

d) 30 × 80 = 3 × (10 × 80)
= 3 × ______
= ______

e) 70 × 600 = 7 × (10 × 600)
= 7 × ______
= ______

f) 60 × 700 = 6 × (10 × 700)
= 6 × ______
= ______

To multiply 40 × 700:
Step 1: Multiply 4 × 7 = 28.
Step 2: Write all the zeros from 40 and 700 in the answer: **4**0 × **7**00 = 28,**000**.

10. Multiply the 1-digit numbers to multiply the tens and hundreds.

a) 8 × 5 = _40_
800 × 50 = _40,000_

b) 2 × 3 = ______
20 × 300 = ______

c) 5 × 2 = ______
50 × 200 = ______

d) 8 × 7 = ______
800 × 70 = ______

e) 4 × 9 = ______
40 × 9,000 = ______

f) 5 × 6 = ______
500 × 600 = ______

g) 40 × 30 = ______

h) 300 × 50 = ______

i) 80 × 500 = ______

j) 800 × 900 = ______

k) 50 × 5,000 = ______

l) 40 × 50,000 = ______

BONUS ▶ 3,000 × 80,000 = ______

11. a) Calculate each product on a calculator.

i) 3,142 × 608
= ______

ii) 2,984 × 497
= ______

iii) 70,162 × 811
= ______

b) Use estimation by rounding to check if your answers in part a) make sense. Explain how you know. Use words such as “close to,” “higher than,” and “lower than.”

NBT4-30 Mental Math

1. Write a product for each array.

a) 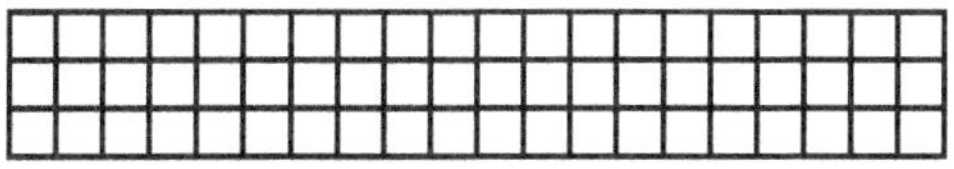

3×20

b) 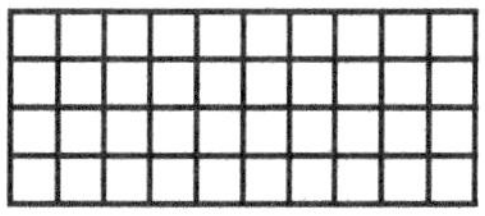

c) 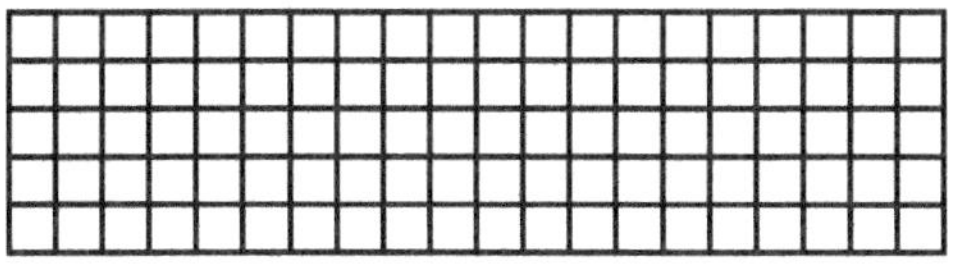

d) 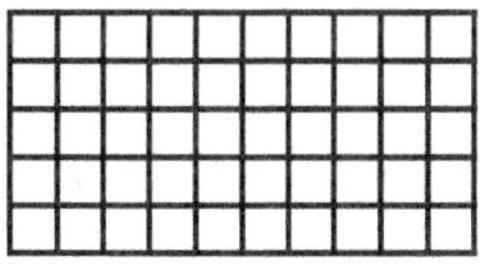

2. Write a product for the whole array and for each part of the array (as shown in part a).

a) 3×24

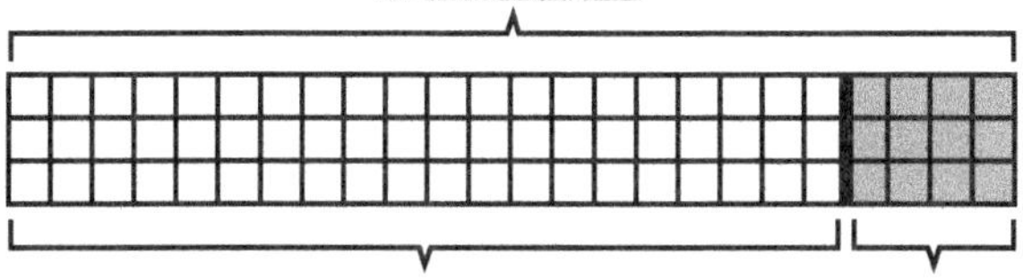

3×20 3×4

b) 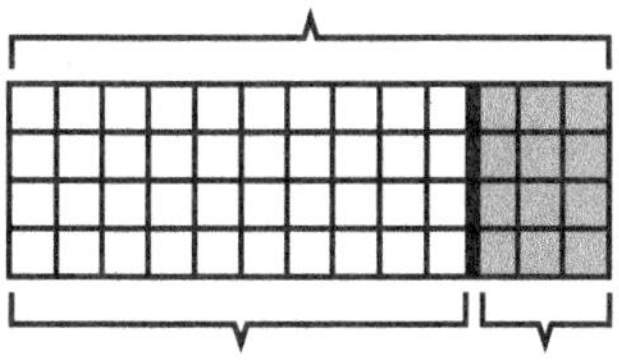

c) 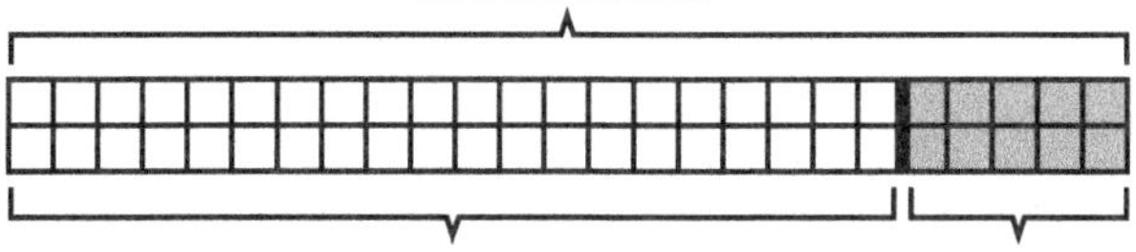

d) 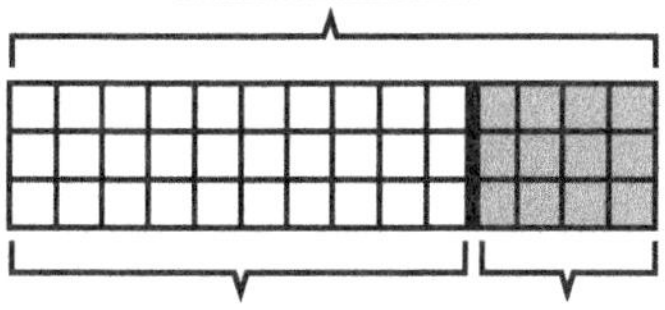

3. Fill in the blanks (as shown in part a).

a) 2×24

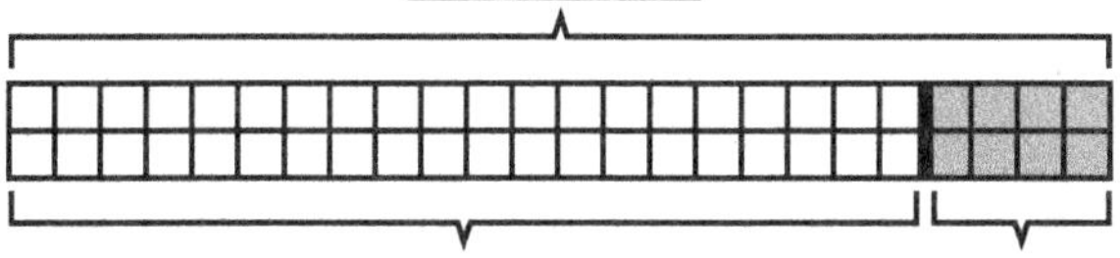

2×20 2×4

$2 \times 24 = (2 \times 20) + (2 \times 4)$

b) 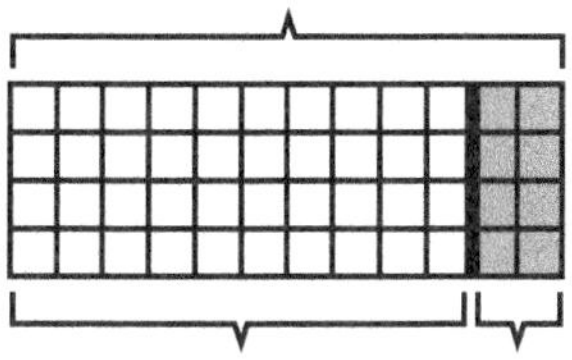

c) 4×25

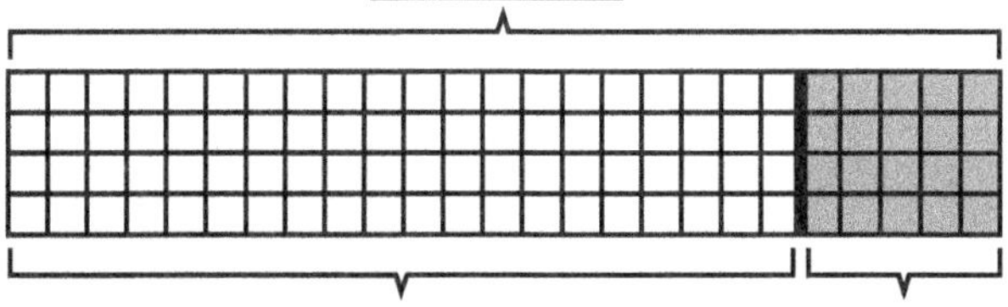

d) 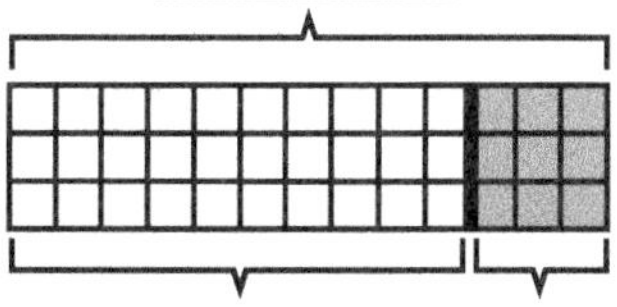

To multiply 3×23, Rosa rewrites 23 as a sum:

$23 = 20 + 3$

She multiplies 20 by 3 and then she multiplies 3 by 3:

$3 \times 20 = 60$ and $3 \times 3 = 9$

Finally she adds the results: $60 + 9 = 69$

The picture shows why Rosa's method works:

$3 \times 23 = (3 \times 20) + (3 \times 3) = 60 + 9 = 69$

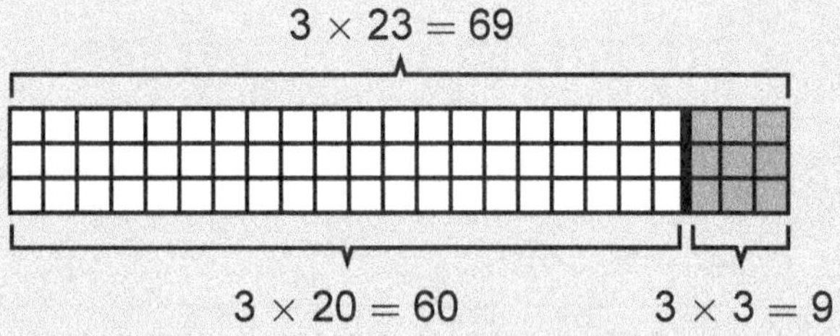

4. Rewrite each multiplication statement as a sum.

a) $2 \times 24 =$ *2 × 20* $+$ *2 × 4* b) $2 \times 23 =$ ____ $+$ ____

c) $3 \times 32 =$ ____ $+$ ____ d) $4 \times 12 =$ ____ $+$ ____

5. Multiply using Rosa's method.

a) $3 \times 13 =$ *3 × 10* $+$ *3 × 3* $=$ *30 + 9* $=$ *39*

b) $3 \times 21 =$ ____ $+$ ____ $=$ ____ $=$ ____

c) $2 \times 14 =$ ____ $+$ ____ $=$ ____ $=$ ____

d) $3 \times 213 =$ *3 × 200* $+$ *3 × 10* $+$ *3 × 3* $=$ *600 + 30 + 9* $=$ *639*

e) $2 \times 231 =$ ____ $+$ ____ $+$ ____ $=$ ____ $=$ ____

f) $2 \times 342 =$ ____ $+$ ____ $+$ ____ $=$ ____ $=$ ____

6. Multiply in your head by multiplying the digits separately.

a) $3 \times 12 =$ ____ b) $2 \times 31 =$ ____ c) $4 \times 12 =$ ____ d) $5 \times 11 =$ ____

e) $4 \times 21 =$ ____ f) $2 \times 43 =$ ____ g) $2 \times 32 =$ ____ h) $3 \times 33 =$ ____

i) $4 \times 112 =$ ____ j) $2 \times 234 =$ ____ k) $3 \times 233 =$ ____ l) $5 \times 111 =$ ____

m) $3 \times 132 =$ ____ n) $2 \times 422 =$ ____ o) $4 \times 212 =$ ____ p) $3 \times 333 =$ ____

7. Yen planted 223 trees in each of 3 rows. How many trees did she plant altogether?

8. Paul put 240 marbles in each of 2 bags. How many marbles did he put in the bags?

NBT4-31 Using Doubles to Multiply

1. Double each number.

a) double 3 is ______ b) double 2 is ______ c) double 6 is ______

d) double 4 is ______ e) double 7 is ______ f) double 8 is ______

2. Double each number mentally by doubling the ones digit and the tens digit separately.

a) double 24 is ______ b) double 14 is ______ c) double 12 is ______

d) double 13 is ______ e) double 51 is ______ f) double 43 is ______

g) double 71 is ______ h) double 84 is ______ i) double 93 is ______

3. Double the ones and tens separately and add the result.

a) double 16 is *20 + 12 = 32* b) double 26 is ______ c) double 37 is ______

d) double 29 is ______ e) double 48 is ______ f) double 19 is ______

g) double 57 is ______ h) double 67 is ______ i) double 89 is ______

If you know 3 times a number, you can double to find 6 times the number.

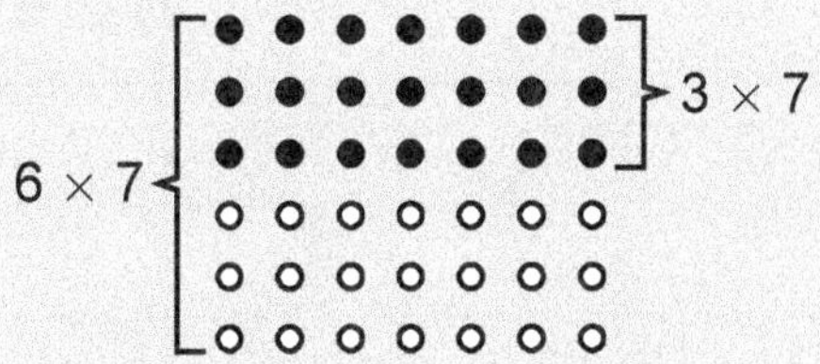

$3 \times 7 = 21$
So $6 \times 7 = 42$

4. Double 3 times the number to find 6 times the number.

a) $3 \times 2 =$ ______ so $6 \times 2 =$ ______

b) $3 \times 5 =$ ______ so $6 \times 5 =$ ______

c) $3 \times 9 =$ ______ so $6 \times 9 =$ ______

d) $3 \times 4 =$ ______ so $6 \times 4 =$ ______

e) $3 \times 6 =$ ______ so $6 \times 6 =$ ______

f) $3 \times 8 =$ ______ so $6 \times 8 =$ ______

5. Double 2 times the number to find 4 times the number. Then find 8 times the number.

a) $2 \times 7 =$ ______ so $4 \times 7 =$ ______ and $8 \times 7 =$ ______

b) $2 \times 8 =$ ______ so $4 \times 8 =$ ______ and $8 \times 8 =$ ______

c) $2 \times 6 =$ ______ so $4 \times 6 =$ ______ and $8 \times 6 =$ ______

d) $2 \times 11 =$ ______

so $4 \times 11 =$ ______

and $8 \times 11 =$ ______

e) $2 \times 9 =$ ______

so $4 \times 9 =$ ______

and $8 \times 9 =$ ______

f) $2 \times 12 =$ ______

so $4 \times 12 =$ ______

and $8 \times 12 =$ ______

6. Double 3 times the number to find 6 times the number. Then find 12 times the number.

a) $3 \times 7 =$ ______

so $6 \times 7 =$ ______

and $12 \times 7 =$ ______

b) $3 \times 8 =$ ______

so $6 \times 8 =$ ______

and $12 \times 8 =$ ______

c) $3 \times 11 =$ ______

so $6 \times 11 =$ ______

and $12 \times 11 =$ ______

d) $3 \times 6 =$ ______

so $6 \times 6 =$ ______

and $12 \times 6 =$ ______

e) $3 \times 9 =$ ______

so $6 \times 9 =$ ______

and $12 \times 9 =$ ______

f) $3 \times 12 =$ ______

so $6 \times 12 =$ ______

and $12 \times 12 =$ ______

7. Use doubling to find 16 times the number.

a) 3

$2 \times 3 = 6$

$4 \times 3 = 12$

$8 \times 3 = 24$

$16 \times 3 = 48$

b) 7

______

______

______

______

c) 9

______

______

______

______

d) 13

______

______

______

______

e) 17

______

______

______

______

f) 19

______

______

______

______

8. Use doubling to calculate the total cost mentally.

a) 2 candies for 42¢ each

b) 2 pencils for 37¢ each

c) 

d) 8 stickers for 7¢ each

e) 12 candies for 9¢ each

BONUS ▶ Use doubling to find 128×13.

NBT4-32 Standard Method for Multiplication (No Regrouping)

Clara uses a chart to multiply 3 × 42:

Step 1: She multiplies the ones digit of 42 by 3. (3 × 2 = 6)

	4	2
×		3
		6

Step 2: She multiplies the tens digit of 42 by 3. (3 × 4 tens = 12 tens)

	4	2
×		3
1	2	6

She regroups 10 tens as 1 hundred. → 1 (hundreds), 2 (tens)

1. Use Clara's method to find the products.

a) 31 × 4	b) 53 × 2	c) 41 × 4	d) 21 × 6	e) 31 × 3
f) 71 × 2	g) 62 × 3	h) 84 × 2	i) 52 × 4	j) 22 × 2
k) 21 × 5	l) 53 × 3	m) 42 × 4	n) 43 × 3	o) 64 × 2
p) 73 × 3	q) 54 × 2	r) 62 × 4	s) 72 × 3	t) 91 × 2
u) 63 × 3	v) 81 × 2	w) 51 × 5	x) 72 × 4	y) 61 × 5
z) 72 × 2	aa) 83 × 3	bb) 91 × 9	cc) 41 × 6	dd) 61 × 8
ee) 92 × 4	ff) 85 × 1	gg) 43 × 2	hh) 61 × 7	ii) 71 × 8

2. Find the following products.

a) 2 × 62 b) 2 × 74 c) 4 × 21 d) 4 × 62 e) 5 × 41 f) 7 × 21

Multiplication with Regrouping

Leo uses a chart to multiply 3 × 24:

Step 1: He multiplies 4 ones by 3. (4 × 3 = 12)

	1	
	2	4
×		3
		2

1 ← He regroups 10 ones as 1 ten.

Step 2: He multiplies 2 tens by 3. (3 × 2 tens = 6 tens)

	1	
	2	4
×		3
	7	2

He adds 1 ten to the result (6 + 1 = 7 tens). → 7

1. Using Leo's method, complete the first step of the multiplication.

a) regroup: *2*; 1 4 × 5; result: ▒ *0*

b) 1 4 × 3

c) 1 5 × 3

d) 3 6 × 2

e) 2 5 × 4

2. Using Leo's method, complete the second step of the multiplication.

a) regroup: *1*; 2 4 × 4; result: *6*

b) regroup: *1*; 1 2 × 5; result: *0*

c) regroup: *2*; 1 4 × 5; result: *0*

d) regroup: *2*; 1 4 × 6; result: *4*

e) regroup: *1*; 2 5 × 3; result: *5*

f) regroup: *1*; 3 5 × 2; result: *0*

g) regroup: *1*; 4 7 × 2; result: *4*

h) regroup: *2*; 1 8 × 3; result: *4*

i) regroup: *2*; 2 7 × 3; result: *1*

j) regroup: *3*; 1 6 × 5; result: *0*

3. Using Leo's method, complete the first and second steps of the multiplication.

a) 2 5 × 2

b) 1 6 × 6

c) 3 5 × 4

d) 3 5 × 3

e) 4 2 × 3

f) 3 4 × 3

g) 3 2 × 5

h) 3 7 × 6

i) 8 2 × 5

j) 2 3 × 7

NBT4-34 Multiplying with the 6, 7, 8, and 9 Times Tables

1. Finish the 3 times table. Double the 3 times table to write the 6 times table.

	1	2	3	4	5	6	7	8	9
the number × 3	*3*	*6*	*9*						
the number × 6	*6*	*12*	*18*						

2. Multiply by 6.

a) (carry *4*) 7 8 × 6 = _ _ *8*
b) 3 5 × 6
c) 9 6 × 6
d) 7 4 × 6
e) 8 5 × 6

f) 5 7 × 6
g) 9 3 × 6
h) 4 9 × 6
i) 2 7 × 6
j) 8 8 × 6

3. Cover the top of this page and multiply. Use grid paper to line up the place values.

a) 37 × 6 b) 98 × 6 c) 79 × 6 d) 85 × 6 e) 46 × 6

4. Finish the 2 times table. Double the 2 times table to write the 4 times table.
Then double again to write the 8 times table.

	1	2	3	4	5	6	7	8	9
the number × 2	*2*	*4*	*6*						
the number × 4	*4*	*8*	*12*						
the number × 8	*8*	*16*	*24*						

5. Multiply by 8.

a) 8 9 × 8
b) 7 6 × 8
c) 5 9 × 8
d) 9 4 × 8
e) 7 8 × 8

6. Multiply by 8. Only look at the times table when you need to. Use grid paper to line up the place values.

a) 99×8 b) 69×8 c) 68×8 d) 87×8 e) 77×8

7. Continue the pattern in the tens digits and the ones digits to write the 9 times table.

$1 \times 9 =$ ______ __9__ $6 \times 9 =$ ______ ______

$2 \times 9 =$ __1__ __8__ $7 \times 9 =$ ______ ______

$3 \times 9 =$ __2__ __7__ $8 \times 9 =$ ______ ______

$4 \times 9 =$ ______ ______ $9 \times 9 =$ ______ ______

$5 \times 9 =$ ______ ______ $10 \times 9 =$ ______ ______

8. Multiply by 9.

a) 79×9 b) 68×9 c) 28×9 d) 75×9 e) 42×9

f) 88×9 g) 66×9 h) 55×9 i) 48×9 j) 93×9

REMINDER ▶ If you know 7×9, then you know 9×7 too.

9. Use $7 \times 7 = 49$ and all the other times tables to write the 7 times table.

	1	2	3	4	5	6	7	8	9
the number × 7									

10. Use grid paper to multiply by 7. Only use the times table when you need to.

a) 36×7 b) 48×7 c) 27×7 d) 81×7 e) 18×7

f) 85×7 g) 76×7 h) 59×7 i) 94×7 j) 39×7

Multiplying a Multi-Digit Number by a 1-Digit Number

Kim multiplies 2×213 in three different ways.

1. With a chart:

	hundreds	tens	ones
	2	1	3
×			2
	4	2	6

2. In expanded form:

$$\begin{array}{r} 200 + 10 + 3 \\ \times\ 2 \\ \hline = 400 + 20 + 6 \\ = 426 \end{array}$$

3. With base ten materials:

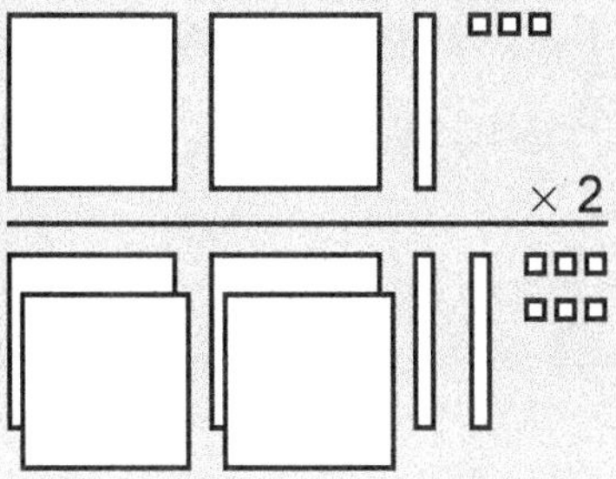

1. Rewrite the multiplication in expanded form. Then multiply.

a) 321×3

_____ + _____ + _____ × 3

= _____ + _____ + _____

= _____

b) 432×2

_____ + _____ + _____ × 2

= _____ + _____ + _____

= _____

2. Draw a picture to show the result of the multiplication.

a) 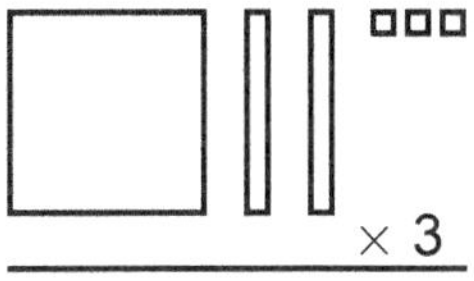

b) 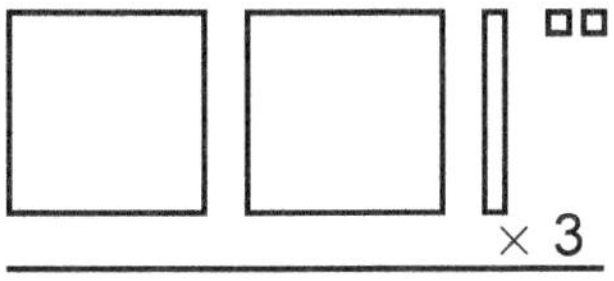

c) 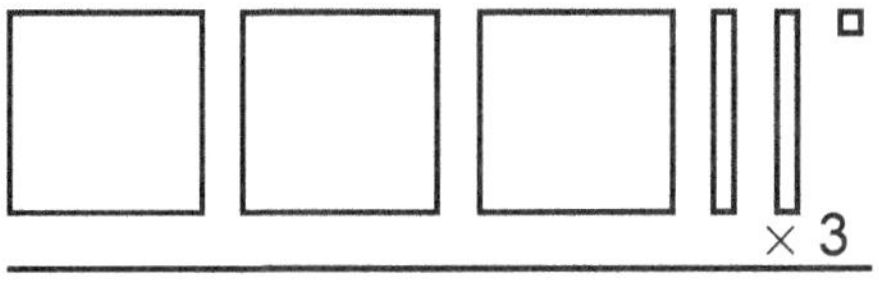

3. Multiply.

a)

1	2	4
×		2

b)

2	1	3
×		3

c)

1	2	2
×		4

d)

3	2	3
×		3

e)

4	1	3
×		2

4. Multiply by regrouping ones as tens.

a)

	1	
1	2	3
×		4
4	*9*	*2*

b)

3	2	5
×		3

c)

1	1	4
×		5

d)

3	1	6
×		2

e)

1	1	5
×		6

5. Multiply by regrouping tens as hundreds.

a)

2	4	1
×		4

b)

1	5	1
×		5

c)

2	4	2
×		3

d)

1	5	2
×		3

e)

2	5	3
×		3

6. Copy these questions onto grid paper. Multiply by regrouping where you need to.

a) 347 × 2 b) 263 × 3 c) 117 × 5 d) 232 × 4 e) 172 × 4 f) 317 × 3

Sometimes, you need to regroup hundreds as thousands. When there are no other thousands, you don't need to show the regrouping on top—you can put the regrouping in the answer right away.

Example:

2			
	5	1	2
×			4
2	0	4	8

← You don't need to write this 2 here, because there are no other thousands to add to it.

7. a) Circle the products you expect to be greater than 1,000.

i) 841 × 2 ii) 283 × 3 iii) 731 × 5 iv) 916 × 4 v) 237 × 4

b) Multiply by regrouping where you need to.

i) 841 × 2 ii) 283 × 3 iii) 731 × 5 iv) 916 × 4 v) 237 × 4

c) Were your predictions in part a) correct? If not, was the mistake in your calculation or your estimation strategy?

Sometimes you need to regroup two or three times.

Example 1:

		2	
	7	1	5
×			4
2	8	6	0

Example 2:

	1	3	
	8	3	6
×			5
4	1	8	0

8. Multiply. You will need to copy questions f) to j) onto grid paper.

a) 523 × 4 b) 631 × 5 c) 264 × 3 d) 153 × 9 e) 278 × 3

f) 4 × 247 g) 5 × 841 h) 7 × 213 i) 8 × 134 j) 3 × 738

9. Complete the 6, 7, 8, and 9 times tables.

	1	2	3	4	5	6	7	8	9
the number × 6									
the number × 7									
the number × 8									
the number × 9									

10. Multiply by regrouping where you need to.

a)

	5	8	1	3
×				6

b)

	2	8	0	9
×				7

c)

	9	6	8	7
×				8

d)

	8	0	7	9
×				8

e)

	8	6	1	5
×				6

f)

	9	7	1	3
×				7

g)

	9	6	8	7
×				9

BONUS ▶

	8	5	4	3	9	0	2	6	1	7
×										8

11. An octopus has 8 arms and 240 suckers on each arm.
How many suckers does an octopus have?

12. Kim can read 1,037 words in an hour.
How many words can she read in 8 hours?

13. A factory produces 2,847 Popsicles in a day.
How many Popsicles does the factory produce in 6 days?

14. Michael made 1,842 shirts. Each shirt has 7 buttons.
How many buttons did he use?

Word Problems with Multiplying

1. Ron bikes 10,372 yards each day. How many yards does he bike in four days?

2. On average, every American uses 147 gallons of water each day.

a) About how much water does each American use in a week?

b) About how much water would a family of 4 use in a day?

3. a) The product of 3 and 2 is 6 because $3 \times 2 = 6$. The sum of 3 and 2 is 5 because $3 + 2 = 5$. Which is greater: the sum or the product?

b) Try finding the sum and the product of different pairs of numbers. (For example, try 3 and 4, 2 and 5, 5 and 6, 1 and 7.) What do you notice? Is the product always greater than the sum?

4. Elisa multiplied two numbers, both not zero. The product was one of the numbers. What was the other number?

5. Write all the pairs of numbers you can think of that multiply to give 20.
BONUS ▶ Find all pairs of numbers that multiply to give 40.

cicada

6. A cicada can burrow into the ground and stay there for 10 years.

a) How many months can a cicada stay in the ground?

b) Sometimes, cicadas stay in the ground for up to 20 years.
How can you use your answer in part a) to find out how many months this is?

7. There are 4 ways to put 6 dots into arrays so that each row contains the same number of dots.

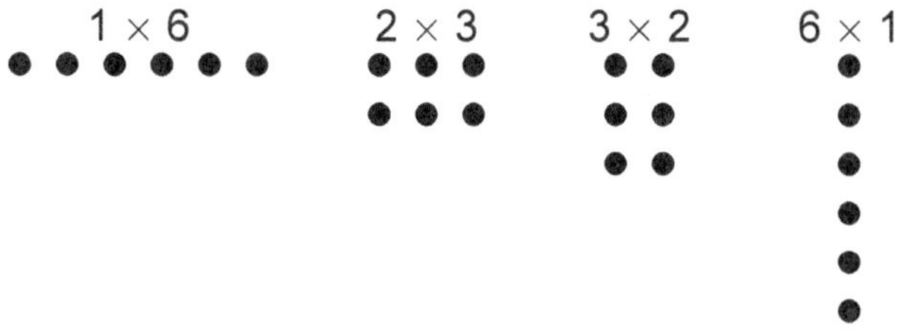

How many ways can you put each number of dots into one or more equal rows? Write a multiplication statement for each array.

a) 4 dots b) 8 dots c) 12 dots d) 16 dots

8. Roger rode a horse around a six-sided field with each side 355 yards long. How far did he ride?

NBT4-37 Multiplying 2-Digit Numbers by Multiples of 10

Erin wants to multiply 20×32. She knows how to find 2×32.
She rewrites 20×32 as $(10 \times 2) \times 32$:

$$\begin{aligned} 20 \times 32 &= (10 \times 2) \times 32 \\ &= 10 \times (2 \times 32) \\ &= 10 \times 64 \\ &= 640 \end{aligned}$$

The picture shows why this works:
a 20×32 array contains the same number of squares as ten 2×32 arrays.

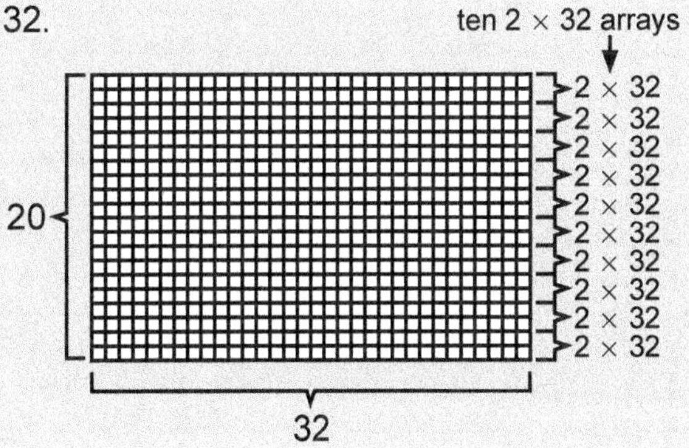

1. Rewrite the product using Erin's method.

a) $20 \times 33 =$ *$10 \times (2 \times 33)$*   b) $20 \times 22 =$ ________

c) $30 \times 13 =$ ________   d) $50 \times 41 =$ ________

2. Find the product.

a) $40 \times 12 =$ *10* × (*4* × *12*)
$=$ *10×48*
$=$ *480*

b) $60 \times 21 =$ ____ × (____ × ____)
$=$ ________
$=$ ________

c) $40 \times 22 =$ ____ × (____ × ____)
$=$ ________
$=$ ________

d) $50 \times 31 =$ ____ × (____ × ____)
$=$ ________
$=$ ________

3. Find the product mentally.

a) $30 \times 22 =$ ____   b) $20 \times 40 =$ ____   c) $20 \times 60 =$ ____   d) $40 \times 32 =$ ____

e) $20 \times 41 =$ ____   f) $30 \times 92 =$ ____   g) $51 \times 20 =$ ____   h) $30 \times 63 =$ ____

i) $60 \times 41 =$ ____   j) $61 \times 50 =$ ____   k) $70 \times 30 =$ ____   l) $80 \times 20 =$ ____

4. Estimate the product. Hint: Round each number to the nearest ten.

a) $27 \times 39 \approx$ *$30 \times 40 = 1{,}200$*   b) $43 \times 51 \approx$ ________

c) $22 \times 47 \approx$ ________   d) $62 \times 41 \approx$ ________

e) $72 \times 49 \approx$ ________   f) $38 \times 17 \approx$ ________

5. Find the product.

a) $30 \times 27 =$ *10 × (3 × 27)* ← rough work here

$=$ *10 × 81*

$=$ *810*

	2	
	2	7
×		3
	8	*1*

b) $50 \times 15 =$ _____ × (_____ × _____)

$=$ __________

$=$ ________

×		

c) $30 \times 24 =$ _____ × (_____ × _____)

$=$ __________

$=$ ________

×		

d) $40 \times 15 =$ _____ × (_____ × _____)

$=$ __________

$=$ ________

×		

You can use a chart to find $40 \times 57 = 10 \times (4 \times 57)$.

Step 1: 10 × (4 × 57)
When you multiply a number by 10, you add a zero. So write a zero in the ones place because you will multiply (4 × 57) by 10.

		5	7
×		4	0
			0

Steps 2 and 3: 10 × (**4** × **57**)
Now multiply 57 by 4.

Regroup the 2 in the hundreds place because you are really multiplying 7 by 40, not 4.

	2		
		5	7
×		4	0
		8	*0*

	2		
		5	7
×		4	0
2	*2*	*8*	*0*

6. Practice the first two steps of the multiplication. Note: In one of the problems, you will not need to regroup the hundreds.

a)

	2		
		1	5
×		5	0
		5	*0*

b)

		2	4
×		3	0
			0

c)

		1	5
×		4	0
			0

d)

		2	5
×		3	0

e)

		1	2
×		4	0

7. Multiply.

a)

			1	3
×			6	0

b)

			5	5
×			2	0

c)

			3	4
×			4	0

d)

			2	5
×			4	0

e)

			4	3
×			5	0

f) 28 × 30 g) 36 × 20 h) 27 × 40 i) 23 × 60 j) 43 × 70

 # Multiplying 2-Digit Numbers by 2-Digit Numbers

To multiply 37 × 25, split 25 into two numbers that are easier to multiply by. The picture shows why this works.

a multiple of 10 ↘ ↙ a 1-digit number

37 × 25 = 37 × **20** + 37 × **5**

= 740 + 185

= 925

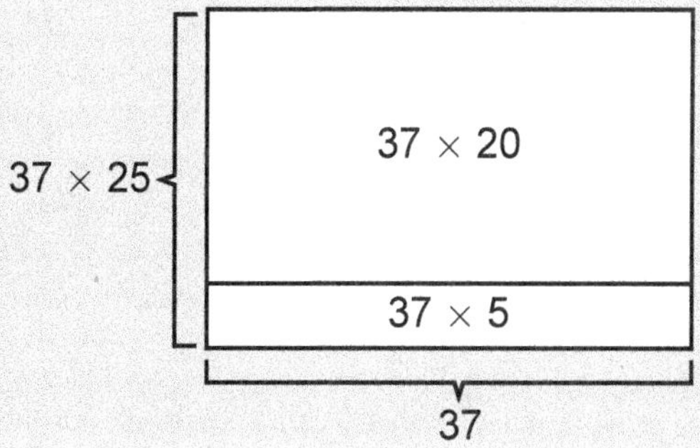

1. Find each product by rewriting the second number as the sum of a 1-digit number and a multiple of 10.

a) 65 × 27

= 65 × (20 + 7)

= 65 × 20 + 65 × 7

= 1,300 + 455

= 1,755

	1			
		6	5	
×		2	0	
1	3	0	0	

	3		
	6	5	
×		7	
4	5	5	

add here

		4	5	5
+	1	3	0	0
	1	7	5	5

b) 54 × 23

= ____ × (____ + ____)

= ____

= ____

= ____

c) 81 × 27

= ____ × (____ + ____)

= ____

= ____

= ____

d) 72 × 45

= ____

= ____

= ____

= ____

You can record the steps in multiplying 2-digit numbers on a grid.

Example: Find 37 × 25.

Step 1: Calculate 37 × 5.

Step 2: Calculate 37 × 20.

Step 3: Add the results.

	1	3	
	3	7	
×	2	5	
1	8	5	← 37 × 5
7	4	0	← 37 × 20
9	2	5	

2. Practice Step 1.

a)

	1		
	1	4	
×	3	4	
	5	6	= 14 × 4

b)

	2	3	
×	1	5	
			= 5 × 23

c)

	2	4
×	1	3

d)

	2	6
×	4	2

e)

	3	4
×	1	3

f)

	2	5
×	4	2

g)

	3	6
×	4	2

h)

	2	4
×	4	5

3. Practice Step 2.

a)

	1	1		
		2	3	
×		4	5	
	1	1	5	
	9	2	0	= 23 × 40

b)

		2		
		3	5	
×		6	4	
	1	4	0	
			0	= 35 × 60

c)

		2	
		2	4
×		3	6
	1	4	4
			0

d)

		1	
		3	5
×		4	3
	1	0	5

e)

		1	
		4	3
×		5	4
	1	7	2

f)

		7	1
×		3	2
	1	4	2

g)

		4	3
×		3	2
		8	6

h)

		1	
		6	4
×		3	3
	1	9	2

4. Practice Steps 1 and 2.

a) Regrouping 56 × 50; Regrouping 56 × 2

		5	6	
×		5	2	
				= 56 × 2
			0	= 56 × 50

b)

		3	5	
×		2	6	

c)

		2	5	
×		3	7	

d)

		2	3	
×		3	4	

e)

		6	5
×		4	3

f)

		4	5
×		3	2

g)

		3	3
×		4	4

h)

		1	5
×		4	6

5. Complete the multiplication by adding the numbers in the last two rows of the chart.

a)

			1	
			1	2
×			3	8
			9	*6*
+		*3*	*6*	*0*
		4	*5*	*6*

b)

		1	*4*	
			2	8
×			2	6
		1	*6*	*8*
+		*5*	*6*	*0*

c)

		4	*2*	
			5	7
×			6	3
		1	*7*	*1*
+	*3*	*4*	*2*	*0*

d)

			8	1
×			3	5
		4	*0*	*5*
+	*2*	*4*	*3*	*0*

6. Multiply.

a)

			2	8
×			3	4
+				

b)

			2	5
×			3	3
+				

c)

			4	3
×			5	2
+				

d)

			6	3
×			2	7
+				

7. Find the products.

a) 27 × 32 b) 56 × 73 c) 85 × 64 d) 19 × 93 e) 74 × 86 f) 64 × 98

NBT4-39 Topics in Multiplication

1. Kyle has 2 stickers. Ravi has 8 stickers.

Ravi has ______ times as many stickers as Kyle.

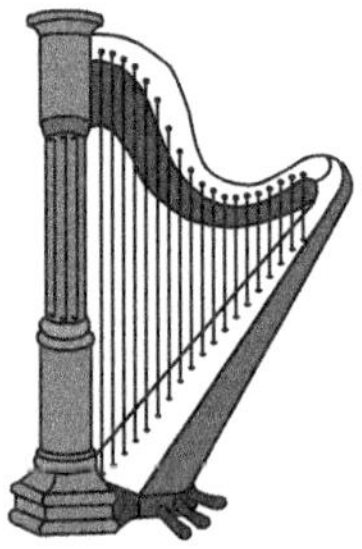

2. A bee has 6 legs. How many legs do 325 bees have?

3. A harp has 47 strings. How many strings do 12 harps have?

4. Explain why the product of two 2-digit numbers must be at least 100.

____

____

5. A hummingbird flaps its wings 15 times a second. How many times does it flap its wings in a minute?

6. How many hours are there in the month of January?

7. Use the digits 3, 4, and 5 to make ...

a) the greatest product

☐ × ☐☐

b) the least product

☐ × ☐☐

8. Use the digits 1, 2, 3, and 4 to make ...

a) the greatest product

☐ × ☐☐☐

b) the least product

☐ × ☐☐☐

9. Find the first four products. Use the pattern in the products to find the products in parts e) and f) without multiplying.

a)

		3	7
×			9

b)

		3	7
×		1	2
+			

c)

		3	7
×		1	5
+			

d)

		3	7
×		1	8
+			

e)

		3	7
×		2	1

f)

		3	7
×		2	4

10. Find the products.

a) 0 × 5 = ______ b) 0 × 7 = ______ c) 0 × 9 = ______ d) 17 × 0 = ______

11. Erin multiplied a number by 5 and got 0. What was the original number? ______

OA4-18 Sets and Sharing

Elisa has 12 glasses of water. A tray holds 3 glasses. There are 4 trays.

Question:	**Answer:**
What has been shared or divided into **sets** or **groups**?	*Glasses*
How many sets are there?	*There are 4 sets of glasses.*
How many of the things being divided are in each set?	*There are 3 glasses in each set.*

1. a)

What has been shared or divided into sets?

____

How many sets? __________

How many in each set? __________

b)

What has been shared or divided into sets?

____

How many sets? __________

How many in each set? __________

2. Using *circles* for sets and *dots* for things, draw a picture to show …

a) 4 sets
6 things in each set

b) 6 groups
3 things in each group

c) 6 sets
2 things in each set

d) 4 groups
5 things in each group

3. Complete the table.

		What has been shared or divided into sets?	How many sets?	How many in each set?
a)	20 toys 4 toys for each child 5 children	*20 toys*	*5*	*4*
b)	7 friends 21 pencils 3 pencils for each friend			
c)	16 students 4 desks 4 students at each desk			
d)	8 plants 24 flowers 3 flowers on each plant			
e)	6 grapefruits in each box 42 grapefruits 7 boxes			
f)	3 school buses 30 children 10 children in each school bus			
g)	6 puppies in each litter 6 litters 36 puppies			
h)	28 markers 4 kids 7 markers for each kid			
i)	4 boxes 24 markers 6 markers in each box			

BONUS ▶ Draw pictures for Questions 3 a), b), and c) using *circles* for sets and *dots* for the things being divided.

Kate wants to share 12 cookies with three friends.
She sets out four plates (one for herself and one for each of her friends).

She puts one cookie at a time on each plate:

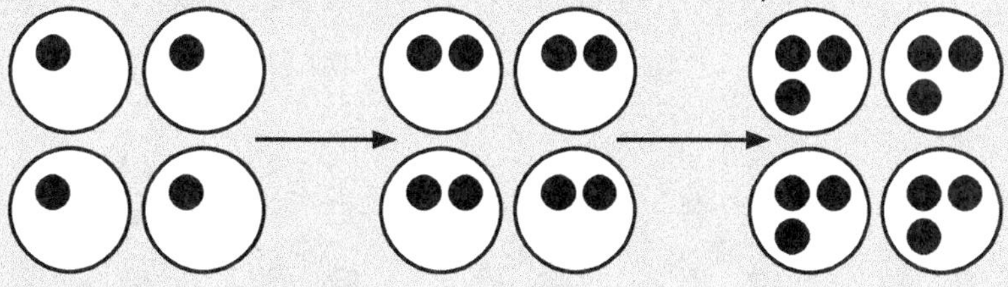

Each plate holds a **set** (or group) of 3 cookies.
When 12 cookies are **divided** (or shared equally) into 4 sets, there are 3 cookies **in each set**.

4. Put an equal number of cookies on each plate the way Kate did.
Draw the plates, then place one cookie at a time.

a) 12 cookies; 3 plates

b) 16 cookies; 4 plates

5. Draw dots for the things being shared or divided equally. Draw circles for the sets.

a) 2 vans; 8 people
How many people in each van?

b) 3 kids; 9 stickers
How many stickers for each kid?

c) 20 flowers; 5 plants
How many flowers on each plant?

d) 12 grapefruits; 6 boxes
How many grapefruits in each box?

6. Five friends shared 20 cherries equally. How many cherries did each friend get?

7. Eileen shared 20 stickers among 3 friends and herself. How many stickers did each person get?

8. There are 16 apples in 8 trees. How many apples are in each tree?

OA4-19 Sharing When You Know the Number in Each Set

Samuel has 30 apples. He wants to give 5 apples to each of his friends.

To find out how many friends he can give apples to, he counts out **sets** (or **groups**) of 5 apples until he has used all 30 apples.

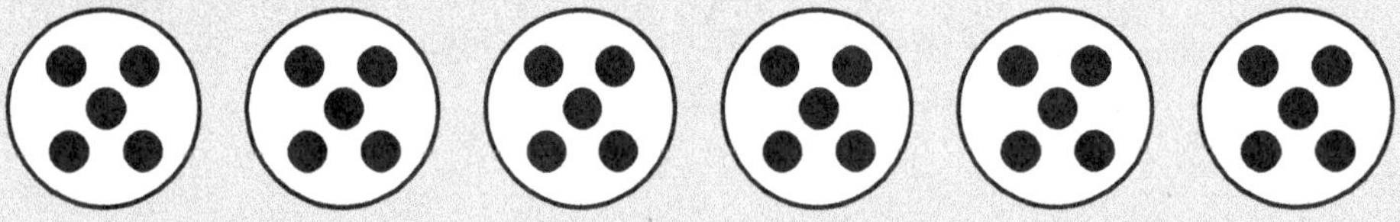

He can give apples to 6 friends. When 30 apples are divided into sets of 5 apples, there are 6 sets.

1. Put the correct number of dots in each set. The first one has been done for you.

a) 
4 dots in each set

b) 
5 dots in each set

c) 
3 dots in each set

2. Draw circles to divide these arrays into …

a) groups of 3
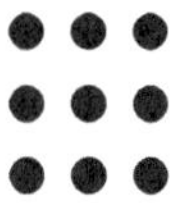

b) groups of 4
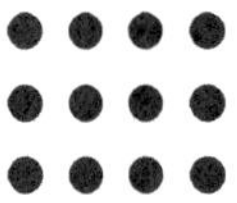

c) groups of 3
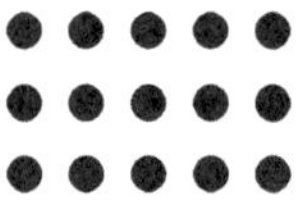

d) groups of 4
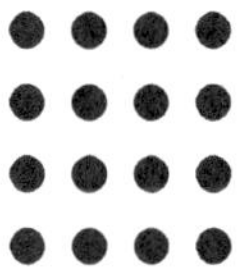

3. Draw dots for the things being shared or divided equally. Draw circles for the sets.

a) 15 apples; 5 apples in each box
How many boxes?

_______ boxes

b) 10 stickers; 2 stickers for each kid
How many kids?

_______ kids

4. Shelly has 18 cookies. She gives 3 cookies to each of her siblings.
How many siblings does she have?

5. Mumtaz has 14 stamps. He puts 2 stamps on each envelope.
How many envelopes does he have?

OA4-20 Two Ways of Sharing

Samuel has 15 cookies. There are two ways he can share or **divide** the cookies equally:

Method 1: Decide how many sets (or groups) **to make.**

Example: Samuel wants to make 3 sets of cookies. He draws 3 circles:
He puts one cookie at a time into the circles until he has placed all 15 cookies.

Method 2: Decide how many will be in each set.

Example: Samuel wants to put 5 cookies in each set. He counts out 5 cookies:
He counts out sets of 5 until he has placed all 15 cookies.

Use Method 1 to do Questions 1, 2, and 3.

1. Share **20** dots equally. How many dots are in each set? Hint: Place one dot at a time.

a) 4 sets:

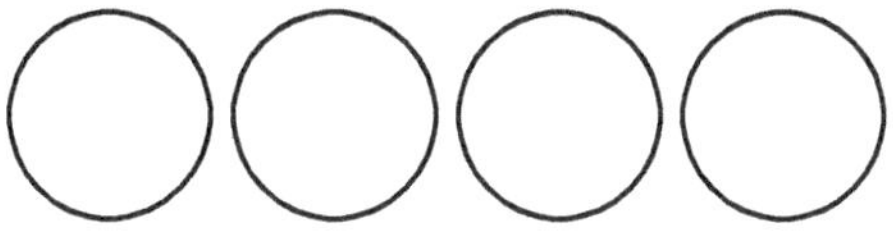

There are ______ dots in each set.

b) 5 sets:

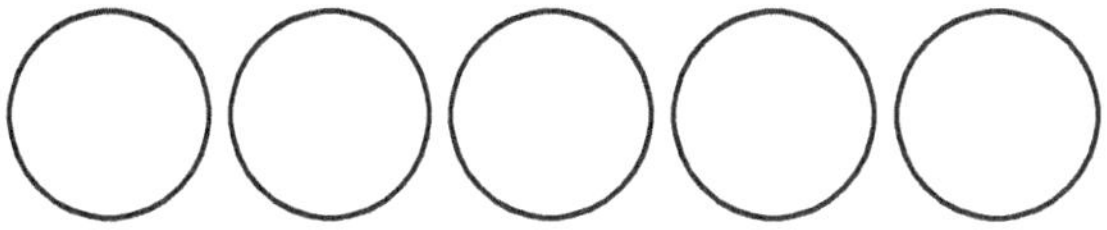

There are ______ dots in each set.

2. Share the triangles equally among the sets. Hint: Count the triangles first.

a)

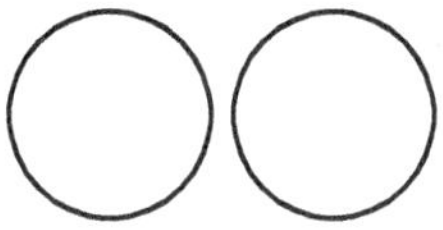

b)

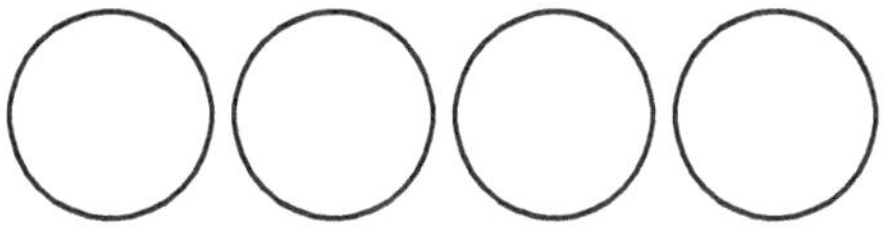

3. Share the squares equally among the sets.

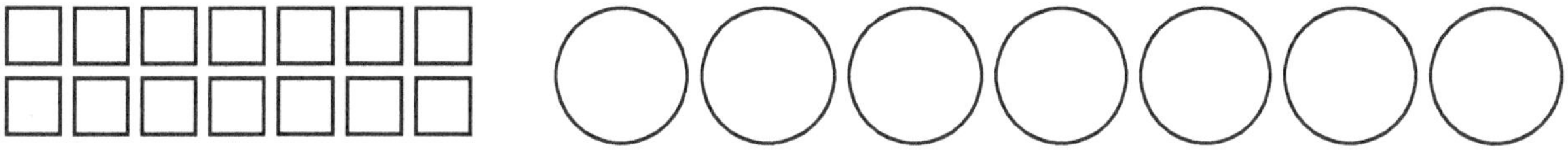

Use Method 2 to do Questions 4 and 5.

4. Group the lines so that there are 3 lines in each set.

a) | | | | | | | | |

There are ______ sets.

b) | | | | | | | | | | | |

There are ______ sets.

c) | | | | | |

There are ______ sets.

5. Group **12** dots so that …

a) there are 6 dots in each set.

b) there are 4 dots in each set.

6. For each part, fill in what you know. Write a question mark for what you don't know.

		What has been shared or divided into sets?	How many sets?	How many in each set?
a)	Vanessa has 25 pencils. She puts 5 pencils in each box.	*25 pencils*	*?*	*5*
b)	30 children are in 10 boats.	*30 children*	*10*	*?*
c)	Ben has 36 stickers. He gives 9 stickers to each of his friends.			
d)	Donald has 12 books. He puts 3 on each shelf.			
e)	15 girls sit at 3 tables.			
f)	30 students are in 2 school buses.			
g)	9 fruit bars are shared among 3 children.			
h)	15 chairs are in 3 rows.			
i)	Each basket holds 4 eggs. There are 12 eggs altogether.			

7. Draw a picture using dots and circles to solve each part of Question 6.

8. Draw a picture using dots and circles to show the answer.

a) 15 dots; 5 sets

____ dots in each set

b) 16 dots; 8 dots in each set

____ sets

c) 15 dots; 5 dots in each set

____ sets

d) 8 dots; 4 sets

____ dots in each set

e) 10 children are in 2 boats.

How many children are in each boat? ____

f) Paul has 12 pencils.
He puts 3 pencils in each box.

How many boxes does he have? ____

g) 4 boys share 12 marbles.

How many marbles does each boy get? ____

h) Pamela has 10 apples.
She gives 2 apples to each friend.

How many friends receive apples? ____

i) 6 children go sailing in 2 boats.

How many children are in each boat? ____

j) Alan has 10 stickers.
He puts 2 on each page.

How many pages does he use? ____

OA4-21 Division, Addition, and Multiplication

Every division equation can be rewritten as an *addition equation* and a *multiplication equation*.

Example: "15 divided into sets of size 3 equals 5 sets" gives

"adding 3 five times equals 15" and "5 groups of 3 equals 15"

$3 + 3 + 3 + 3 + 3 = 15$

$5 \times 3 = 15$

1. Draw a picture and write addition and multiplication equations for each division equation.

a) $8 \div 2 = 4$

$2 + 2 + 2 + 2 = 8$

$4 \times 2 = 8$

b) $12 \div 6 = 2$

____

____

c) $12 \div 3 = 4$

____

____

2. Draw a picture and write a division equation for each multiplication or addition equation.

a) $3 \times 4 = 12$

$12 \div 4 = 3$

b) $3 \times 6 = 18$

____

c) $5 + 5 + 5 + 5 = 20$

____

d) $2 \times 5 = 10$

____

e) $5 \times 3 = 15$

____

f) $9 + 9 = 18$

____

OA4-22 Dividing by Skip Counting

You can divide by skip counting on a number line. Example: Solve the problem **15 ÷ 3 = ?.**

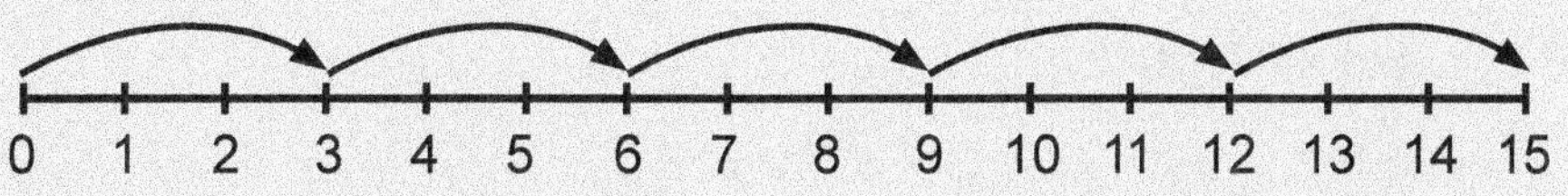

It takes 5 skips of size 3 to get 15: **3 + 3 + 3 + 3 + 3 = 15**, so **15 ÷ 3 = 5.**

1. Draw a picture and complete the division equation.

a)

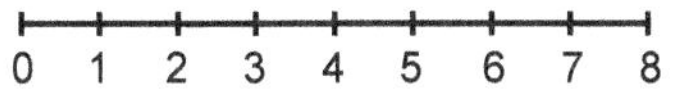

8 ÷ 2 = ________

b)

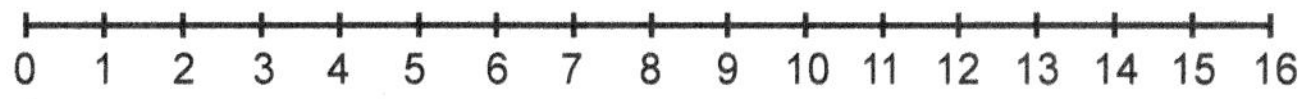

16 ÷ 8 = ________

2. What division equation does the picture represent?

a)

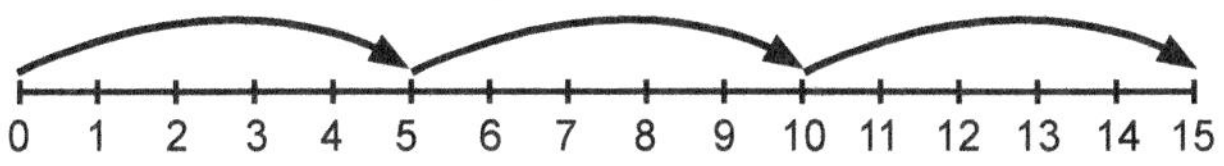

____

b)

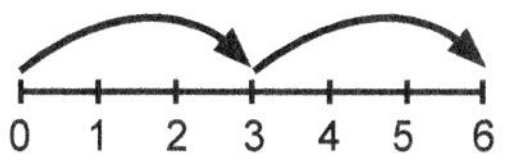

____

You can also divide by skip counting on your fingers.

Example: To find **45 ÷ 9**, skip count by 9s until you reach 45.

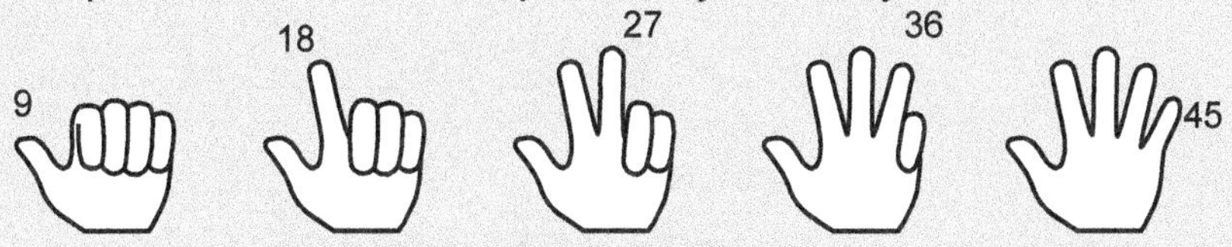

The number of fingers you have up when you stop is the answer. So **45 ÷ 9 = 5.**

3. Find the answers by skip counting on your fingers.

a) 14 ÷ 2 = ___7___ b) 18 ÷ 3 = ________ c) 20 ÷ 5 = ________

d) 36 ÷ 6 = ________ e) 48 ÷ 8 = ________ f) 63 ÷ 7 = ________

4. Use your answers from Question 3 to complete the equations.
Was each answer correct?

a) Does 2 × [7] = _14_? ✓ b) Does 3 × [ ] = _18_? c) Does 5 × [ ] = _____?

d) Does 6 × [ ] = _____? e) Does _____ × [ ] = _____? f) Does _____ × [ ] = _____?

5. 30 students sit in 6 rows. How many students are in each row?

The Two Meanings of Division

Daniel bought 12 fish from a pet store. He has 4 fish bowls.

How many fish can Daniel put in each fish bowl? Daniel counts by 4s to find out:

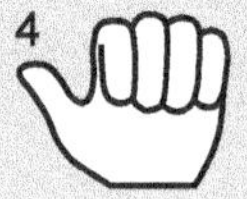

"I could put one fish in each bowl." (4 are placed)

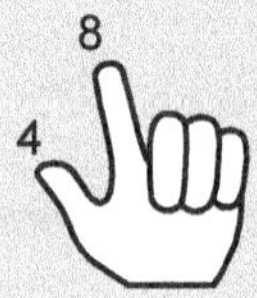

"I could put one more in each bowl." (8 are placed)

"I could put one more in each bowl." (12 are placed)

He has raised 3 fingers, so he knows that **12 ÷ 4 = 3**. He puts 3 fish in each fish bowl.

1. Count the way Daniel did to divide the objects into the number of sets given. Draw a circle around each set. The first one has been done for you.

a) 3 equal sets:

b) 5 equal sets:

c) 2 equal sets:

d) 4 equal sets:

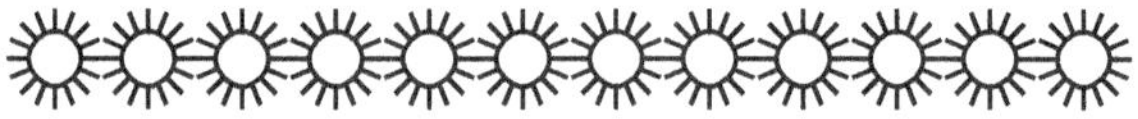

e) 7 equal sets:

f) 2 equal sets:

g) 3 equal sets:

h) 6 equal sets:

BONUS ▶

i) 3 equal sets:

j) 5 equal sets:

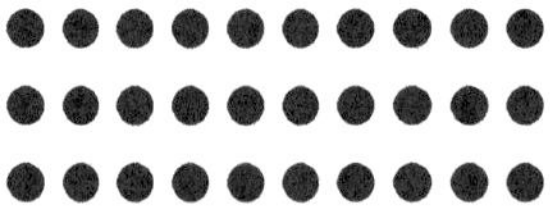

k) 4 equal sets:

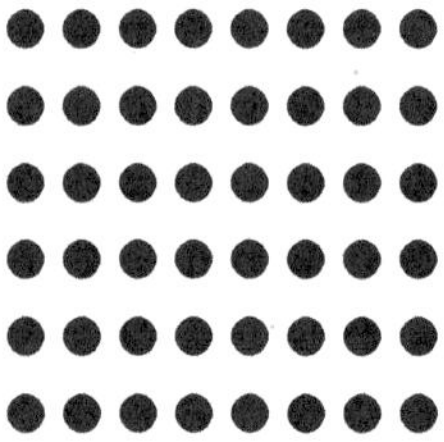

2. Arya has 16 fish and 4 fish bowls. How many fish can she put in each bowl?

Write a division equation for your answer. ______________________

Here are two ways to describe the picture below.

When 15 things are divided into 5 sets, there are 3 things in each set: **15 ÷ 5 = 3.**

When 15 things are divided into sets of size 3, there are 5 sets: **15 ÷ 3 = 5.**

3. Fill in the blanks. Then write two division equations.

a) 

____ lines ____ sets

____ lines in each set

____ ÷ ____ = ____

____ ÷ ____ = ____

b) 

____ lines ____ sets

____ lines in each set

____

____

c) 

____ lines ____ sets

____ lines in each set

____

____

4. Fill in the blanks. Then write two division equations.

a) 

____ squares ____ sets

____ squares in each set

____

____

b) 

____ triangles ____ sets

____ triangles in each set

____

____

c) 

____ stars ____ sets

____ stars in each set

____

____

5. Solve the problem by drawing a picture. Then write a division equation for your answer.

a) 12 triangles; 4 sets

____

How many triangles in each set? ________

b) 6 squares; 3 squares in each set

____

How many sets? ________

6. Solve each problem by drawing a picture. Write a division equation for your answer.

a) 20 people; 5 cars
How many people in each car?

b) 12 children; 3 boats
How many children in each boat?

OA4-24 Division and Multiplication

Remember: $10 \div 2 = 5$ tells us that $10 \div 5 = 2$ and $5 \times 2 = 10$ tells us that $2 \times 5 = 10$.
Also, every *division equation* can be rewritten as a *multiplication equation.*

Example: "10 divided into sets of size 2 equals 5 sets" or $\mathbf{10 \div 2 = 5}$

can be rewritten as "5 sets of size 2 equals 10" or $\mathbf{5 \times 2 = 10}$

1. Write two multiplication equations and two division equations for each picture.

a) 

____
____
____
____

b) 

____
____
____
____

c) 

____
____
____
____

How many fish? ______

How many sets? ______

How many fish in each set? ______

d) 

____
____
____
____

How many snails? ______

How many sets? ______

How many snails in each set? ______

2. Find the answer to the division problem by first finding the answer to the multiplication problem.

a) $4 \times \boxed{5} = 20$
$20 \div 4 = \boxed{5}$

b) $6 \times \boxed{} = 12$
$12 \div 6 = \boxed{}$

c) $5 \times \boxed{} = 20$
$20 \div 5 = \boxed{}$

d) $6 \times \boxed{} = 30$
$30 \div 6 = \boxed{}$

e) $9 \times \boxed{} = 45$
$45 \div 9 = \boxed{}$

f) $7 \times \boxed{} = 21$
$21 \div 7 = \boxed{}$

g) $3 \times \boxed{} = 24$
$24 \div 3 = \boxed{}$

h) $6 \times \boxed{} = 24$
$24 \div 6 = \boxed{}$

3. Fill in the blanks for each picture.

a) 

____ lines

____ lines in each set

____ sets

b) 

____ lines in total

____ sets

____ lines in each set

c) 

____ lines in each group

____ groups

____ lines

d) 

____ lines in each set

____ sets

____ lines altogether

e) 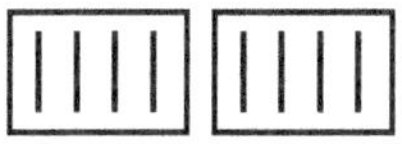

____ lines

____ lines in each set

____ sets

f) 

____ lines in total

____ groups

____ lines in each group

g) 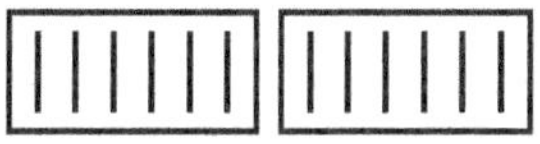

____ lines

____ lines in each set

____ sets

h) 

____ lines in total

____ sets

____ lines in each set

i) 

____ lines in each group

____ groups

____ lines

4. Draw a picture of …

a) 16 lines altogether; 4 lines in each set; 4 sets

b) 8 lines; 4 lines in each set; 2 sets

c) 6 sets; 3 lines in each set; 18 lines in total

d) 12 lines; 2 sets; 6 lines in each set

5. Draw a picture *and* write two division equations and two multiplication equations for …

a) 20 lines; 5 sets; 4 lines in each set

b) 15 lines; 5 lines in each set; 3 sets

6. Draw a picture to find the missing piece of information.

a) *5* lines in each set

____ sets

15 lines altogether

b) *18* lines

____ lines in each set

3 sets

c) ____ lines in total

3 groups

4 lines in each group

OA4-25 Knowing When to Multiply or Divide

1. Multiply or divide to find the missing information (?) in each row.

	Total number of things	Number of sets	Number in each set	Multiplication or division equation
a)	?	6	3	$6 \times 3 = 18$
b)	20	4	?	$20 \div 4 = 5$
c)	15	?	5	
d)	10	2	?	
e)	?	4	6	
f)	21	7	?	

2. Write a multiplication or division equation to solve the problem.

a) 18 things in total
3 things in each set

$18 \div 3 = 6$

How many sets?

6

b) 5 sets
4 things in each set

____

How many things in total?

_____

c) 15 things in total
5 sets

____

How many things in each set?

_____

d) 8 groups
3 things in each group

____

How many things in total?

_____

e) 6 things in each set
12 things in total

____

How many sets?

_____

f) 5 groups
10 things in total

____

How many in each group?

_____

g) 5 things in each set
4 sets

____

How many things in total?

_____

h) 4 things in each set
6 sets

____

How many things in total?

_____

i) 16 things in total
8 sets

____

How many things in each set?

_____

3. Fill in the table. Use a question mark to show what you don't know. Then write a multiplication or division equation in the last column.

		Total number of things	Number of sets	Number in each set	Multiplication or division equation
a)	20 people 4 vans	20	4	?	*20 ÷ 4 = 5* How many people in each van? *5*
b)	3 marbles in each jar 6 jars				How many marbles? ________
c)	15 flowers 5 pots				How many flowers in each pot? ________
d)	4 chairs at each table 2 tables				How many chairs? ________
e)	18 pillows 6 beds				How many pillows on each bed? ________
f)	18 houses 9 houses on each block				How many blocks? ________

The **fact family** for the multiplication equation **3** × **5** = **15** is

$3 \times 5 = 15$ $5 \times 3 = 15$ $15 \div 3 = 5$ $15 \div 5 = 3$

4. Complete the fact family for each equation.

a) $5 \times 2 = 10$

____

____

____

b) $4 \times 3 = 12$

____

____

____

c) $12 \div 2 = 6$

____

____

____

d) $8 \div 4 = 2$

____

____

____

MD4-1 Centimeters

A **centimeter** (cm) is a unit of measurement for **length** (or **height** or **thickness**).

Midori counts the number of centimeters between the black arrows by counting the number of "hops" it takes to move between them.

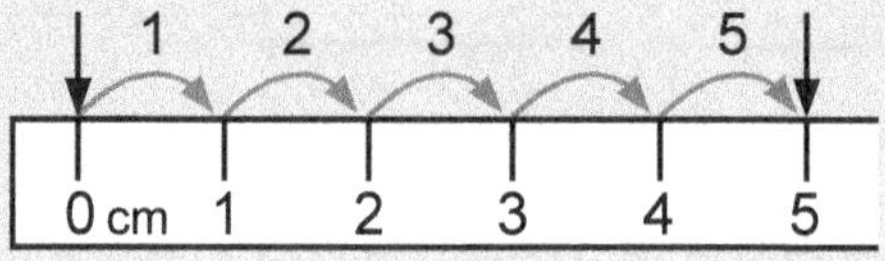

5 cm

1. Measure the distance between the arrows.

a)

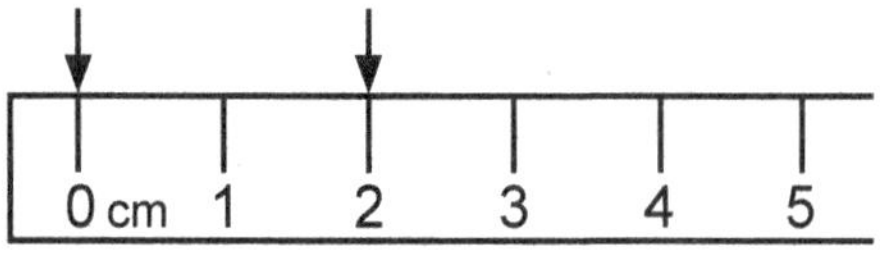

_____ cm

b)

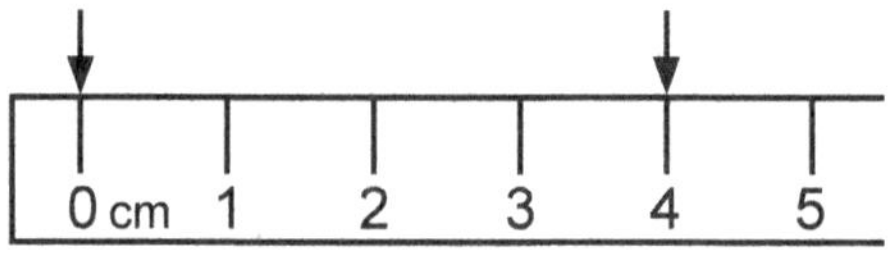

_____ cm

2. Measure the distance between the arrows. Count carefully! The first arrow is not at the beginning of the ruler.

a)

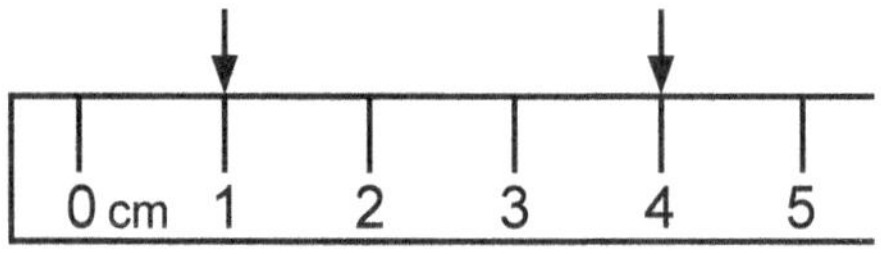

_____ cm

b)

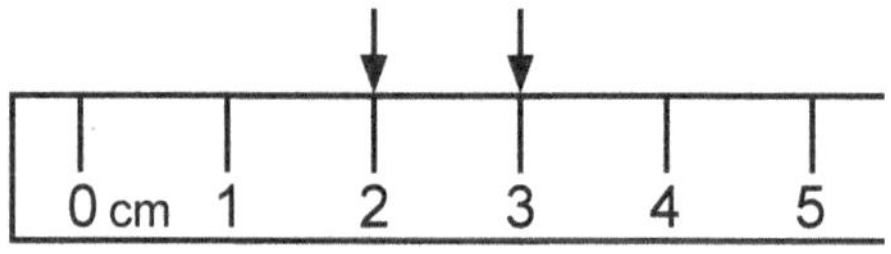

_____ cm

3. Measure the distance between the arrows.

a)

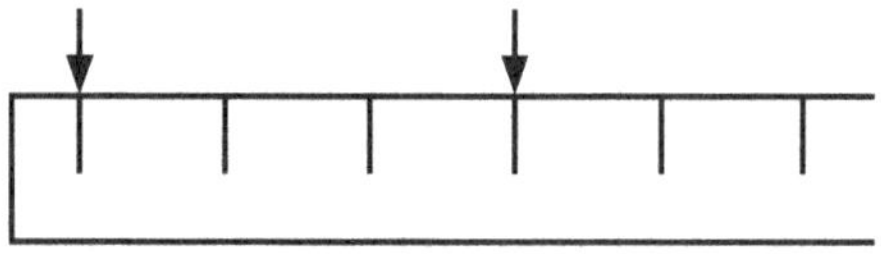

_____ cm

b)

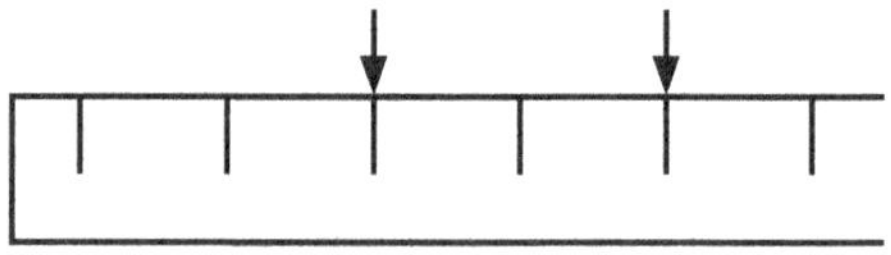

_____ cm

4. Measure the length of each line segment or object.

a)

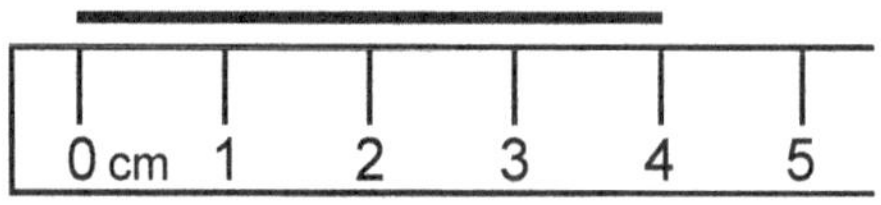

_____ cm

b)

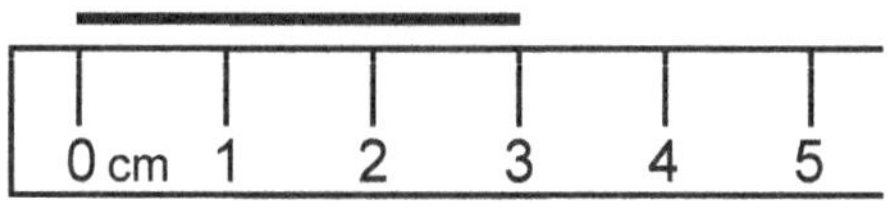

_____ cm

c)

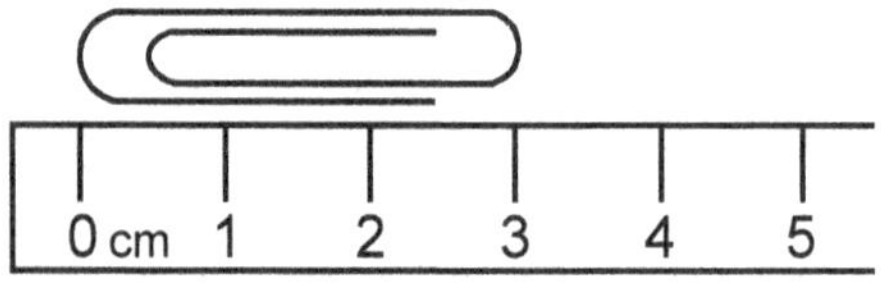

_____ cm

d)

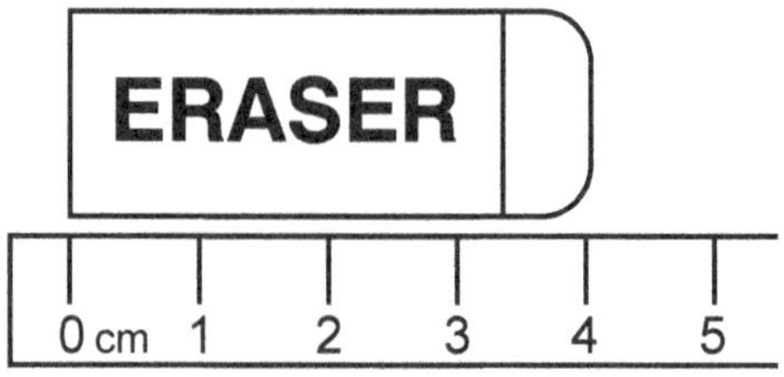

_____ cm

5. Measure the length of each line segment or object.

a)

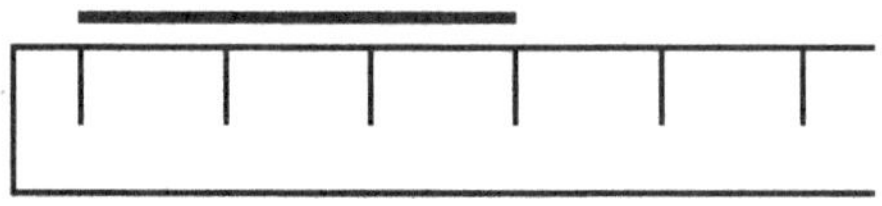

_____ cm

b)

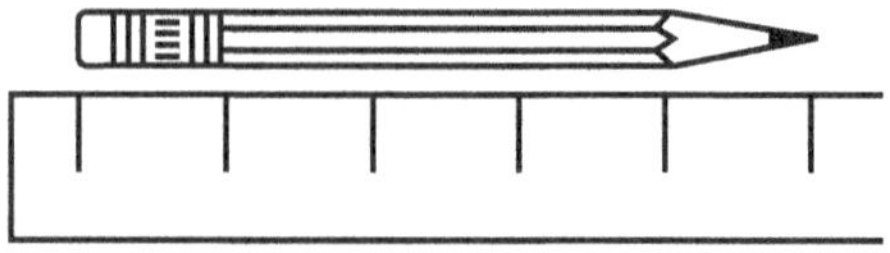

_____ cm

6. Measure the length of each strip using a ruler.

a) ______ cm

b) ______ cm

c) ______ cm

d) ______ cm

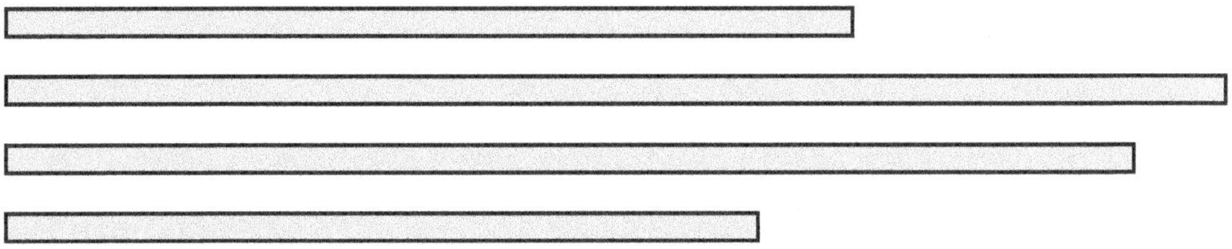

7. Measure the length of each picture using a ruler.

a)  ______ cm

b) 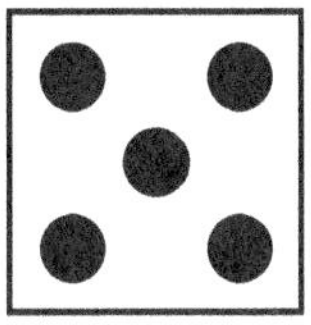 ______ cm

8. Measure all the sides of each shape.

a) 

______ cm (top)
______ cm (left)
______ cm (right)
______ cm (bottom)

b) 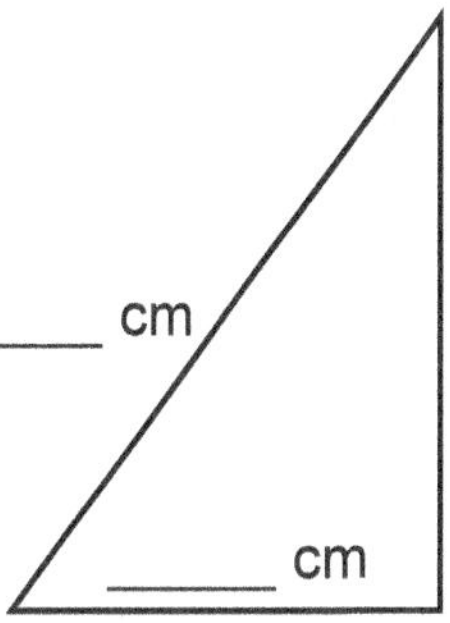

______ cm
______ cm
______ cm

9. On each ruler, draw two arrows to show the given distance. The first question is done for you.

a) 4 cm apart

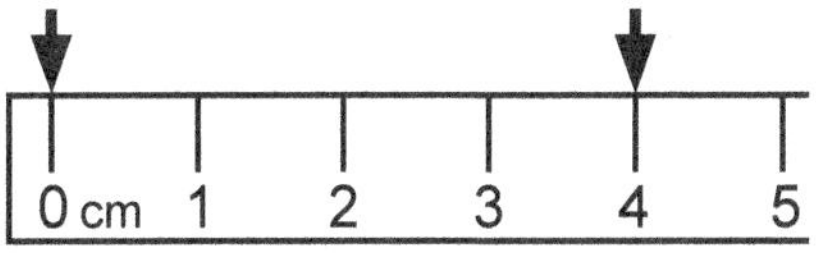

b) 3 cm apart

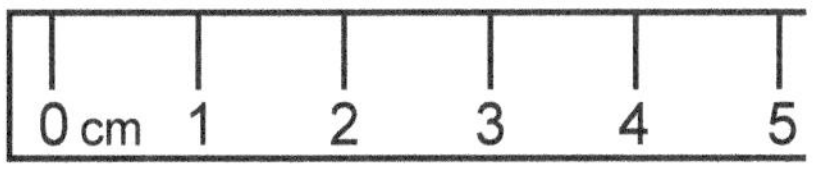

c) 5 cm apart

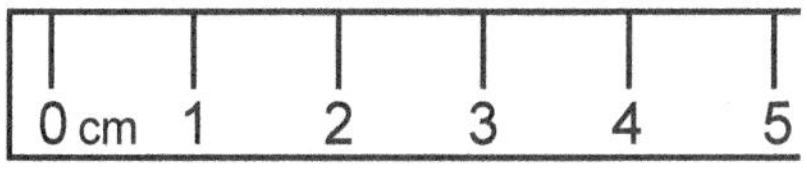

10. Draw a line segment that is …

a) 1 cm long

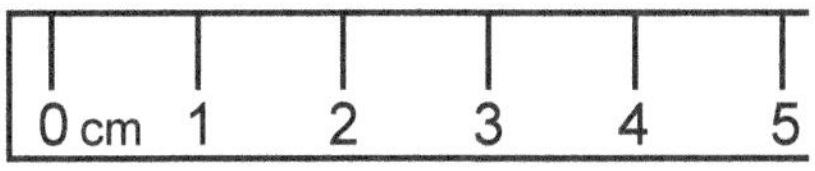

b) 4 cm long

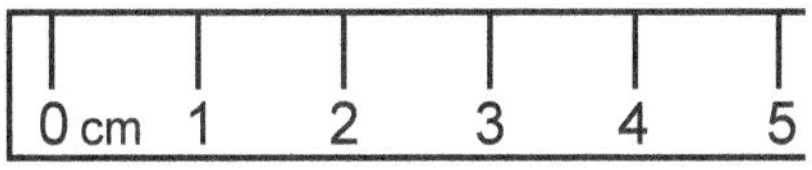

c) 2 cm long

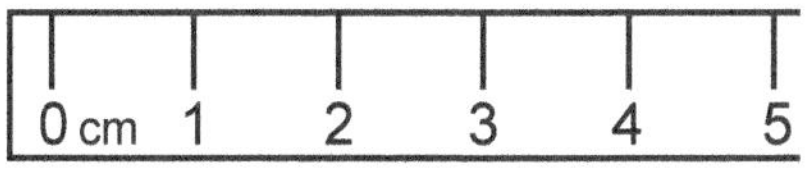

11. Draw a line segment this is …

a) 3 cm long
b) 5 cm long
c) 10 cm long

12. Draw each object to the exact measurement.

a) a caterpillar, 4 cm long
b) a leaf, 11 cm long
c) a pencil, 8 cm long

13. On grid paper, draw a rectangle with a length of 5 cm and a width of 2 cm.

MD4-2 Millimeters

A **millimeter** (mm) is another unit of measurement for **length** (or **height** or **thickness**).

If you look at a ruler with millimeter measurements, you can see that 1 cm is equal to 10 mm.

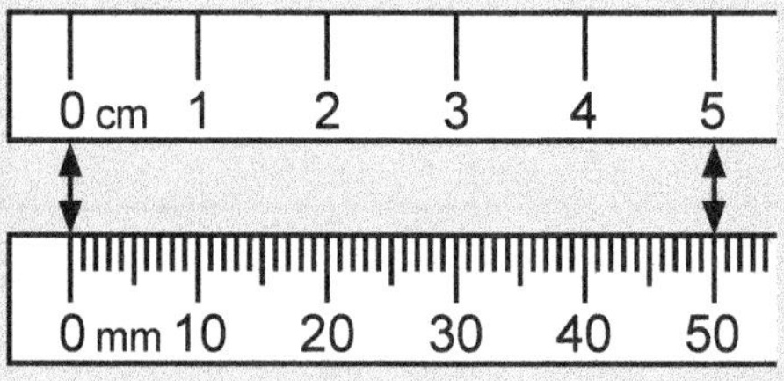

1. Fill in the measurements in millimeters.

cm	1	2	3	4	5	6	7	8
mm	*10*							

2. To change a measurement from centimeters (cm) to millimeters (mm), what number do you have to multiply by? _______

3. Fill in the numbers that are missing from the tables.

a)

cm	**mm**
7	
8	
12	

b)

cm	**mm**
15	
20	
25	

c)

cm	**mm**
32	
57	
200	

d)

cm	**mm**
112	
257	
736	

4. Convert the centimeters to millimeters. Then circle the greater measurement.

a) 5 cm   (70 mm)
   50 mm

b) 83 cm   910 mm

c) 45 cm   53 mm

d) 2 cm   12 mm

e) 60 cm   6,200 mm

f) 72 cm   420 mm

A nickel is about 2 mm high. So a stack of five nickels would be about 1 cm high.

1 nickel = 2 mm

5 nickels = 10 mm = 1 cm

5. How many nickels would be in a stack …

a) 2 cm high? _______   b) 3 cm high? _______   c) 5 cm high? _______   d) 10 cm high? _______

Mei-Ling wants to measure a line that is 23 mm long.

It is hard to count every millimeter. Mei-Ling counts by 10s until she reaches 20. Then she counts on by 1s.

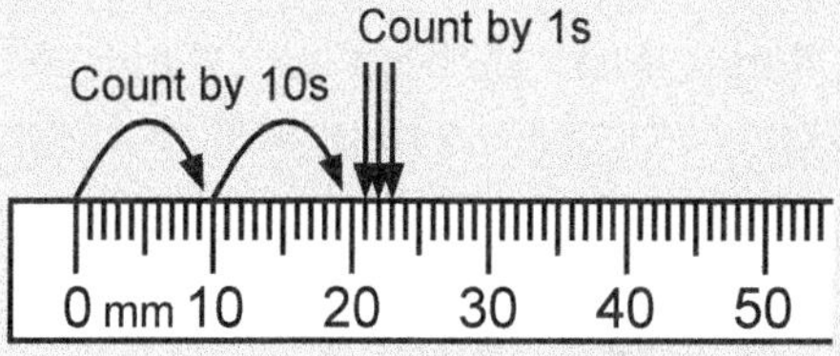

6. What is the distance between the two arrows?

a)

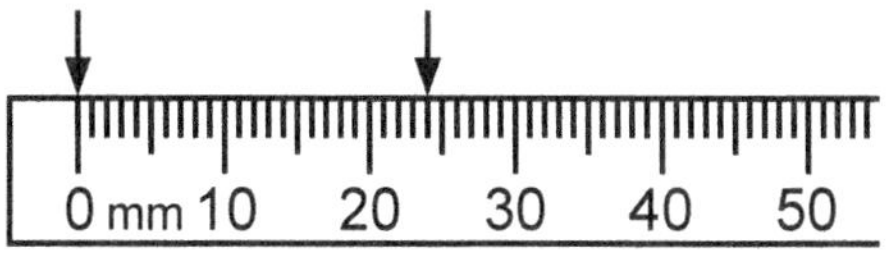

_______ mm

b)

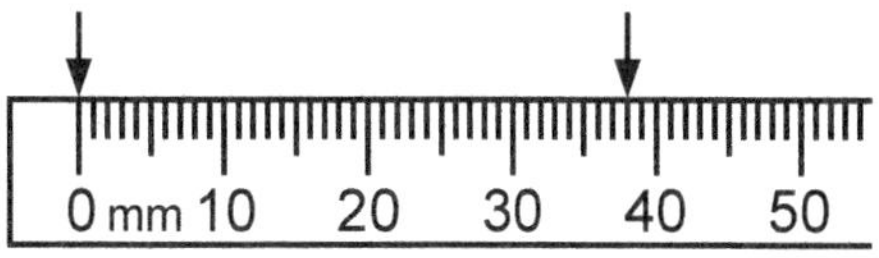

_______ mm

7. Find the length of each strip.

a)

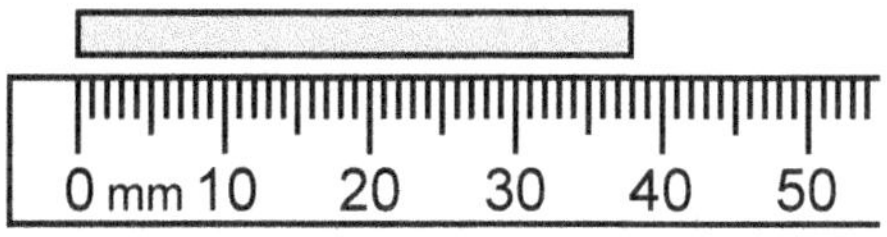

_______ mm

b)

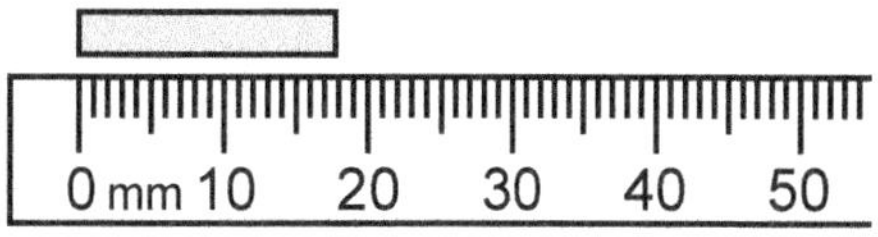

_______ mm

8. Draw a second arrow to show where a line segment of the given length would end.

a) 32 mm

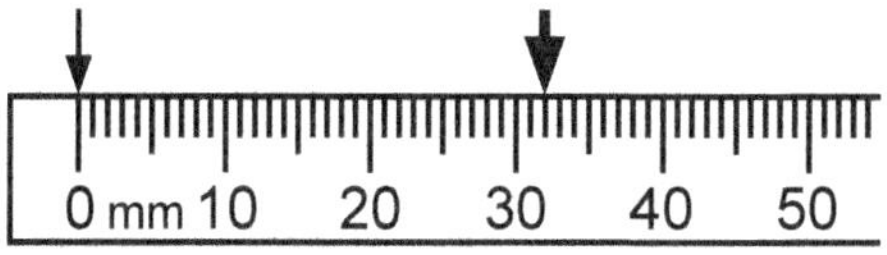

b) 18 mm

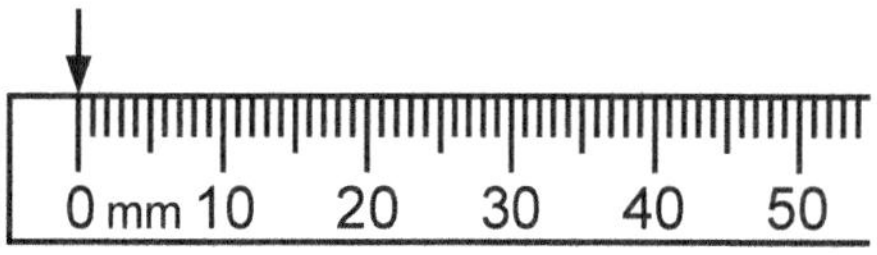

c) 26 mm

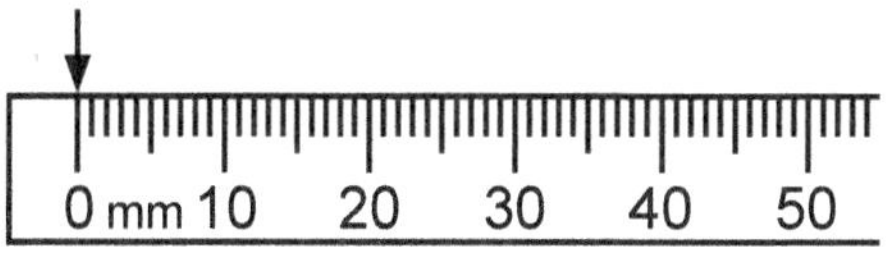

d) 19 mm

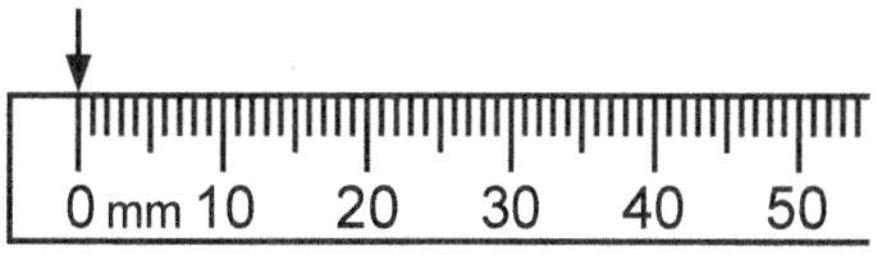

9. Draw a line segment of the given length. Start at the "0" mark of the ruler.

a) 16 mm

b) 41 mm

10. Use a ruler to draw the following objects to the exact millimeter.

a) A line 20 mm long b) A line 27 mm long c) A pencil 50 mm long d) A beetle 32 mm long

MD4-3 Centimeters and Millimeters

1. Your finger is about 1 cm (or 10 mm) wide. Measure each picture with your finger, then convert the measurement to millimeters.

a) 

The eraser measures about ______ fingers.

So the eraser is close to ______ mm long.

b) 

The crayon measures about ______ fingers.

So the crayon is close to ______ mm long.

c) 

The pencil measures about ______ fingers.

So the pencil is close to ______ mm long.

d) 

The tack measures about ______ fingers.

So the tack is close to ______ mm long.

2. Estimate if each strip is **less than** or **more than** 30 mm long. Put a check mark in the correct column.

		Less than 30 mm	More than 30 mm
a)			
b)			
c)			
d)			

3. How good were your estimates? Measure the length of each strip in Question 2.

a) _______ mm   b) _______ mm   c) _______ mm   d) _______ mm

4. Estimate if the distance between the lines is **less than** 20 mm or **more than** 20 mm. Then measure the **actual** distance in millimeters.

		Less than 20 mm	More than 20 mm	Actual distance
a)				
b)				
c)				
d)				

This rectangle is 23 mm long.
It is about 2 cm long.

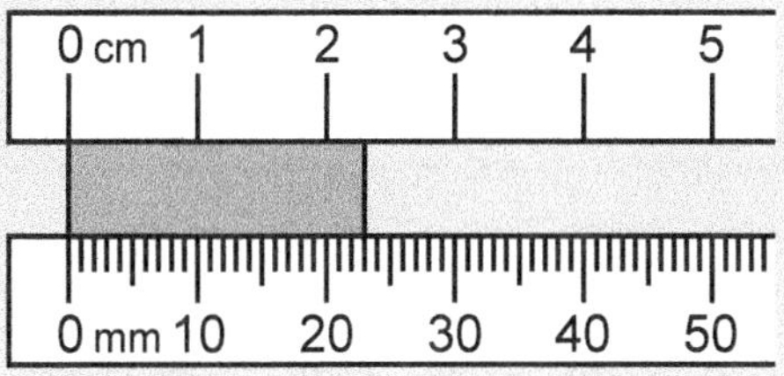

This rectangle is 28 mm long.
It is about 3 cm long.

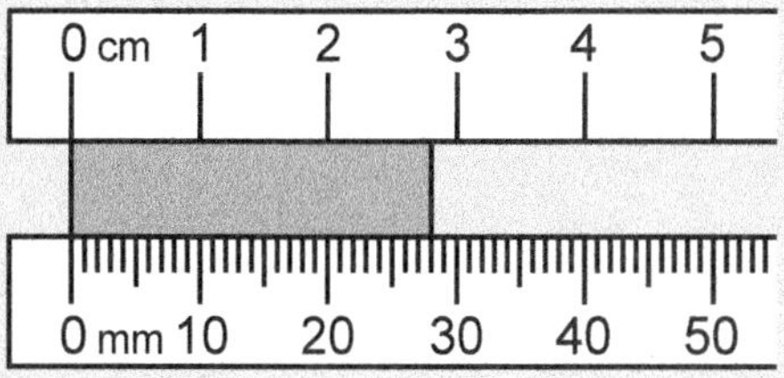

5. Measure the following line segments in centimeters and millimeters.

a)

_______ mm

about _______ cm

b)

_______ mm

about _______ cm

c)

_______ mm

about _______ cm

d) 

_______ mm

about _______ cm

6. Measure the sides of the rectangles in centimeters. Then measure the distance between the opposite corners along the dashed line in centimeters and millimeters.

a) ______ cm

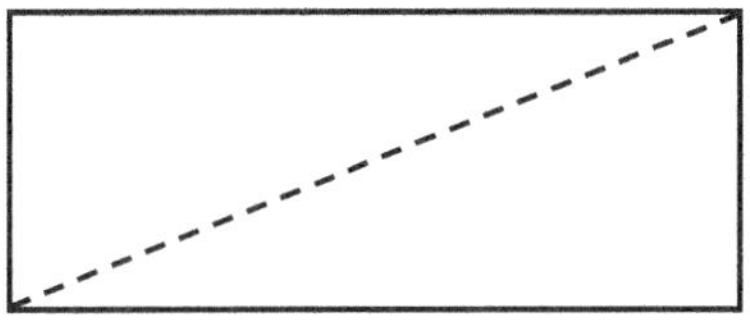

______ cm

Dashed line = about _______ cm

= _______ mm

b) ______ cm

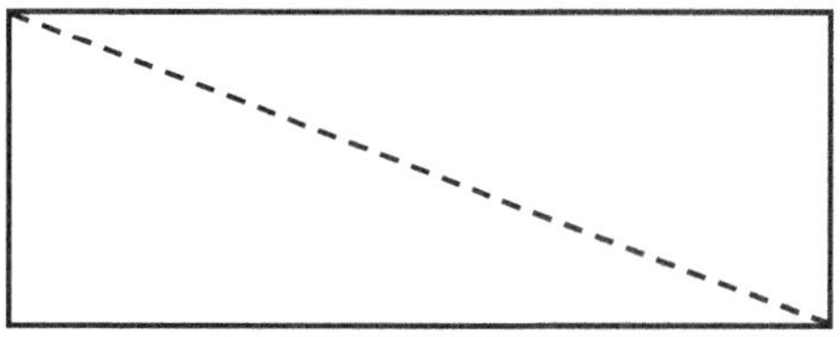

______ cm

Dashed line = about _______ cm

= _______ mm

7. a) Estimate the width and the length of each rectangle (in cm). Then convert the estimates to millimeters.

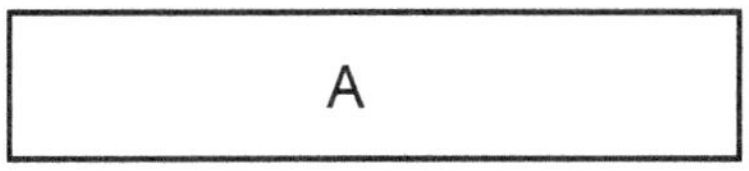

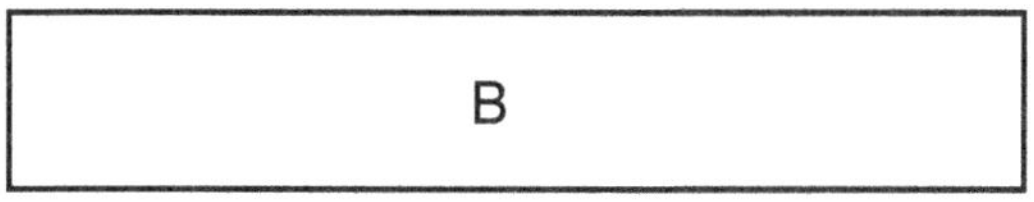

A: Length _______ cm, about _______ mm

Width _______ cm, about _______ mm

B: Length _______ cm, about _______ mm

Width _______ cm, about _______ mm

b) Measure the width and length of the rectangles exactly (in mm) with a ruler.

A: Length = _______ mm

Width = _______ mm

B: Length = _______ mm

Width = _______ mm

c) How close were your estimates in a)?

MD4-4 Centimeters and Millimeters (Advanced)

1. Using a ruler, draw a second mark so that the pair of marks are separated by the distance given. Then complete the chart.

		Distance Apart	
		cm	**mm**
a)		4	40
b)		3	
c)			80
d)		7	

2. Draw a line segment with a length between …

a) 3 cm and 4 cm. How long is your line segment in mm? _________

b) 4 cm and 5 cm. How long is your line segment in mm? _________

c) 5 cm and 6 cm. How long is your line segment in mm? _________

3. Write a measurement in millimeters that is between …

a) 6 cm and 7 cm _________ b) 7 cm and 8 cm _________ c) 12 cm and 13 cm _________

4. Write a measurement in centimeters that is between …

a) 67 mm and 75 mm _________ b) 27 mm and 39 mm _________

c) 52 mm and 7 cm _________ d) 112 mm and 13 cm _________

5. Draw a line segment with a length that is an exact number of centimeters between …

a) 45 mm and 55 mm b) 65 mm and 75 mm

6. Peter says 5 mm is longer than 2 cm because 5 is greater than 2.
Is this correct? Explain.

7. Each leaf has a different length. Measure the lengths to identify each leaf.

Elm: 4 cm Maple: 5 cm Willow: 6 cm Oak: 7 cm

____

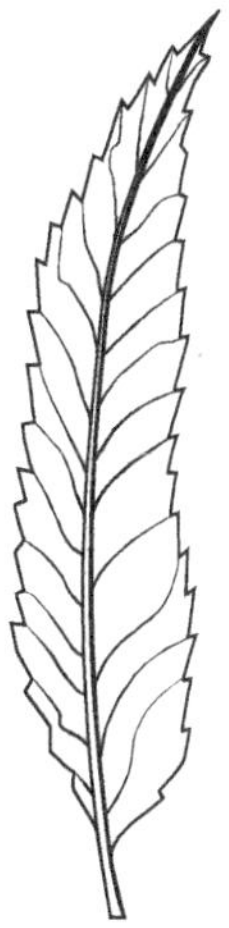

____

____

____

8. Which line is longer, *A* or *B*? Guess, then measure to check.

a)

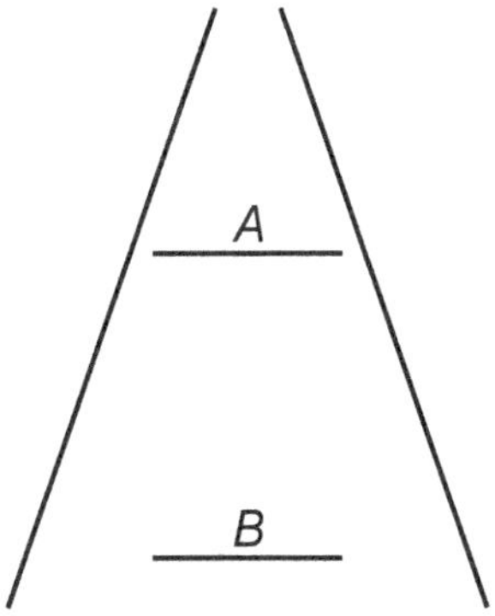

b)

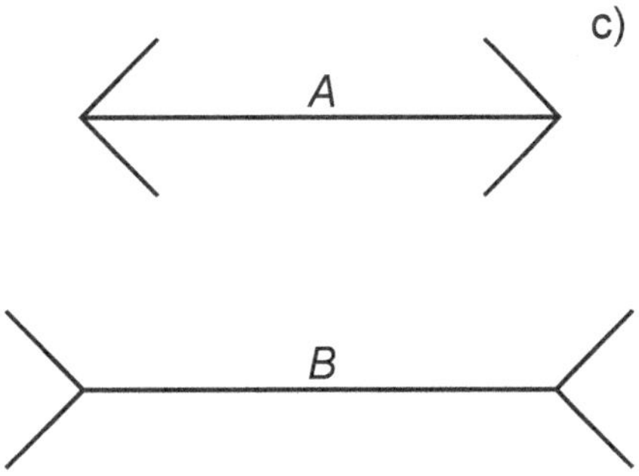

c)

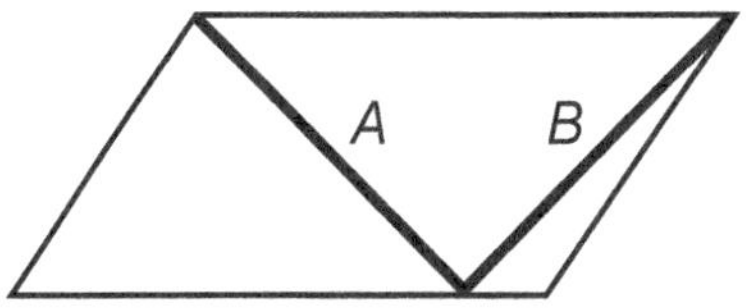

MD4-5 Meters

A **meter** (m) is a unit of measurement for **length** (or **height** or **thickness**) equal to 100 cm.

A meter stick is about 100 cm long. 

1. a) Measure the length of your classroom in giant steps. Try to make the giant steps the same length.

Length = _________ giant steps

b) Measure the length of your classroom in meter sticks. Length = _________ meter sticks

c) Is your giant step longer than a meter or shorter than a meter? _________

d) Can you use giant steps to estimate distance in meters? _________

2. a) Stretch your arms out. The distance between the tips of your fingers is called your *arm span*.

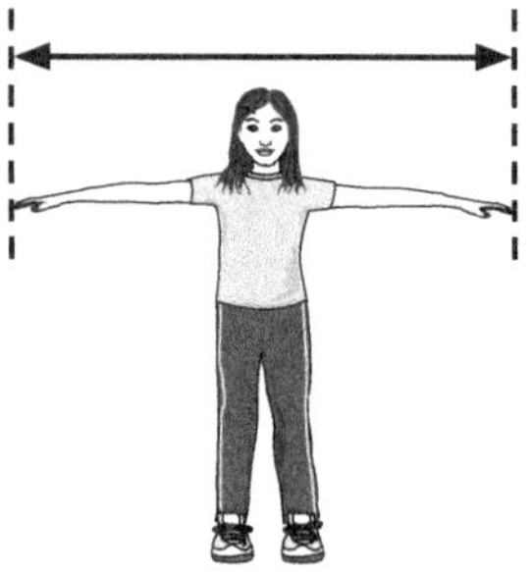

Ask a friend to measure your arm span with a piece of string.

Arm span = _________ cm

Is your arm span more or less than a meter? _________

b) Stretch your arms out. Fold them as shown. The distance between your elbows is called your *elbow span*.

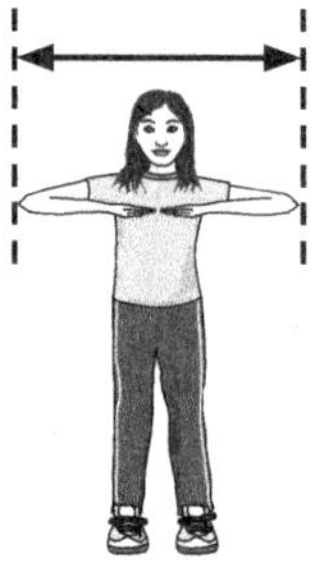

Ask a friend to measure your elbow span with a piece of string.

Elbow span = _________ cm

Is your elbow span more or less than a meter? _________

c) Stretch your arms out. Fold one arm as shown. The distance from one elbow to the tips of the fingers on the other hand is called your *arm-and-elbow span.*

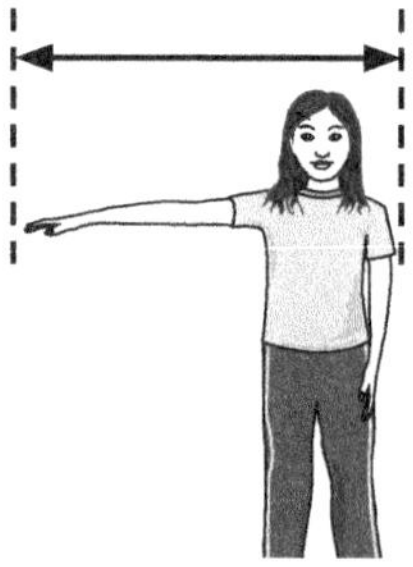

Ask a friend to measure your arm-and-elbow span with a piece of string.

Arm-and-elbow span = _________ cm

Is your arm-and-elbow span more or less than a meter? _________

d) Which distance is closest to 1 meter? _____________________

3. a) Measure your height in centimeters. Height = _________ cm

Are you taller than 1 meter? _________

b) Measure the distance from your armpit to the floor. _________ cm

Is this distance more than 1 meter? _________

c) Which distance is better for estimating height in meters? _____________________

4. Estimate each distance. Then measure the actual distance with a meter stick or measuring tape.

a) The length of a blackboard is ...

Estimate: about _______ m   Actual: about _______ m

b) The distance from the floor to the door handle is ...

Estimate: about _______ m   Actual: about _______ m

5. Fill in the measurements in centimeters.

m	1	2	3	4	5	6	7	8
cm	*100*							

6. To change a measurement from meters (m) to centimeters (cm),

what number do you have to multiply by? _________

7. Fill in the numbers that are missing from the tables.

a)

m	**cm**
9	
10	
11	

b)

m	**cm**
20	
25	
32	

c)

m	**cm**
359	
412	
500	

8. Convert the measurement in meters to centimeters.
Then circle the greater measurement.

a) 500 cm   (7 m) *700 cm}   b) 830 cm   91 m   c) 245 cm   5 m

d) 2,222 cm   12 m   e) 60 m   6,200 cm   f) 72 m   4,203 cm

9. Write a measurement in centimeters that is between ...

a) 6 m and 7 m _________   b) 7 m and 8 m _________   c) 12 m and 13 m _________

10. Write a measurement in meters that is between ...

a) 670 cm and 750 cm _________   b) 270 cm and 390 cm _________

MD4-6 Meters (Advanced)

1. Continue the pattern to fill in the table.

m	1	2	3	4	5	6
dm	10	20				
cm	100	200				
mm	1,000	2,000				

2. a) 1 cm = _______ mm b) 1 m = _______ cm c) 1 m = __________ mm

3. Convert the measurements.

a)

m	cm
1	
14	
80	

b)

m	cm
2	
19	
21	

c)

m	cm
3	
65	
106	

4. Sheena measured the height of her bedroom window with both a meter stick and a measuring tape.

- When she measured with the meter stick, the window was 2 m with 15 cm extra.
- When she measured with the measuring tape, the measurement was 215 cm.

Is there a difference in the two measurements? Explain.

____

____

5. Convert the measurements in centimeters to mixed measurements.

a) 513 cm = __*5*__ m __*13*__ cm b) 217 cm = _______ m _______ cm

c) 367 cm = _______ m _______ cm d) 481 cm = _______ m _______ cm

e) 706 cm = _______ m _______ cm f) 303 cm = _______ m _______ cm

6. Convert the mixed measurements to measurements in centimeters.

a) 3 m 1 cm = __*301*__ cm b) 4 m 51 cm = _______ cm

c) 3 m 45 cm = _______ cm d) 8 m 2 cm = _______ cm

e) 9 m 7 cm = _______ cm f) 7 m 50 cm = _______ cm

MD4-7 Kilometers and Meters

We measure large distances in **kilometers**. 1 km = 1,000 meters.

1. a) Count by 100s to find out how many times you need to add 100 to make 1,000.

100 , ________ , ________ , ________ , ________ , ________ , ________ , ________ , ________ , ________

b) A football field is about 100 m long.

How many football fields long is a kilometer? ________

2. a) Skip count by 50s to find out how many times you need to add 50 to make 1,000.

b) An Olympic swimming pool is 50 m long.

How many swimming pools long is a kilometer? ________

3. a) How many 10s do you need to make each number? Count by 10s to find out.

Number	100	200	300	400	500	600
Number of 10s						

b) Using the pattern in the table, how many times would you need to add 10 to make 1,000? ________

4. A school bus is about 10 m long. How many school buses lined end to end would equal …

a) close to a kilometer? ________

b) close to 2 km? ________

5. You can travel 1 km if you walk for 15 minutes at a regular speed. Name a place (a store, a park, a friend's house) that is about 1 km from your school or from your home.

____

6. Fill in the table.

km	1	2	3	4	5	6	7	8
m	*1,000*							

7. To change a measurement from kilometers (km) to meters (m), what number do you have to multiply by? ________

8. Convert the measurement in kilometers to meters. Then circle the greater measurement.

a) 500 m   (7 km) *7,000 m*   b) 8,300 m   91 km   c) 24,567 m   5 km

d) 8,888 m   8 km   e) 60 km   6,200 m   f) 72 km   45,203 m

9. a) Write a measurement in meters that is between 5 km and 6 km. _________

b) Write a measurement in kilometers that is between 3,790 m and 4,258 m. _________

10. A track is 400 m long. Fill in the T-table.

a) Khalid ran around the track twice.

How many meters did he run? _________

Did he run a kilometer? _________

b) Khalid wants to run 1,500 m. About how many times must he run around the track?

____

c) How many times must Khalid run around the track to cover 2 km? _________

Laps around the track	**Distance covered (m)**
1	*400*
2	

11. The number beside each black line on the map indicates the length of the road (driving distance) between the cities.

a) The driving distance between …

i) Cleveland, OH, and Philadelphia, PA, is _______ km.

ii) Philadelphia, PA, and Binghamton, NY, is _______ km.

iii) Binghamton, NY, and Buffalo, NY, is _______ km.

iv) Buffalo, NY, and Cleveland, OH, is _______ km.

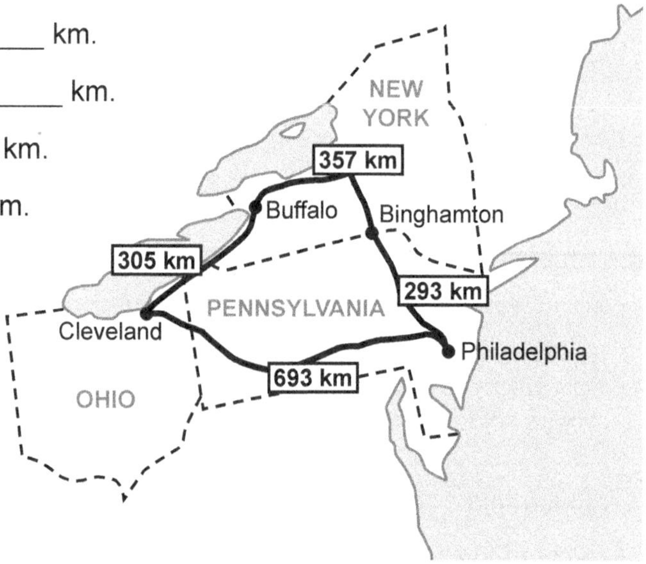

b) How far would you travel if you drove from …

i) Buffalo to Cleveland to Philadelphia?

_______ km

ii) Philadelphia to Binghamton to Buffalo?

_______ km

iii) Cleveland to Buffalo to Binghamton?

_______ km

MD4-8 Ordering and Assigning Appropriate Units

1. Jeremy's classroom is 5 m long.

a) How many centimeters long is Jeremy's classroom? _______ cm

b) How many millimeters long is Jeremy's classroom? _______ mm

c) Which unit (m, cm, or mm) gives the simplest measurement? _______

d) Would you measure Jeremy's classroom in kilometers? Explain.

____

____

2. A table is 63 cm wide.

a) About how many meters wide is the table? _______ m

b) Which units give more useful information about the width of the table: meters or centimeters? _______

The unit that gives the best way to write a measurement is called the **most appropriate** unit. It makes the number simple and provides the most information about the object.

3. Circle the measurement that uses the most appropriate unit for each object.

a) A cereal box is 190 mm 19 cm wide.

b) An airplane is about 70,000 mm 7,000 cm 70 m long.

c) The distance from New York, NY, to Detroit, MI, is about 1,000,000 m 1,000 km.

The thickness of a penny is about 1 millimeter (mm).

The width of your finger is about 1 centimeter (cm).

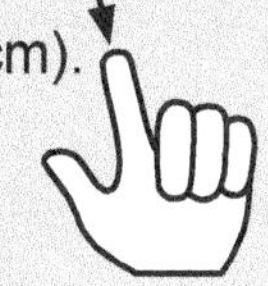

The height of a 4-year-old child is about 1 meter (m).

The distance you can walk in 15 min is about 1 kilometer (km).

4. Match the word with the short form. Then match the most appropriate unit of measurement with the object.

a)

mm	kilometer	length of a book
cm	centimeter	length of a street
m	millimeter	height of a room
km	meter	length of an ant

b)

km	meter	height of a door
cm	millimeter	distance to Lynn, MA
m	kilometer	thickness of a pencil
mm	centimeter	length of a postage stamp

5. Circle the measurement that best fills the blank.

a) The thickness of a piece of construction paper is about _______.

1 mm 1 cm 1 m 1 km

b) Schools might close if more than _______ of snow fell overnight.

50 cm 50 m 50 km

c) An average adult bicycle is about _______ long.

2 mm 2 cm 2 m 2 km

d) It is fewer than _______ from Boston, MA, to Washington, DC.

800 mm 800 cm 800 m 800 km

6. Which unit of measurement (mm, cm, m, or km) will make the statement correct?

a) The classroom door is about 2 _______ high.

b) Your shoe is close to 20 _______ long.

c) The Statue of Liberty is about 93 _______ high.

d) A cell phone is about 9 _______ thick.

e) The width of a maple leaf is about 16 _______.

f) The Moon is about 380,000 _______ away.

7. What unit would you use to measure each distance: meters (m) or kilometers (km)? Explain one of your answers below.

a) From your home to the school: _______

b) From your classroom to the cafeteria: _______

c) Around the schoolyard: _______

d) Between Denver, CO, and Dallas, TX: _______

____

____

8. Which unit of measurement would you use for the following?

a) Length of a subway car: _______

b) Length of your hair: _______

c) Distance traveled on a flight from Los Angeles, CA, to Chicago, IL: _______

9. Choose an object in your classroom. Which unit of measurement would be best to measure the object? Explain.

MD4-9 Length (Review)

REMINDER ▶ 1 cm = 10 mm 1 m = 100 cm 1 km = 1,000 m

1. Fill in the tables.

a)

m	cm
1	
2	
3	
25	

b)

cm	mm
1	
2	
3	
37	

c)

km	m
1	
2	
3	
75	

2. Mark the measurements on the number line. (First convert meters to centimeters.)

A. 150 cm **B.** 2 m **C.** 1 m

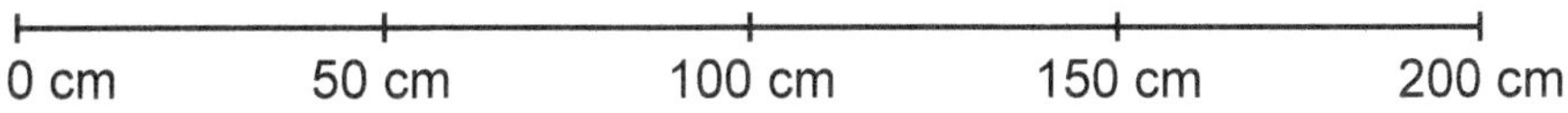

3. The table shows the lengths of some animals at the zoo.

a) Mark the lengths of **L**, **R**, **B**, and **W** on the number line.

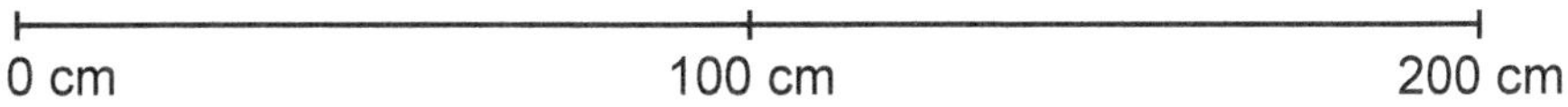

b) How many centimeters longer than a lynx is a wolf? _______

Animal	Length
Lynx: **L**	150 cm
Rabbit: **R**	50 cm
Beaver: **B**	100 cm
Wolf: **W**	2 m

4. A fence is made of four parts joined end to end. Each part is 32 cm long.

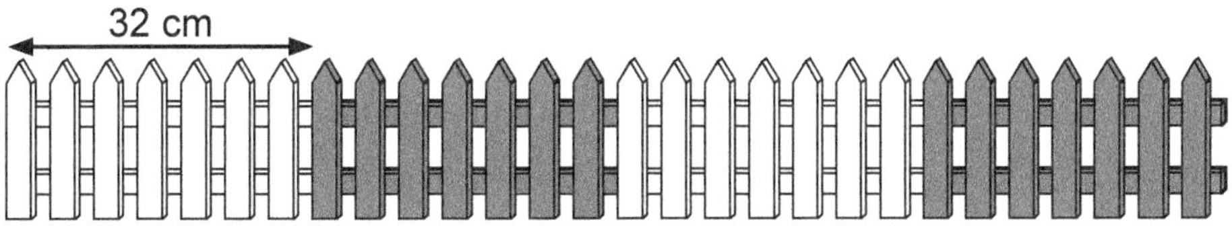

a) How long is the fence in centimeters? _______

b) Is the fence longer or shorter than a meter? _____________

5. The distance from Joan's home to school is 600 m. The distance from school to the library is 700 m. Joan walked to school and continued to the library.

a) How many meters did she walk? _______

b) Is her walk longer than a kilometer or shorter than a kilometer? _____________

c) How many meters longer or shorter than a kilometer is Joan's walk? _______

MD4-10 Perimeter

A figure is made with toothpicks. Count the number of toothpicks on the outside of the figure:

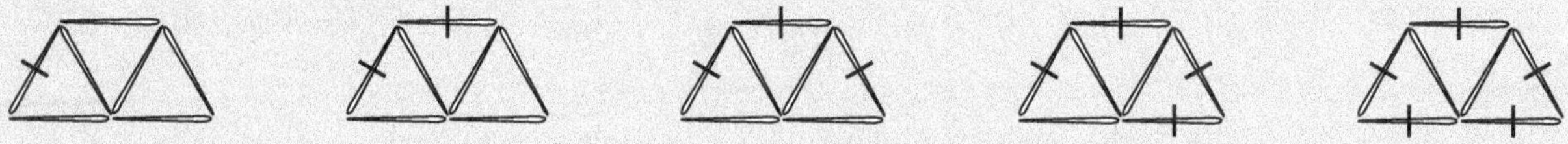

1 2 3 4 5

1. Count the number of toothpicks on the outside of the figure. Mark the toothpicks as you count. Write your answer in the blank.

a)  _____ b) 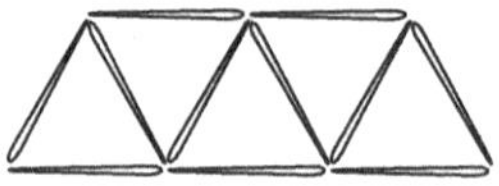 _____ c) 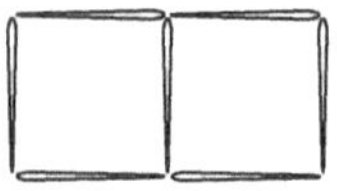 _____

2. Count the number of edges on the **outside** of the figure. Mark the edges as you count.

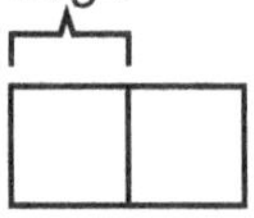

a) 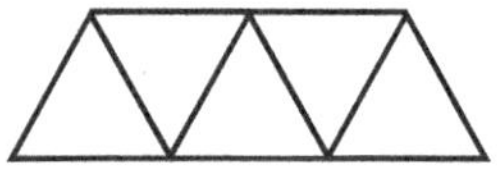 _____ b) 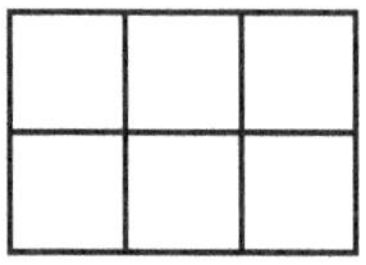 _____ c) 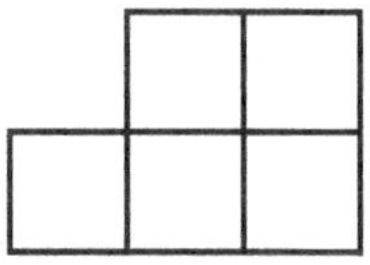 _____

The distance around the outside of a shape is called the **perimeter** of the shape. The perimeter of this figure, measured in toothpicks, is 5 toothpicks.

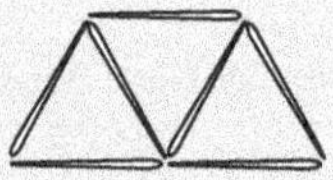

3. Each edge is 1 cm long. Find the perimeter in centimeters.

a) 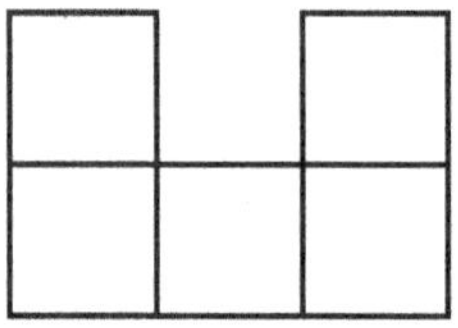 _____ cm

b) 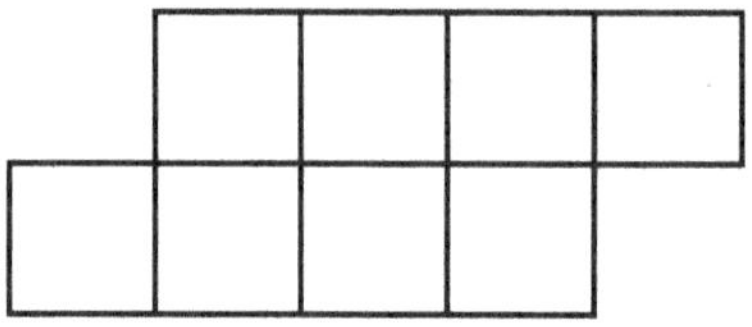 _____ cm

c) 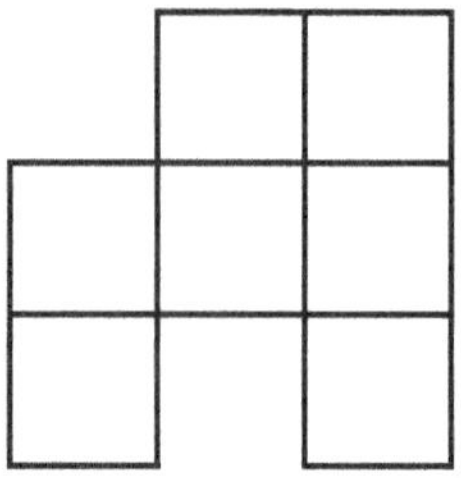 _____ cm

4. Write the perimeter of each figure in the sequence (each edge is 1 unit).

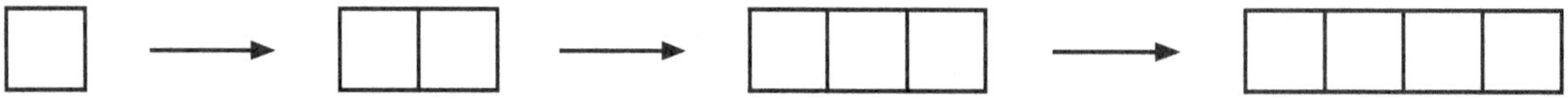

____ ____ ____ ____

a) How does the perimeter change each time a square is added?

____

b) What would the perimeter of the 6th figure be? __________

5. Write the perimeter of each figure in the sequence.

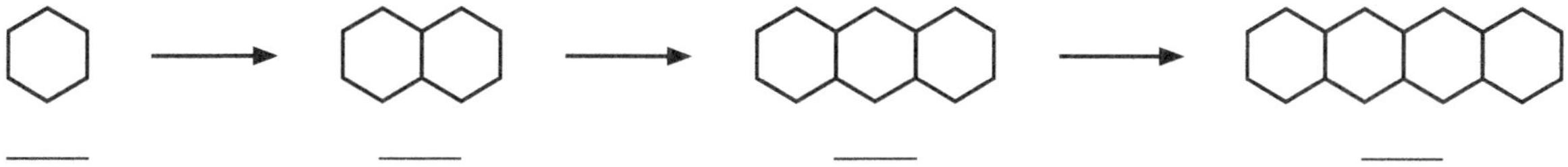

a) How does the perimeter change each time a hexagon is added?

____

b) What would the perimeter of the 6th figure be? __________

6. a) Perimeter: _______

Add one square so that the perimeter of the figure increases by 2.

New perimeter: _______

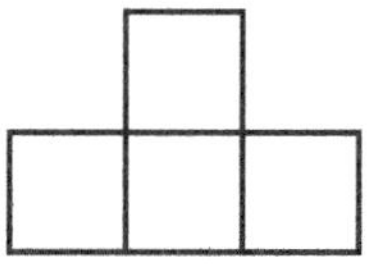

b) Perimeter: _______

Add one square so that the perimeter of the figure stays the same.

New perimeter: _______

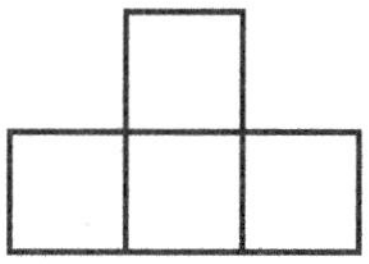

7. Draw your own figure and find its perimeter.

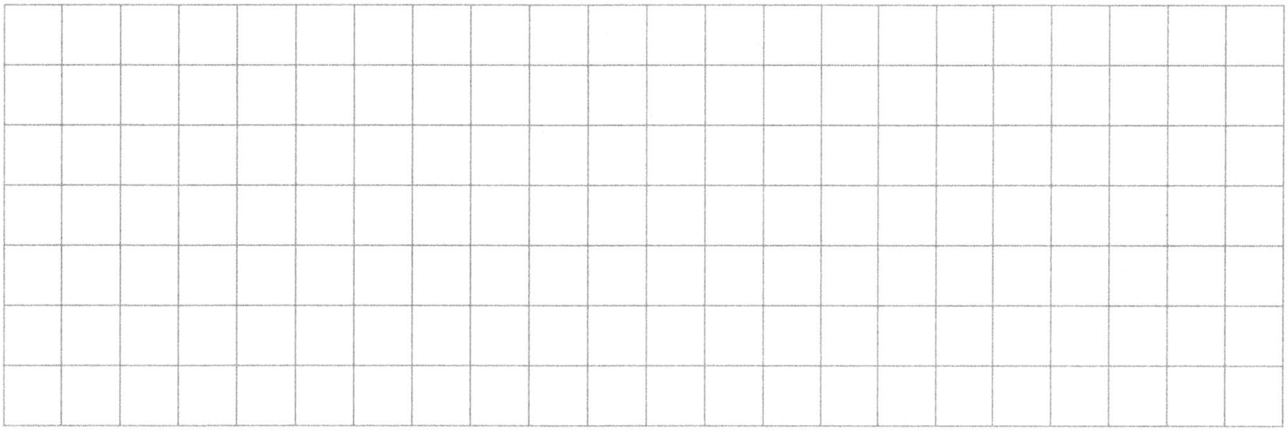

8. The pictures (**A** and **B**) show two ways to make a rectangle using four squares.

A

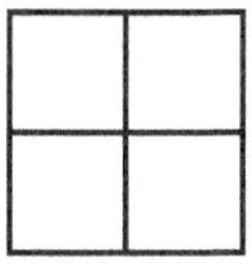

B

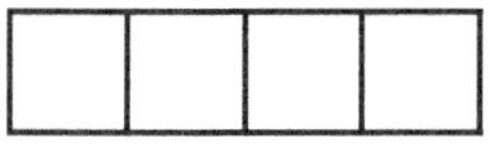

a) Which figure has the shorter perimeter? How do you know?

b) Are there any other ways to make a rectangle using 4 squares?

9. On grid paper, show all the ways you can make a rectangle using …

a) 6 squares   b) 10 squares   c) 9 squares

MD4-11 Exploring Perimeter

1. The pictures show the designs for two gardens. Find the perimeter of each garden by writing an addition equation.

a)

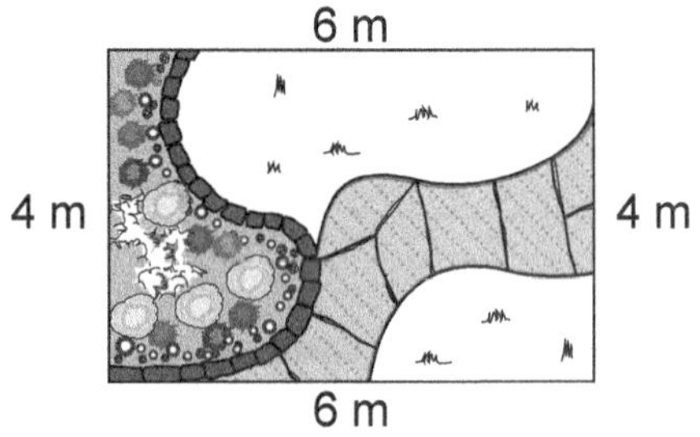

____

b)

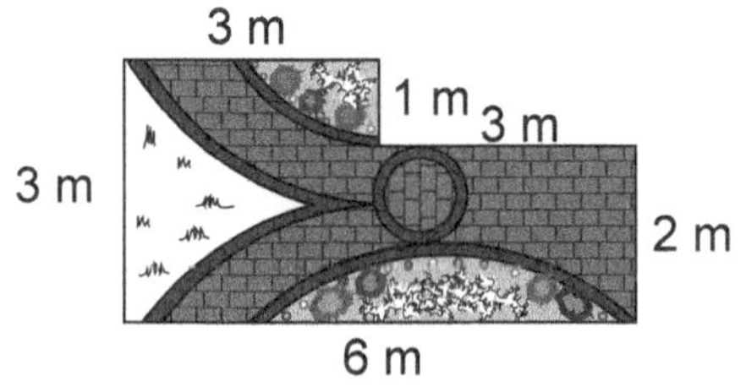

____

2. Each edge is 1 cm long. Write the total length of each side beside the figure (one side is done for you in part a). Then write an addition equation and find the perimeter.

a)

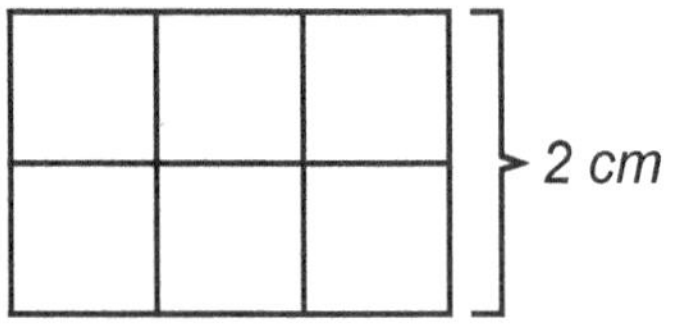

Perimeter: ______________________

b)

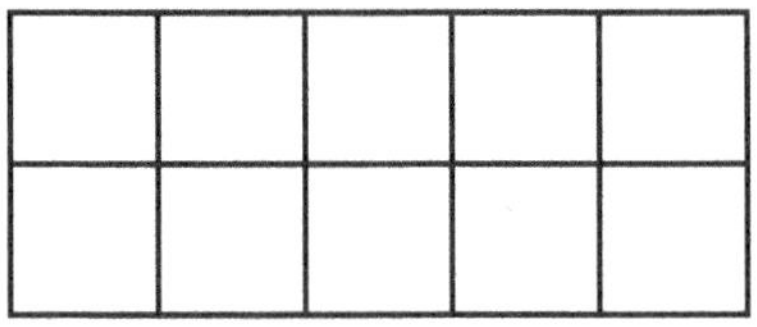

Perimeter: ______________________

c)

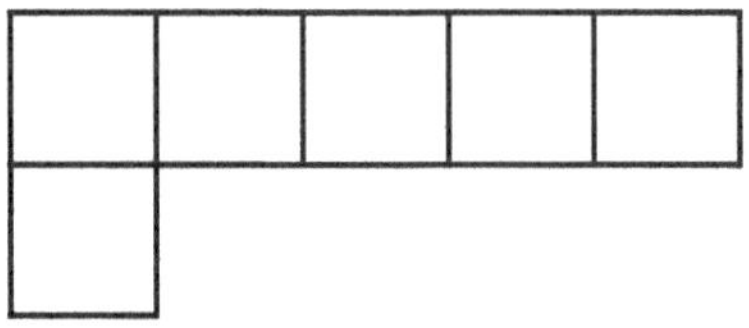

Perimeter: ______________________

d)

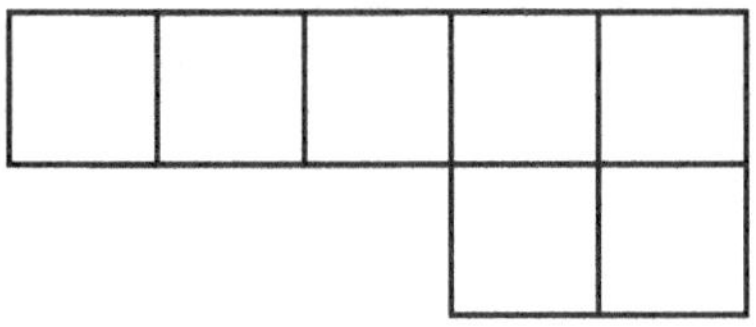

Perimeter: ______________________

3. Each edge is 1 unit long. Write the length of each side beside the figure (don't miss any edges!). Then use the side lengths to find the perimeter.

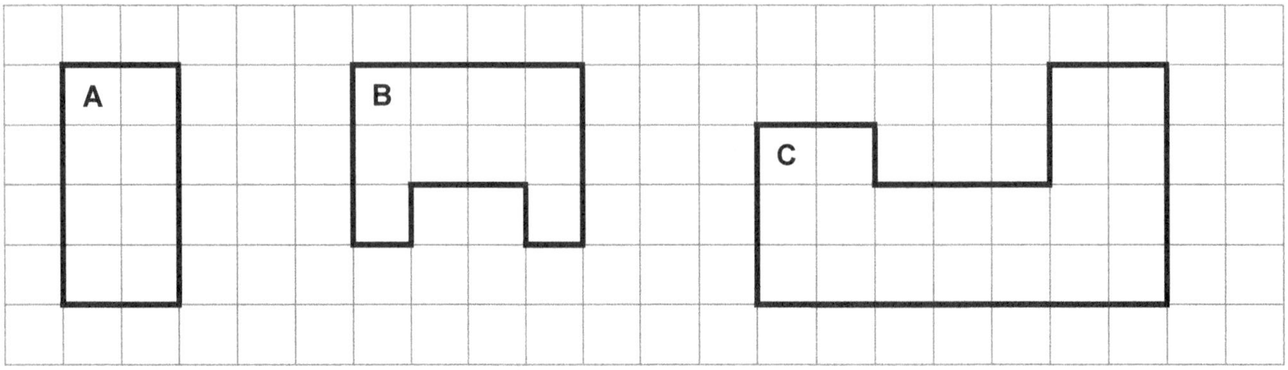

4. On grid paper, draw your own figures and find their perimeters. Try drawing letters or other shapes!

A rectangle has perimeter 12 m. Each side is an exact number of meters long.

What are the dimensions of the rectangle? Let's try different widths. Try 1 m first.

The widths add to 2 m.
The missing lengths are 12 m − 2 m = 10 m altogether.
Each length is 10 m ÷ 2 = 5 m.

5. a) The widths add to _______ m.

b) The missing lengths are 12 m − _______ m = _______ m altogether.

c) Each length is _______ m ÷ 2 = _______ m.

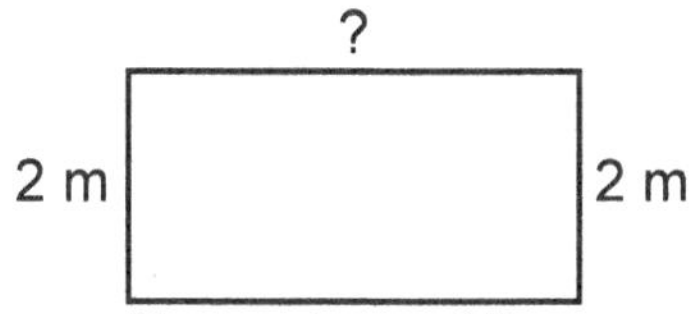

Perimeter = 12 m

6. a) The widths add to _______ m.

b) The missing lengths are ____________________________ altogether.

c) Each length is ____________________________ m.

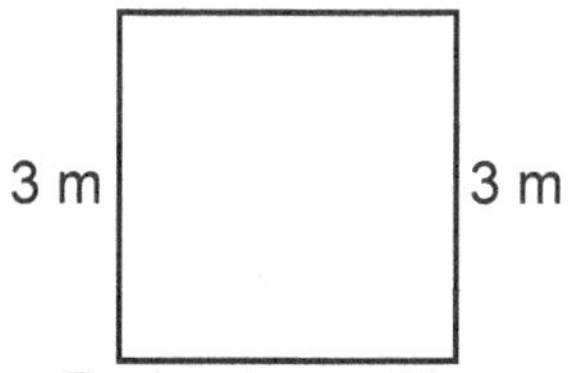

Perimeter = 12 m

7. Find the missing sides. (The pictures are not drawn to scale.)

a) Perimeter = 14 m

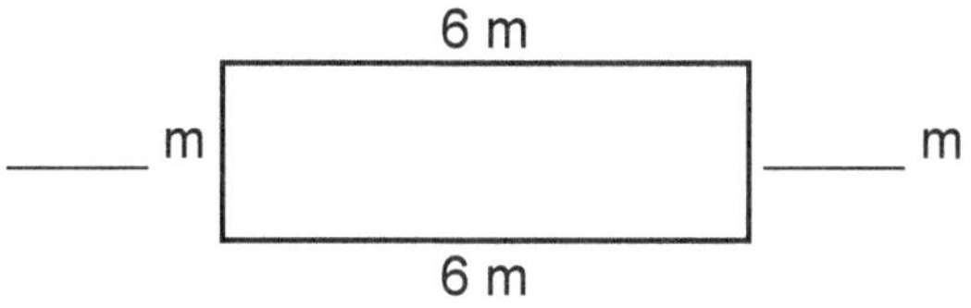

b) Perimeter = 14 cm

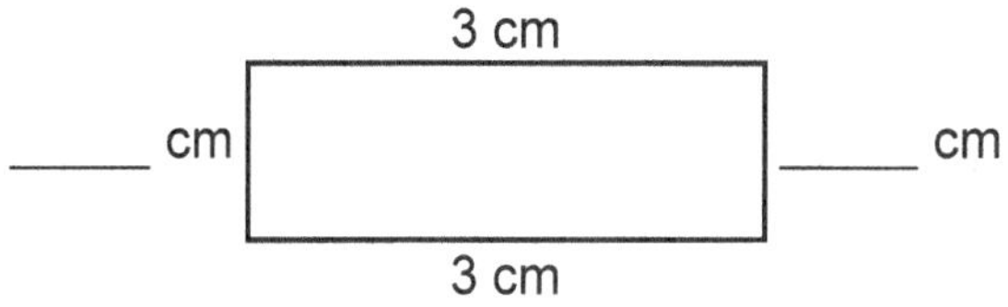

c) Perimeter = 10 cm

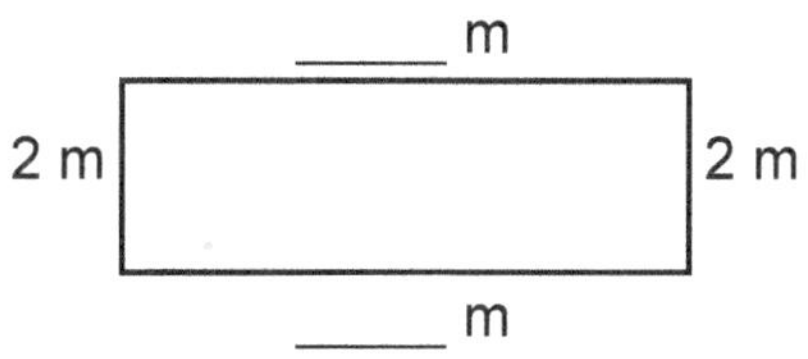

d) Perimeter = 14 m

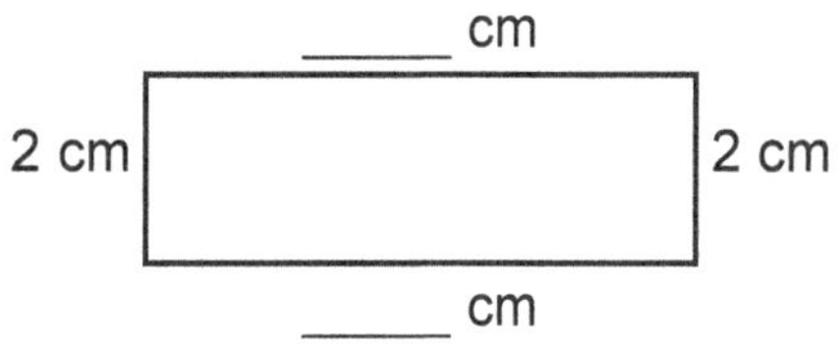

8. Find all rectangles with the given perimeter (with lengths and widths that are exact numbers of units).

Perimeter = 6 units	
Width	**Length**

Perimeter = 10 units	
Width	**Length**

Perimeter = 16 units	
Width	**Length**

Perimeter = 18 units	
Width	**Length**

9. Write a rule for finding the perimeter of a rectangle from its width and length.

MD4-12 Measuring Perimeter

1. Measure the perimeter of each figure in centimeters. Use a ruler.

a) 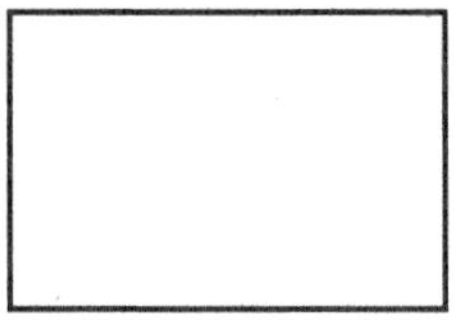

____

b) 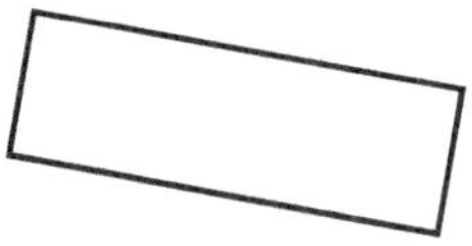

____

c) 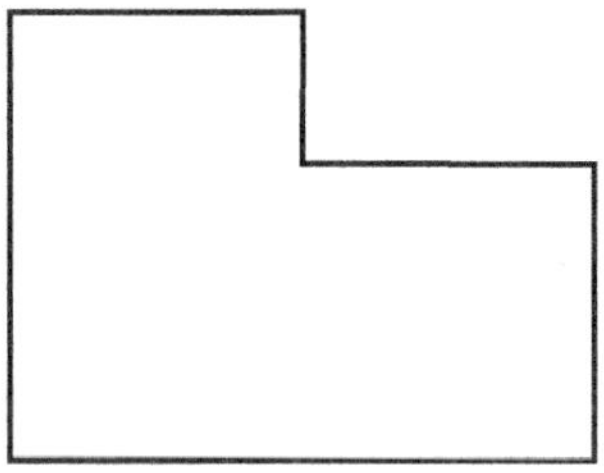

____

2. a) Find the perimeter of each figure (include the units).

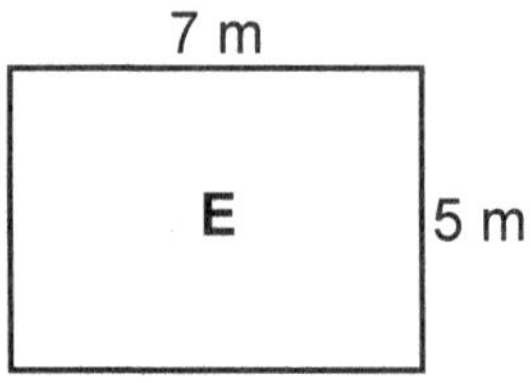

Perimeter: ______

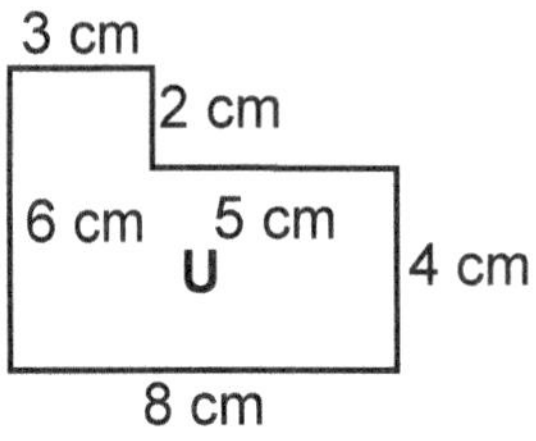

Perimeter: ______

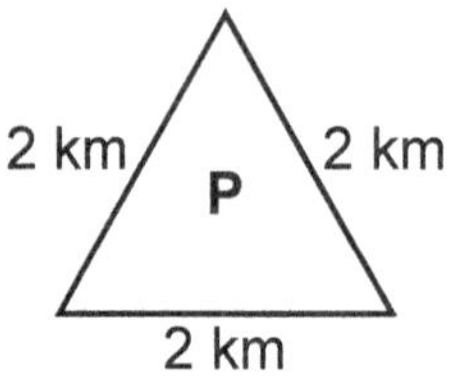

Perimeter: ______

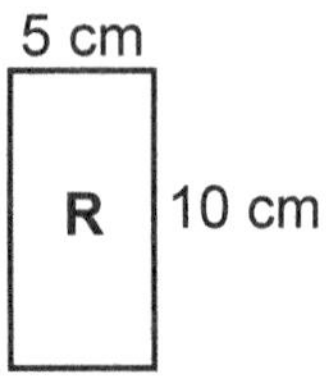

Perimeter: ______

b) Write the letters from the figures in order from greatest to least perimeter. They should spell a country in South America. Watch the units!

______ ______ ______ ______

3. Estimate the perimeter of each figure in centimeters. Then measure the actual perimeter with a ruler.

a) 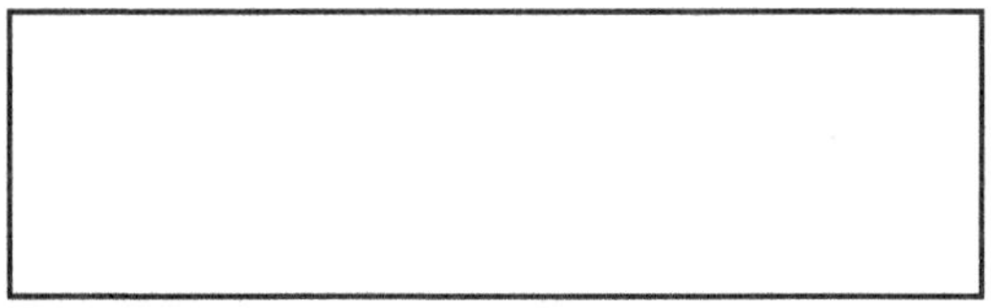

Estimated Perimeter: ____________

Actual Perimeter: ____________

b) 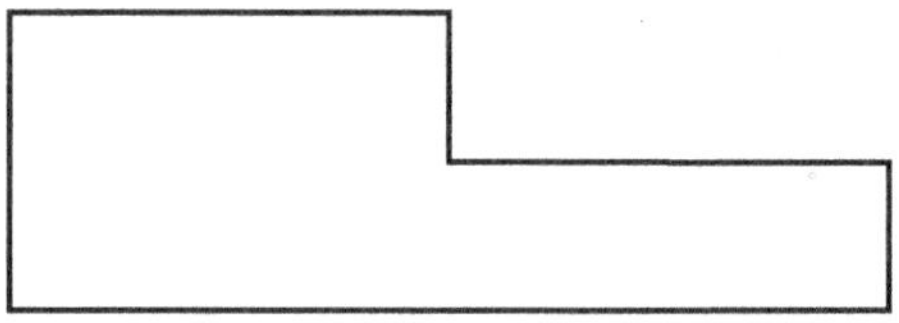

Estimated Perimeter: ____________

Actual Perimeter: ____________

4. a) Estimate the perimeter of your JUMP Math book in centimeters.
Hint: The width of your hand, with fingers spread slightly, is about 10 cm.

Estimated Perimeter: ____________

b) Measure the perimeter with a ruler.

Actual Perimeter: ____________

5. a) About how many bicycles, parked end to end, would fit along the width of your classroom? _______

b) A bicycle is about 2 m long. About how many meters wide is your classroom? _______

c) About how many meters long is your classroom? _______

d) What is the perimeter of your classroom? about _______

6. The length of a *square* room is about 3 bicycles. A bike is about 2 m long.

a) About how many meters long is the room? _______

b) What is the perimeter of the room? about _______

7. What unit (cm, m, or km) would you use to measure the perimeter of ...

a) a house? _______ b) a book? _______

c) a schoolyard? _______ d) a nature park? _______

e) a calculator? _______ f) a city? _______

g) a basketball court? _______ h) a country? _______

8. Estimate the perimeter of a room in your home. Explain how you estimated the perimeter.

9. a) A square has sides 5 cm. What is its perimeter?
b) How could you find the perimeter of a square without drawing a picture?
c) A square has perimeter 12 cm. How long is one side? Explain.

10. Sally arranged four squares (each with sides 1 m) to make a poster.
She wants to make a border from ribbon for her poster.
Ribbon costs 15¢ for each meter.
How much will the border cost?

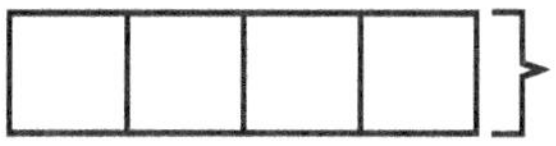

11. How could you measure the perimeter of a round object (like a plate or a can) using a strip of paper and a ruler?

12. Can two different shapes have the same perimeter? Use grid paper to explain.

13. Emma says the rule "2 × (length + width)" gives the perimeter of a rectangle. Is she correct?

MD4-13 Telling Time to the Minute

Each division on the clock stands for 1 minute.

The minute hand is pointing between the 4 and the 5.
Count by 5s until you reach the 4: twenty minutes have passed.
Then count on by ones: two minutes have passed.

20 + 2 = 22 minutes have passed

It is **7:22** or **twenty-two minutes after seven.**

1. How many minutes past the hour is it?

a) 

24 minutes past

b) 

_________ minutes past

c) 

_________ minutes past

d) 

_________ minutes past

e) 

_________ minutes past

f) 

_________ minutes past

2. What time is it?

a) 

_____ minutes past _____

b) 

_____ minutes past _____

c) 

_____ minutes past _____

3. Write the exact time.

a)

6 : 24

b)

____ : ____

c)

____ : ____

d)

____ : ____

e)

____ : ____

f)

____ : ____

BONUS ▶

g)

h)

i)

j)

k)

l)

The minute hand is pointing between the 8 and the 9.
To say how many minutes to the hour:

Count by 5s until you reach the 9. Then count on by ones.

15 + 2 = 17 minutes are left before the next hour.

It is **seventeen minutes to seven**.

4. How many minutes to the hour is it?

a)

___*24*___ minutes to 7

b)

__________ minutes to 9

c)

__________ minutes to 1

5. What time is it?

a)

______ minutes to ______

b)

______ minutes to ______

c)

______ minutes to ______

d)

______ minutes past ______

e)

______ minutes to ______

f)

______ minutes past ______

6. Tell the time two ways.

a) 

_____ minutes past _____

_____ minutes to _____

b) 

_____ minutes past _____

_____ minutes to _____

c) 

_____ minutes past _____

_____ minutes to _____

REMINDER▶ 1 hour = 60 minutes

It is 4:35. This is 35 minutes past 4.

How much time is left till 5 o'clock?

60 − 35 = 25, so it is 25 minutes to 5.

7. Tell the time two ways.

a) 

_____ minutes past _____

_____ minutes to _____

b) 

_____ minutes past _____

_____ minutes to _____

c) 

_____ minutes past _____

_____ minutes to _____

8. Write the time in numbers.

a) twenty minutes after five __5__ : __20__

b) quarter past eleven _____ : _____

c) three fifty-six _____ : _____

d) eight thirty _____ : _____

e) forty-one minutes after seven _____ : _____

f) quarter to nine _____ : _____

BONUS ▶

g) twenty-three minutes to four _____ : _____

h) nineteen minutes to twelve _____ : _____

BONUS ▶ Write the time shown on the clock three different ways.

a) ______________________________

b) ______________________________

c) ______________________________

MD4-14 Elapsed Time

1. Draw arrows to show how the minute hand moved from the start time to the end time.

a) 

b) 

c) 

2. Count by 5s to find out how much time has elapsed.

a) 8:10 to 8:25

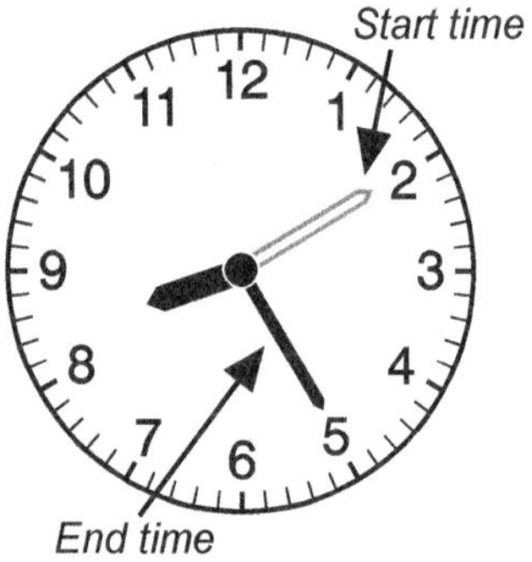

15 minutes ______

b) 3:15 to 3:40

______

c) 10:25 to 10:55

______

d) 7:35 to 8:00

______

e) 3:40 to 4:00

______

f) 9:25 to 10:00

______

g) 8:35 to 9:05

______

h) 4:30 to 5:10

______

i) 6:20 to 7:15

______

3. Count by 5s to show how much time has elapsed between ...

a) 6:50 and 7:25

6:50 (0), *6:55* (5), ______ (10), ______ (15), ______, ______, ______, ______, ______

Elapsed time: ______________________

b) 4:45 and 5:05

______, ______, ______, ______, ______, ______, ______, ______, ______

Elapsed time: ______________________

c) 12:35 and 1:05

______, ______, ______, ______, ______, ______, ______, ______, ______

Elapsed time: ______________________

d) 2:45 and 3:20

Elapsed time: ______________________

e) 9:15 and 10:10

Elapsed time: ______________________

4. It is now 5:10. Mohamed started playing at 4:25. How long has he been playing? ______________

5. The clock shows the time Kelly started reading. At what time did she finish reading? Count by 5s and draw an arrow on the clock to show the time she finished.

a) Kelly read for 20 minutes.

Kelly finished at________

b) Kelly read for 15 minutes.

Kelly finished at________

c) Kelly read for 25 minutes.

Kelly finished at________

Jake started reading at 1:20. He read for 30 minutes. When did he finish reading?

1:20 ← start time

+ 0:30 ← elapsed time = 30 minutes = 0 hours 30 minutes = 0:30

1:50

Jake finished reading at 1:50.

6. Add to find the end time.

a) 3:23 + 0:20

b) 8:22 + 0:11

c) 1:48 + 5:00

d) 6:40 + 2:15

e) 3:42 + 8:09

7. Regroup 60 minutes as 1 hour.

a) 2:65
3:05

b) 7:71

c) 5:80

d) 2:92

e) 1:105

8. Add and regroup to find the end time.

a) 3:23 + 1:40 = *4:63* = *5:03*

b) 8:22 + 0:51

c) 9:48 + 1:30

d) 6:40 + 2:25

e) 3:42 + 1:05

9. a) Kyla goes to bed at 7:45 p.m. Jake's bedtime is 30 minutes later.

What time does Jake go to bed? ____________

b) Ann put chicken in the oven at 4:50 p.m. It should bake for 1 hour and 40 minutes.

At what time should she take it out? ____________

10. Subtract to find the elapsed time.

a) 3:43 − 3:20 = *0:23*

b) 8:22 − 7:21

c) 11:48 − 5:30

d) 6:40 − 2:25

e) 3:42 − 1:05

To subtract 1:40 from 4:23, regroup 1 hour as 60 minutes:

4:23 − 1:40 ⟶ ~~4~~:23 (*3:83*) − 1:40 = *2:43*

11. Regroup 1 hour as 60 minutes.

a) ~~3~~:~~2~~0 *2:80*

b) 7:21

c) 5:30

d) 2:35

e) 11:45

12. Regroup, then subtract to find the elapsed time.

a) ~~5~~:~~2~~3 (*4:83*) − 1:27 = *3:56*

b) 8:22 − 7:41

c) 11:23 − 5:52

d) 6:40 − 3:59

e) 3:05 − 1:42

13. Cyril started reading at 3:30. He finished at 4:25. How long was he reading for?____________

BONUS ▶ Muffins need to bake for 22 minutes. You want them to be ready at 6:00 p.m.

When should you put the muffins into the oven?____________

MD4-15 Elapsed Time (Advanced)

1. Find how much time has passed between the times in bold (intervals are not shown to scale).

a)

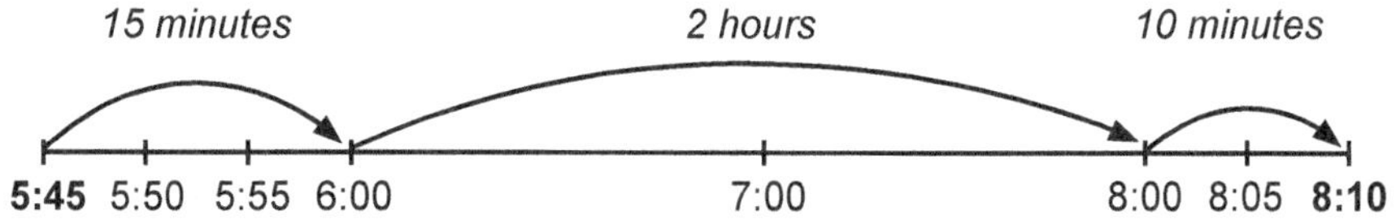

Elapsed time: *2 hours 25 minutes*

b)

Elapsed time: ______________________

c)

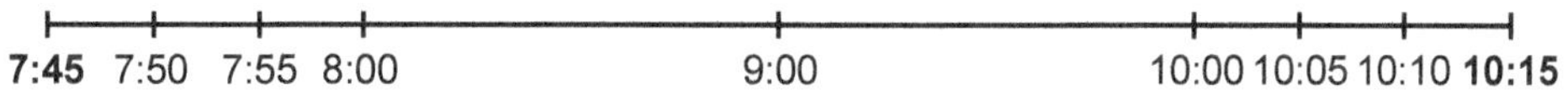

Elapsed time: ______________________

2. Find how much time has passed between the times in bold. Regroup 60 minutes as 1 hour.

a)

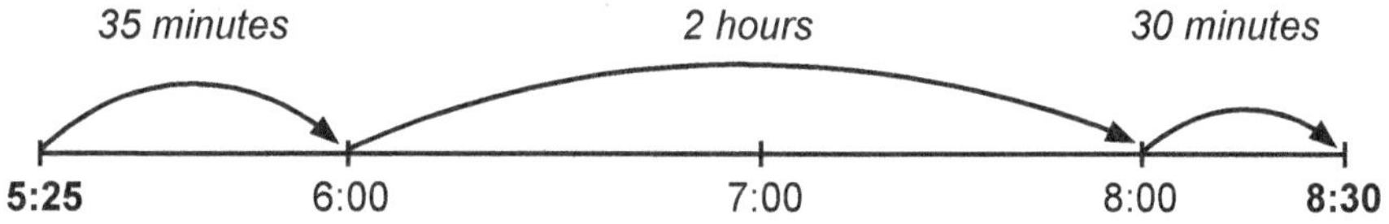

Elapsed time: *2 hours 65 minutes = 3 hours 5 minutes*

b)

Elapsed time: ______________________

c)

Elapsed time: ______________________

3. Draw a timeline to find out how much time has elapsed between …

a) 7:40 and 10:10 b) 4:35 and 6:05 c) 8:50 and 10:10

MD4-16 Time Intervals

1. a) Fill in the table.

weeks	1	2	3	4	5	6	7
days	*7*						

b) What number do you multiply by to get the number of days from the number of weeks? ________

2. A month can have 28, 29, 30, or 31 days. About how many weeks are in 1 month? ________________

3. Change the time expressed in weeks and days to days only.

a) 2 weeks 3 days

$=$ *14* days $+$ *3* days

$=$ *17* days

b) 2 weeks 5 days

$=$ ____ days $+$ ____ days

$=$ ____ days

c) 3 weeks 2 days

$=$ ____ days $+$ ____ days

$=$ ____ days

4. Janice wants to know how long it took her plant to grow a certain height. Help her find the time in days.

Height of Janice's plant	**Time After Planting** *(in weeks and days)*	**Rough Work**	**Time After Planting** *(in days)*
2 cm	0 weeks and 4 days	$0 \times 7 = 0$ $0 + 4 = 4$	*4*
4 cm	1 week and 1 day	$1 \times 7 = 7$ $7 + 1 = 8$	
6 cm	1 week and 5 days		
8 cm	2 weeks and 2 days		
10 cm	2 weeks and 6 days		
12 cm	3 weeks and 3 days		

a) Complete the table.

b) How long did it take the plant to grow 2 cm? ________________

c) How long (in days) did it take the plant to reach 11 cm? ________________ Explain.

____

____

____

d) How long (in days) will it take the plant to reach 14 cm? ________________

1 hour = 60 minutes   1 minute = 60 seconds

5. Fill in the tables.

hours	1	2	3	4	5	6	7	8
minutes	*60*							

minutes	1	2	3	4	5	6	7	8
seconds	*60*							

6. a) To change a measurement from hours to minutes, what number do you have to multiply by? ________

b) To change a measurement from minutes to seconds, what number do you have to multiply by? ________

c) 1 hour = ________ minutes = ____________ seconds

7. Fill in the numbers that are missing from the following tables.

hours	minutes
7	
8	

hours	minutes
15	
20	

minutes	seconds
32	
57	

minutes	seconds
112	
257	

8. Convert the multiple-unit measurements to minutes.

a) 3 hours = ___*180*___ minutes,

so 3 hours 10 minutes = ___*190*___ minutes

b) 4 hours = ________ minutes,

so 4 hours 25 minutes = ________ minutes

c) 2 hours = ________ minutes,

so 2 hours 43 minutes = ________ minutes

d) 10 hours = ________ minutes,

so 10 hours 12 minutes = ________ minutes

9. Convert the multiple-unit measurements to seconds.

a) 3 minutes = ___*180*___ seconds,

so 3 minutes 7 seconds = ___*187*___ seconds

b) 4 minutes = ________ seconds,

so 4 minutes 40 seconds = ________ seconds

c) 5 minutes = ________ seconds,

so 5 minutes 4 seconds = ________ seconds

d) 8 minutes = ________ seconds,

so 8 minutes 12 seconds = ________ seconds

MD4-17 Topics in Time

1 year = 365 days and 1 year = about 52 weeks

Note: There are 366 days in a leap year.

1. Order the units from smallest (1) to largest (5).

day	minute	week	year	hour
☐	1	☐	☐	☐

2. Fill in the tables.

a)

days	hours
1	24
2	
3	

b)

weeks	days
1	7
2	
3	

c)

years	weeks
1	52
2	
3	

d)

years	days
1	365
2	
3	

3. Which interval is longer? Explain.

a) 70 minutes OR 1 hour 20 minutes

b) 3 hours 10 minutes OR 170 minutes

c) 4 minutes 24 seconds OR 285 seconds

d) 10 minutes OR 650 seconds

4. Tom worked for 1 hour 55 minutes. Jo worked 20 minutes longer. How long did Jo work?

A **decade** is 10 years. A **century** is 100 years.

5. Fill in the tables.

decades	1	2	3	4
years	*10*			

centuries	1	2	3	4
years	*100*			

6. Fill in the blanks.

a) 60 years = ______ decades

b) 800 years = ______ centries

c) 12 decades = ______ years

d) 40 decades = ____centuries

7. Which interval is longer? Explain.

a) 7 decades OR 85 years

b) 8 centuries OR 670 years

8. The United States became independent in 1776.

a) About how many centuries ago was this?

b) About how many decades ago was this?

G4-1 Introduction to Classifying Data

Data is facts or information. For example, your age is a piece of data, and so is your name.

Data can be organized into **categories**. We use attributes to sort data. Some attributes are:
• Gender (boy or girl) • Age (age 9 or age 10) • Length of Hair (long hair or short hair)

1. *Animals:* sparrow butterfly goldfish swan shark beetle goose ant

a) Circle the animals that are birds.

b) Underline the animals that are fish.

c) How many animals are in each category? Birds ____ Fish ____ Insects ____

2. Count how many are in each category.

Foods: ham apple banana milk yogurt strawberry cheese chicken grapes

Categories: Fruit ____ Meat ____ Dairy products ____

3. Match the data with the correct category.

A. Chicago, Dallas, Boston ____ pizza toppings

B. baseball, soccer, tennis ____ coins

C. cheese, pepperoni, mushrooms ____ trees

D. maple, oak, beech ____ cities in the USA

E. nickel, dime, quarter ____ sports

4. Put a check mark next to the category that describes each group of numbers.

a) 7, 9, 52, 11, 6, 33
- ☐ greater than 4
- ☐ less than 4

b) 19, 11, 3, 5, 21, 7
- ☐ even numbers
- ☐ odd numbers

c) $\frac{1}{2}, \frac{3}{4}, \frac{1}{4}, \frac{2}{5}, \frac{5}{10}$
- ☐ whole numbers
- ☐ fractions

5. Describe how the numbers were sorted. 1, 5, 3, 7, 9 0, 2, 8, 4, 6

Venn Diagrams

We can use circles to sort objects by their properties.
Objects inside a circle have the property, and objects outside the circle do not.

Use these shapes for Questions 1, 2, and 3.

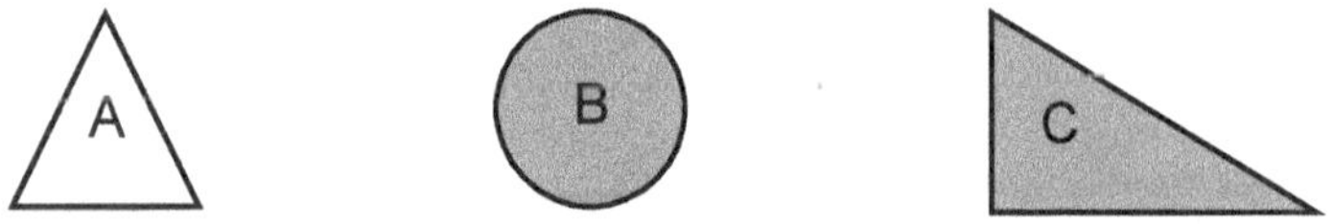

1. Put the letters from each shape inside or outside the circle.

a) 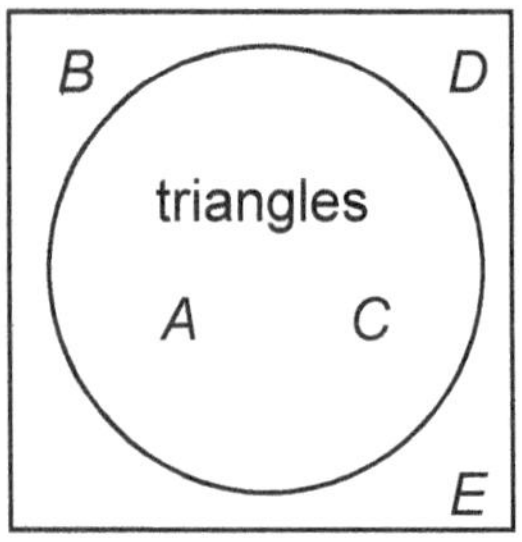

b) 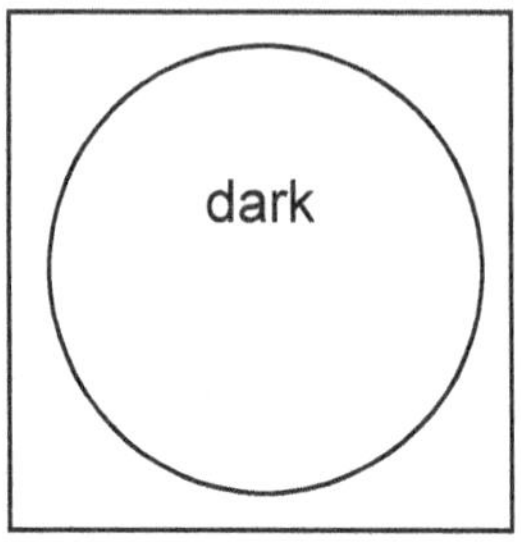

c) 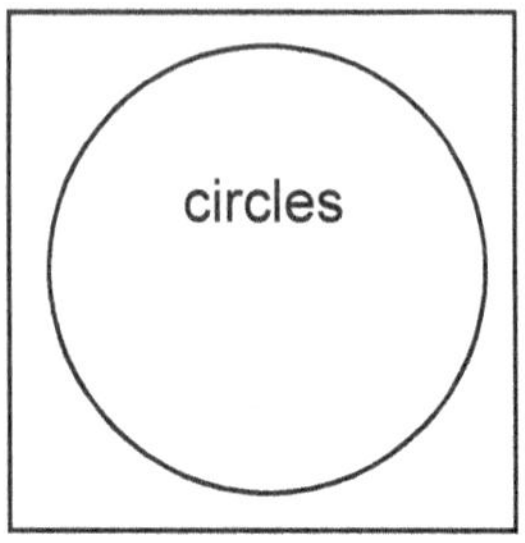

Objects can be in more than one circle at the same time.
The overlapping circles or ovals are called a **Venn diagram**.

2. a) Shade the area that is **inside** both ovals. Put the correct letter in that area.

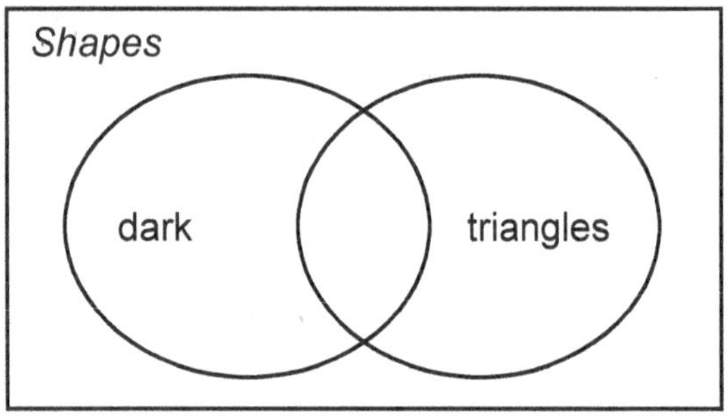

b) Shade the area that is **outside** both ovals. Put the correct letter in that area.

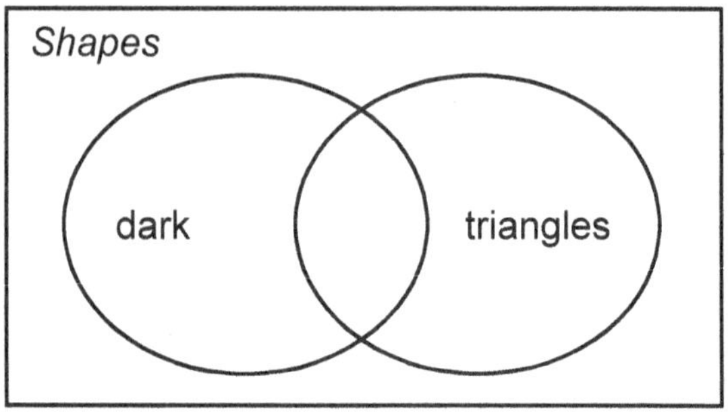

3. Complete the Venn diagrams.

a) 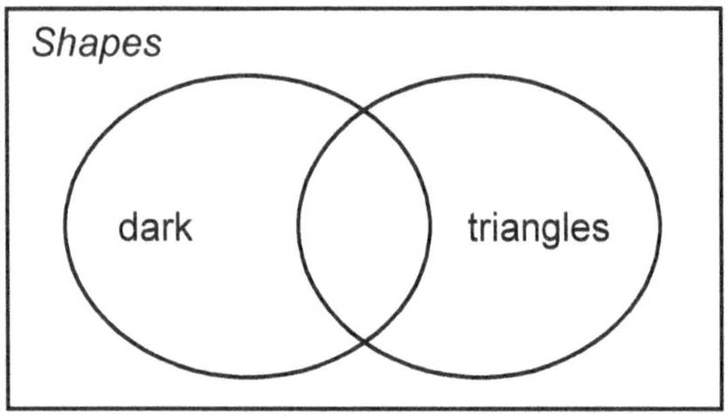

b) 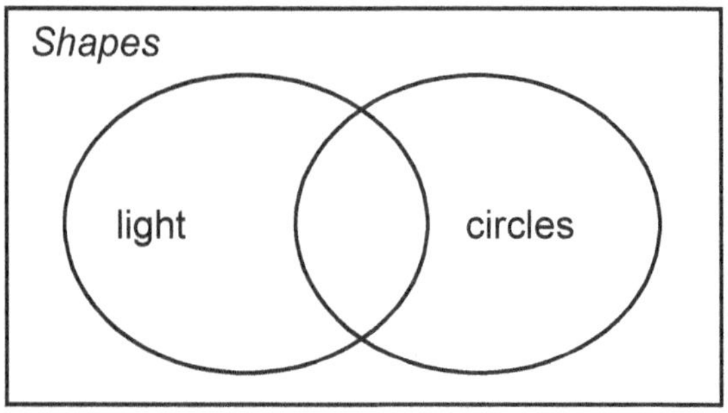

4. Complete the Venn diagram.

A. bat B. dog C. owl D. cat E. mosquito F. flamingo G. sparrow H. bee

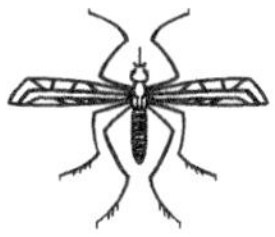

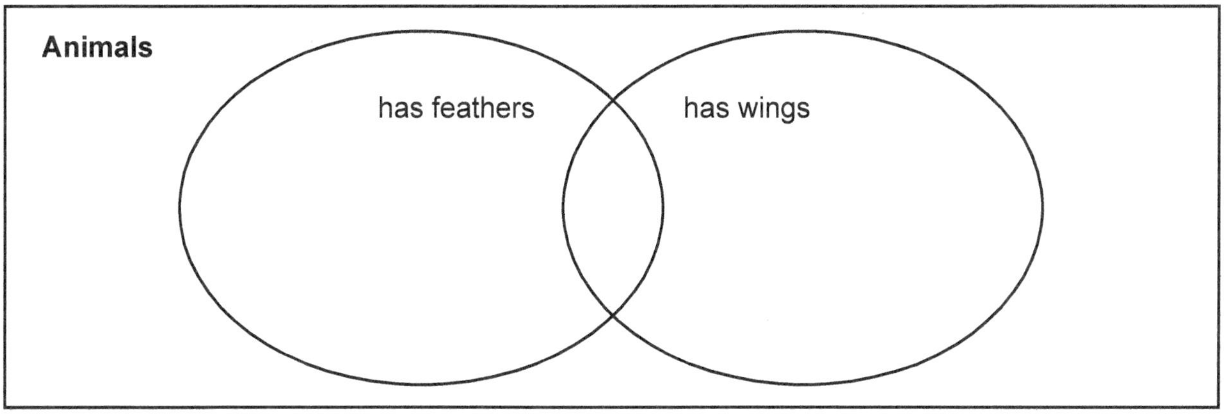

One part of the Venn diagram is empty. Explain what that means. ______________________________

____

5. Complete the Venn diagrams.

a) A. rice B. hat C. sit D. rat

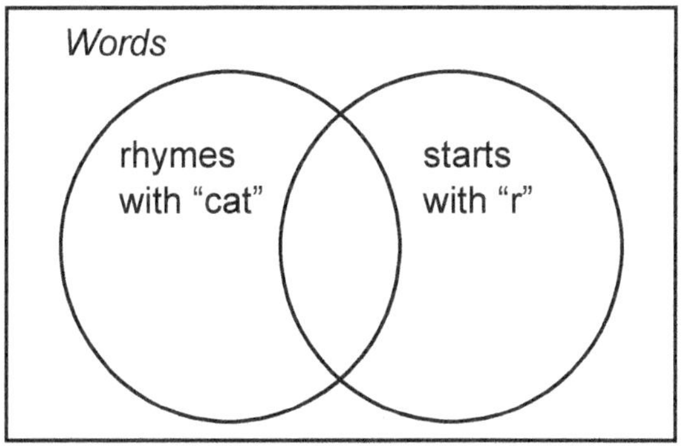

b) A. human B. chair C. fish D. worm

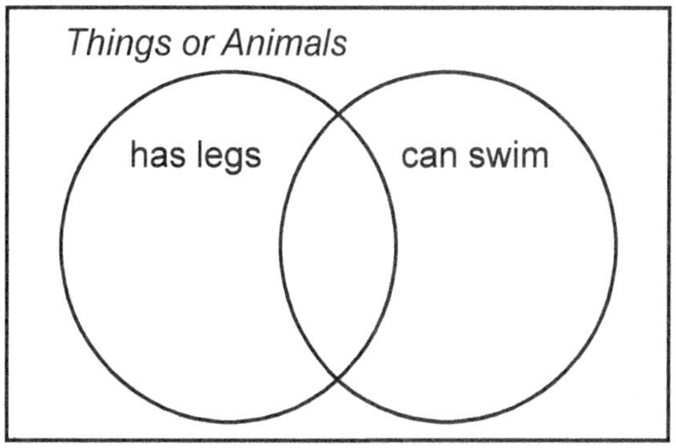

c) A. cat B. listen C. watch D. fly

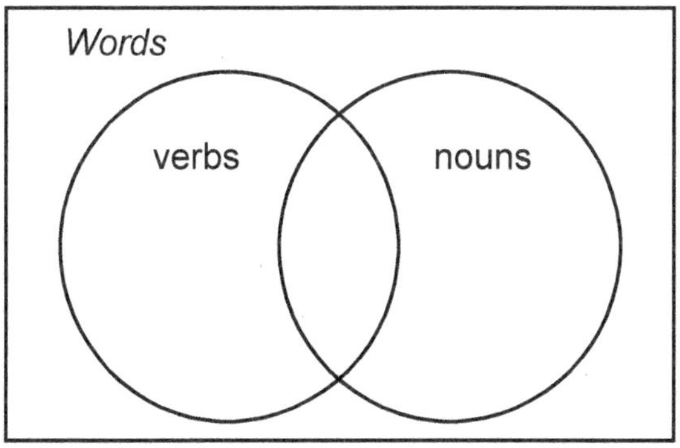

d) A. Utah B. Asia C. Boston D. USA

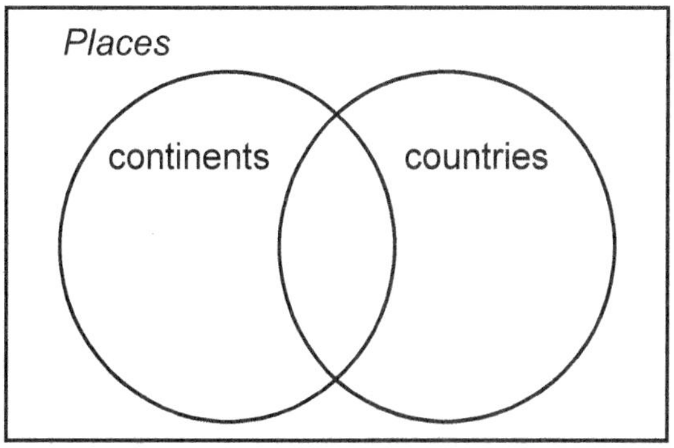

G4-3 Sides and Vertices of 2-D Shapes

All 2-D (flat) shapes have **sides** (or edges) and **vertices** (the corners where the sides meet).

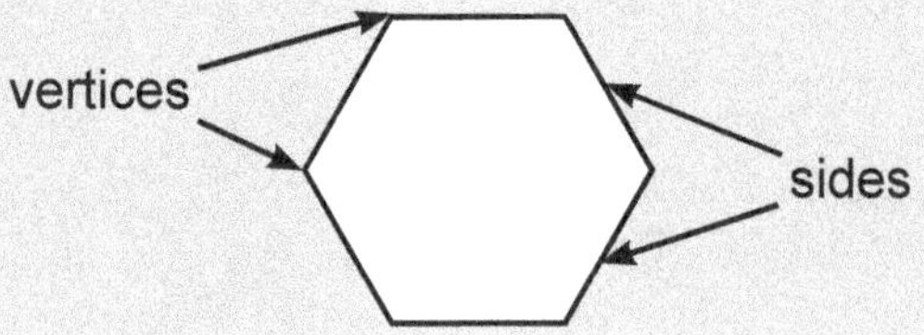

1. Count the number of sides and vertices in each shape. Put a check mark on each side and circle each vertex as you count.

a) 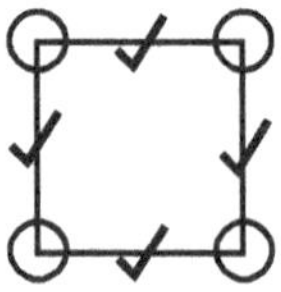

__4__ sides

__4__ vertices

b) 

_____ sides

_____ vertices

c) 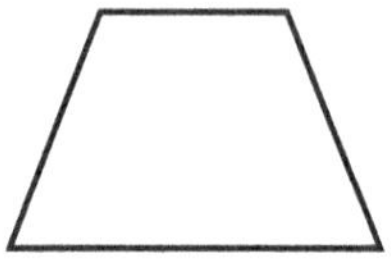

_____ sides

_____ vertices

d) 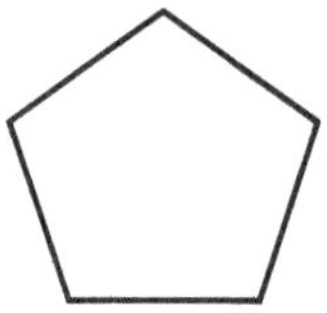

_____ sides

_____ vertices

e) 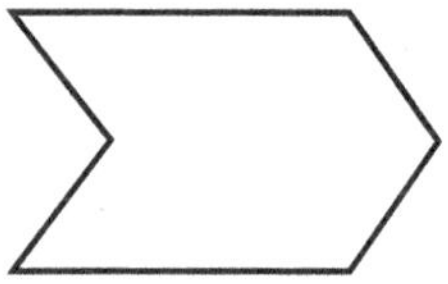

_____ sides _____ vertices

f) 

_____ sides _____ vertices

g) 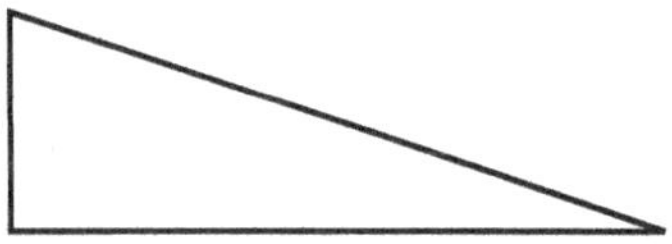

_____ sides _____ vertices

BONUS ▶

h) 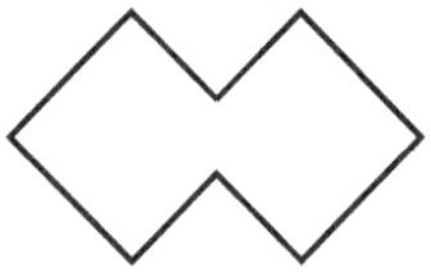

_____ sides _____ vertices

i) 

_____ sides _____ vertices

j) 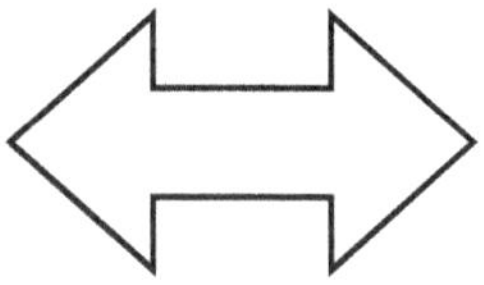

_____ sides _____ vertices

k) 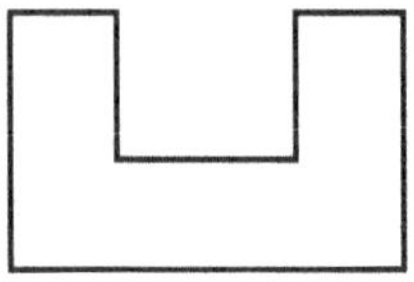

_____ sides _____ vertices

l) 

_____ sides _____ vertices

m) 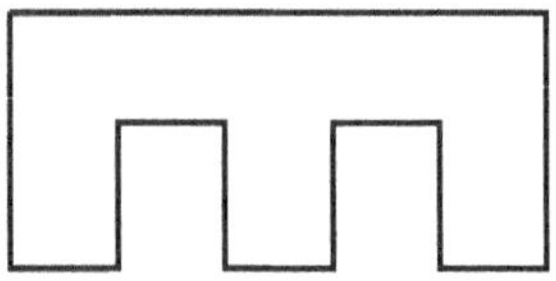

_____ sides _____ vertices

A **polygon** is a 2-D shape with only straight sides.

2. These shapes have both straight and curved sides. Fill in the missing numbers.

a) 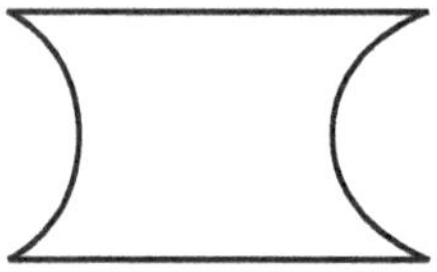

_____ curved sides

_____ straight sides

b) 

_____ curved sides

_____ straight sides

c) Are these shapes polygons? Explain.

Polygons are named according to how many sides they have.

3 sides	triangle	5 sides	pentagon
4 sides	quadrilateral	6 sides	hexagon

3. Count the sides. Then name the shape.

a) 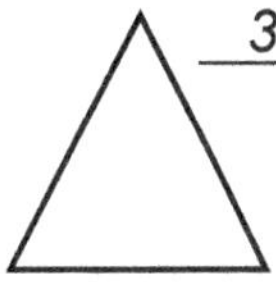 _3_ sides

triangle

b) 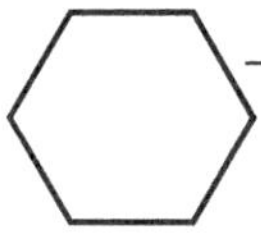 ____ sides

____

c) 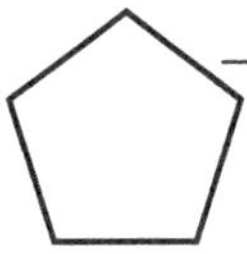 ____ sides

____

d) 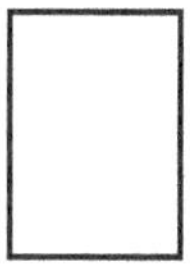 ____ sides

____

4. Find the number of sides and complete the chart.

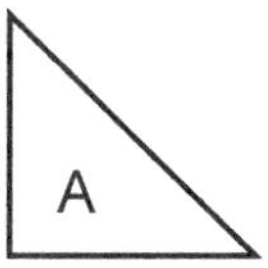

_3_ sides

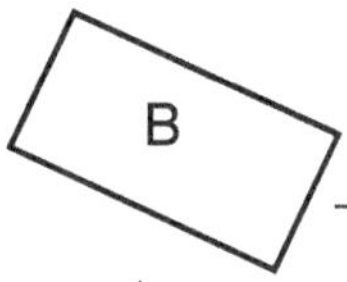

____ sides

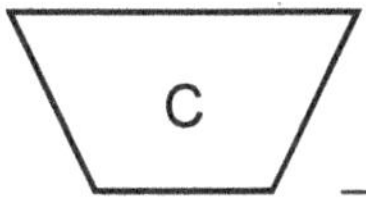

____ sides

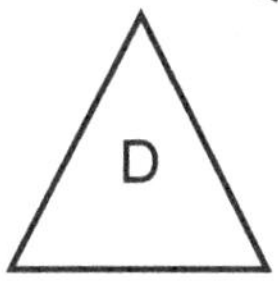

____ sides

Name	**Shapes**
Triangle	*A,*
Quadrilateral	

5. Complete the chart. Find as many shapes as you can for each shape name.

Name	**Shapes**
Triangle	
Quadrilateral	
Pentagon	
Hexagon	

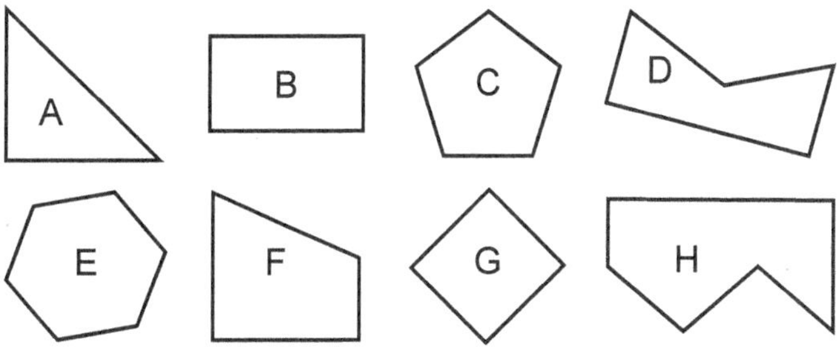

6. Use a ruler. Draw a polygon with …

a) 3 sides b) 4 sides

c) 5 sides d) 6 sides

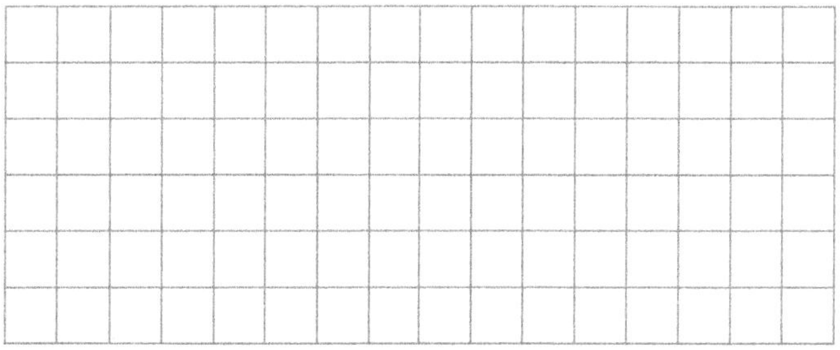

7. a) Count the vertices in the polygons you drew above. What do you notice?

b) Can you draw a polygon in which the number of sides does not equal the number of vertices?

G4-4 Right Angles

In mathematics, square corners are called **right angles**.

A rectangle has 4 right angles.

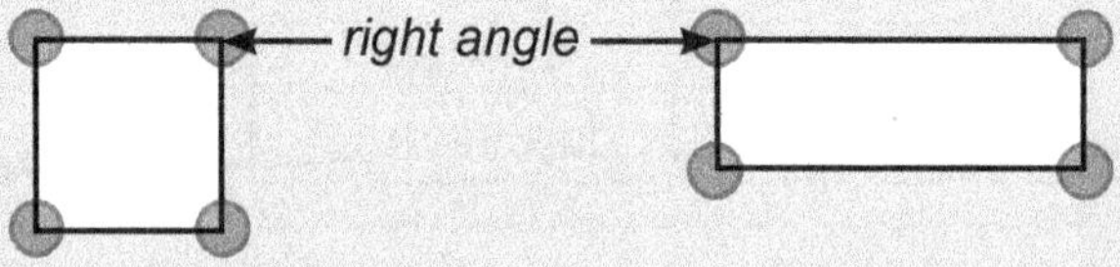

To check if an angle is a right angle, compare it with a corner of a piece of paper.

1. Circle the right angles. Check your answers with the corner of a piece of paper.

a) 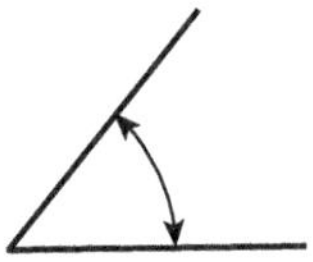

b) 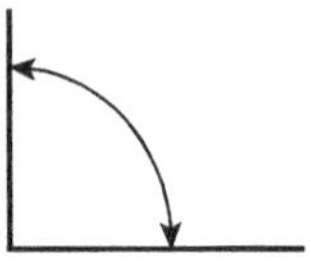

c) 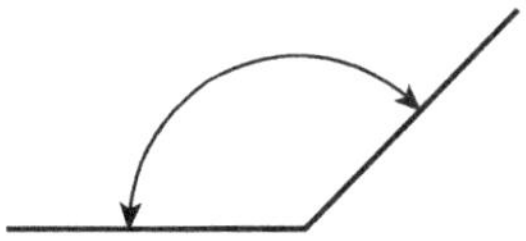

d) 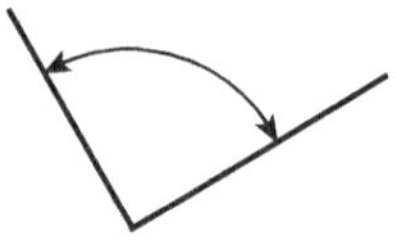

e) 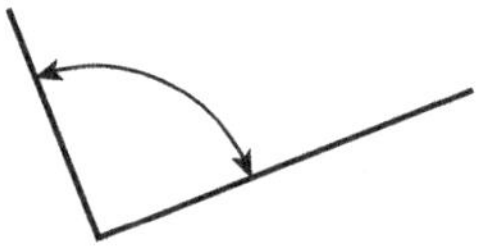

f) 

g) 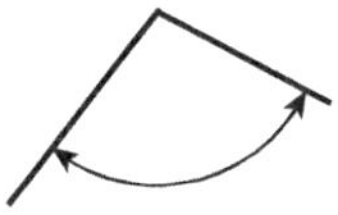

h) 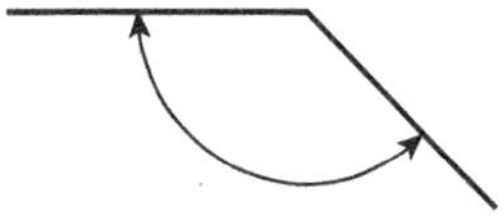

Mathematicians use a small square to mark right angles.

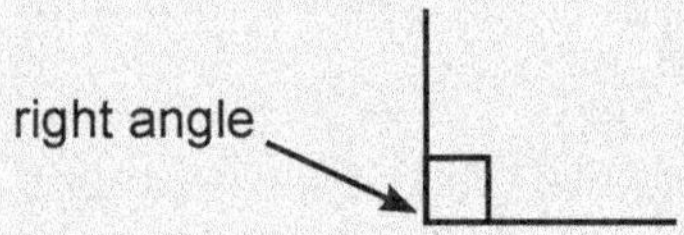

2. Mark the right angles with a small square.

a) 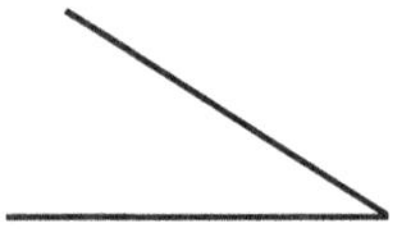

b) 

c) 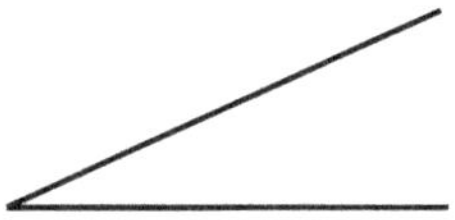

d) 

e) 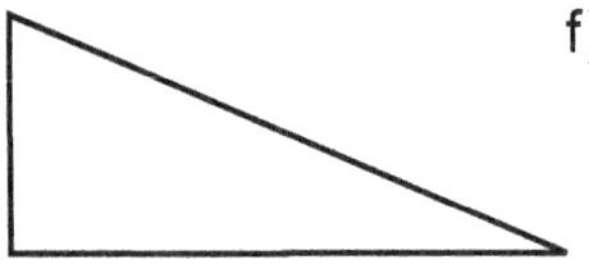

f) 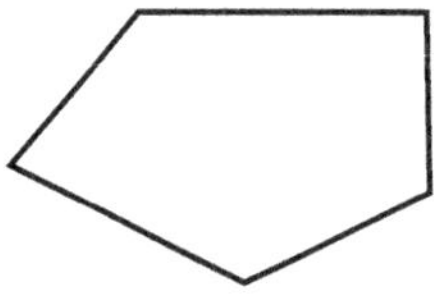

g) 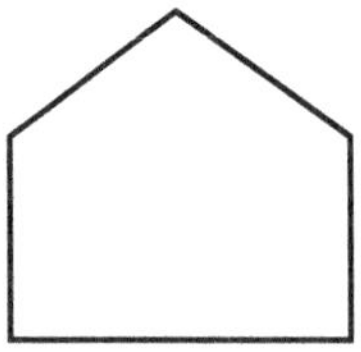

h) 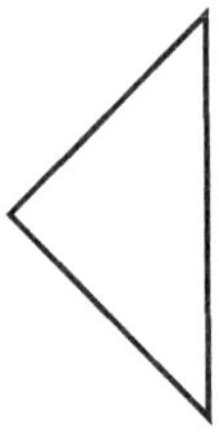

3. Circle the shape that has no right angle.

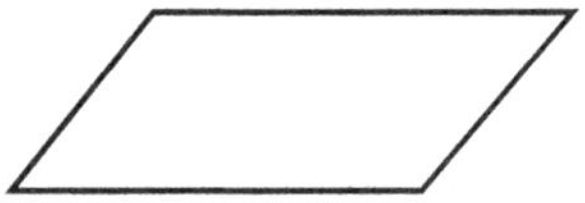

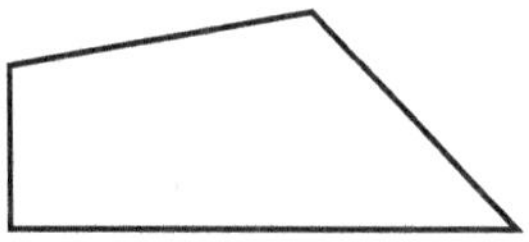

4. Draw two right angles, facing different directions. Mark them with a small square.

5. a) Draw 3 letters of the alphabet that have at least one right angle. Mark all the right angles.

b) Draw more letters with right angles. Which letters have the most right angles?

When two lines make a right angle, they are called **perpendicular lines**.

6. The two lines are perpendicular. Check all the angles with a piece of paper. Mark all the right angles with a small square.

a) 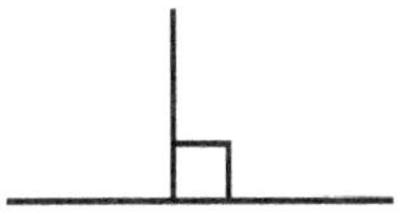

b) 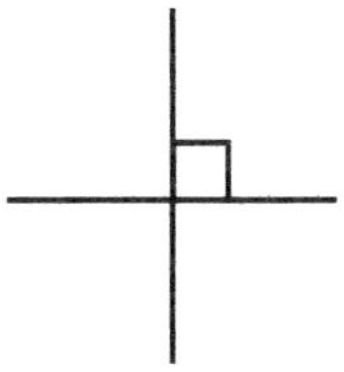

c) 

7. Circle the pairs of perpendicular lines.

8. Check if each angle is a right angle. Mark all the right angles.

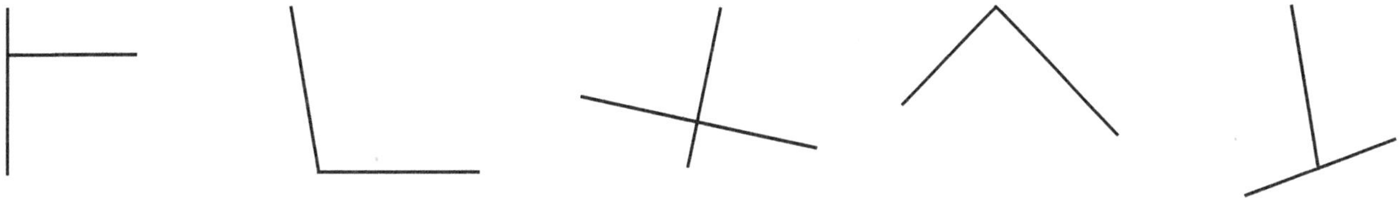

9. Which quadrilaterals have pairs of perpendicular sides? Mark the perpendicular sides with small squares.

a) rectangle

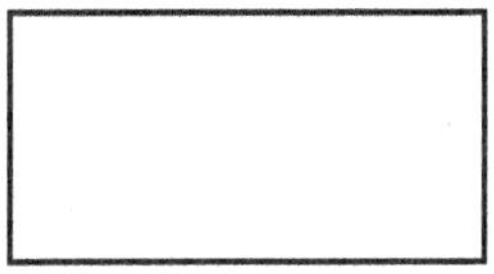

b) square

c) rhombus

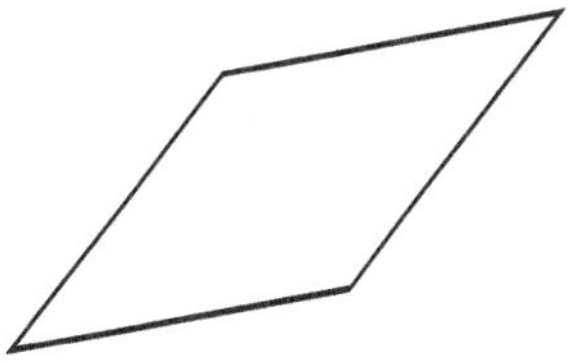

d) parallelogram

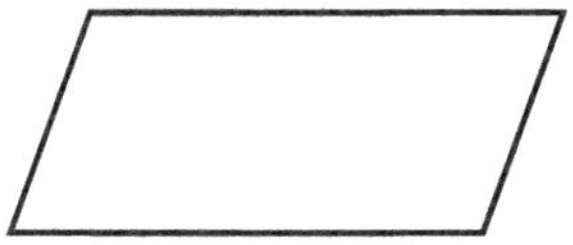

10. Find all pairs of perpendicular sides in each shape.

a) 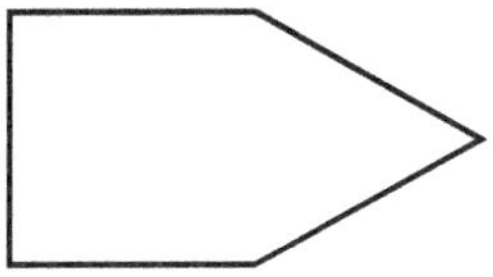

b) 

c) 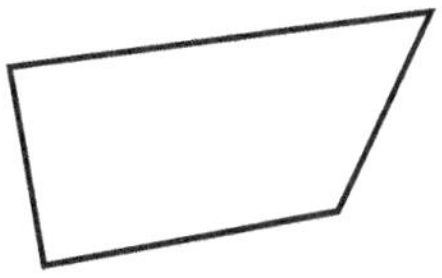

d) 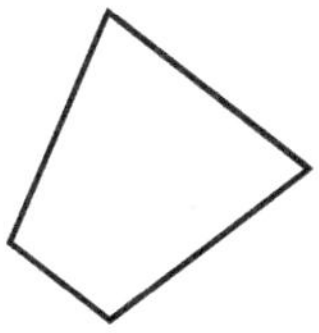

G4-5 Parallel Lines

Parallel lines are like the long, straight rails on a railroad track.
Parallel lines are:

- Straight
- Always the same distance apart

You can extend lines in both directions as much as you want.
No matter how long they are, parallel lines will never meet.

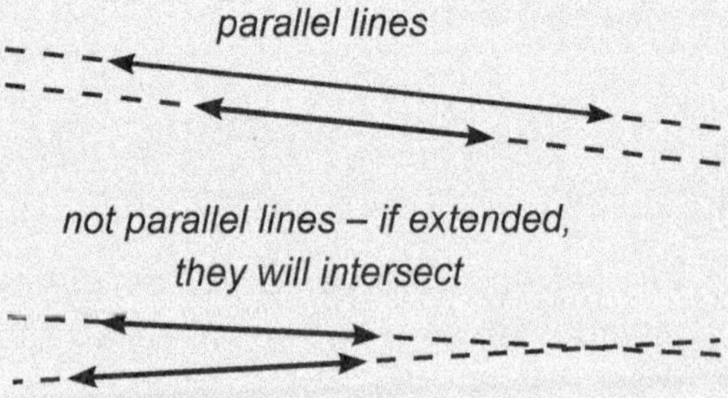

1. Extend the lines to check if they intersect. Then circle parallel lines.

a) 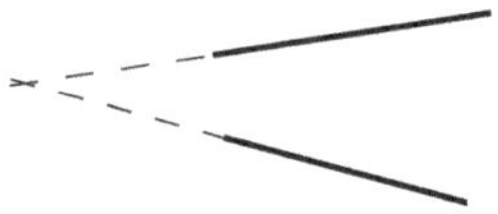

b) 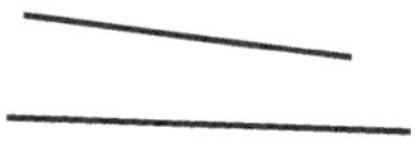

c) 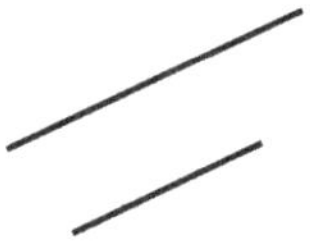

Mathematicians mark parallel lines with arrows, like this: 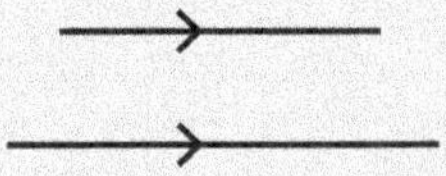

2. Mark any pairs of lines that are parallel with arrows.

a) 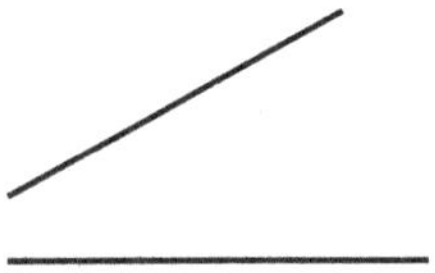

b) 

c) 

d) 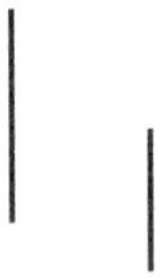

e) 

f) 

g) 

h) 

3. Draw a line parallel to each line below. Use a ruler!

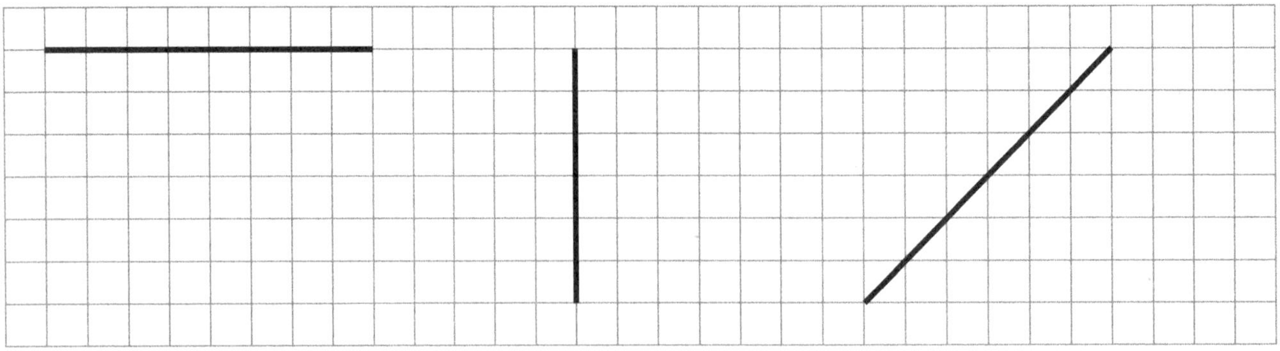

BONUS ▶ Select one pair of lines in Question 2 that are not parallel.
How do you know these lines are not parallel?

4. The line segments are parallel. Join the dots to make a quadrilateral. Use a ruler.

a) 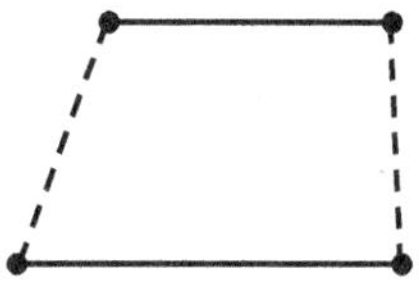

b) 

c) 

d) 

5. Each shape has one pair of parallel sides. Mark opposite sides that are not parallel with an **X**.

a) 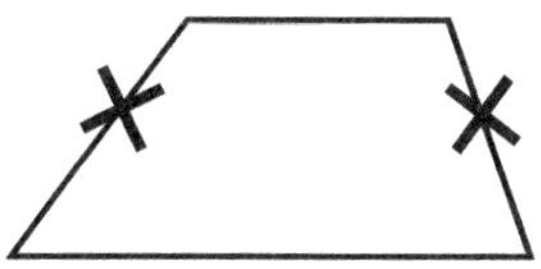

b) 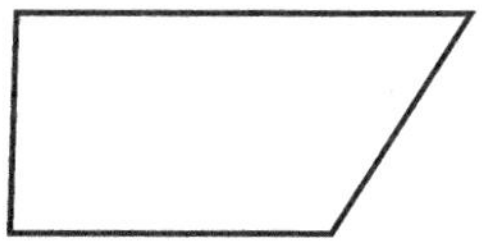

c) 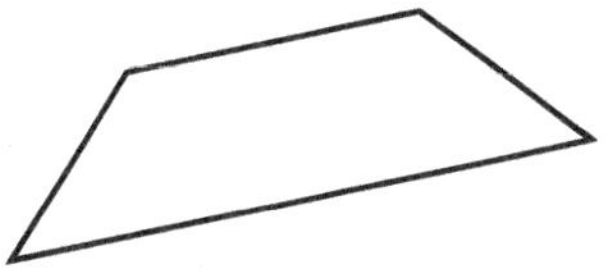

d) 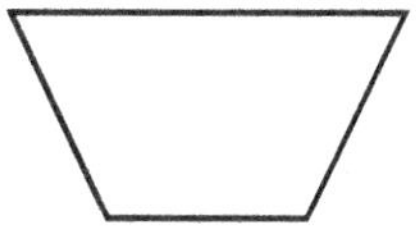

e) 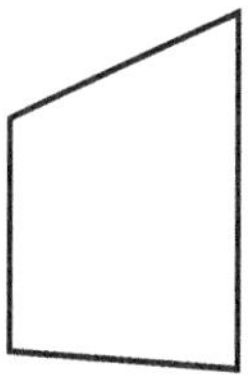

f) 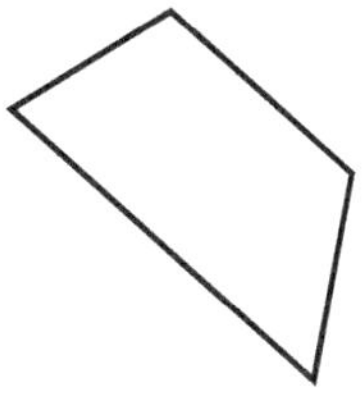

g) 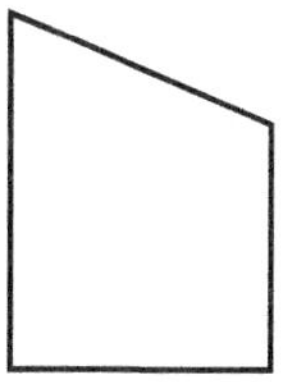

h) 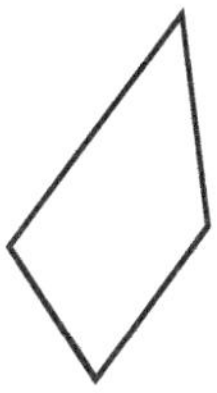

If there is more than one pair of parallel sides in a figure, use a different number of arrows for each pair.

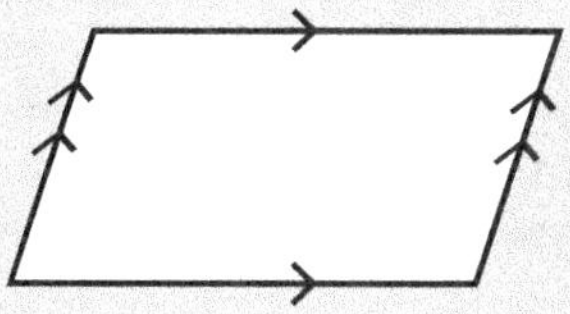

6. Use arrows to mark all the pairs of parallel sides in each figure. Write the number of pairs in the blank.

a) 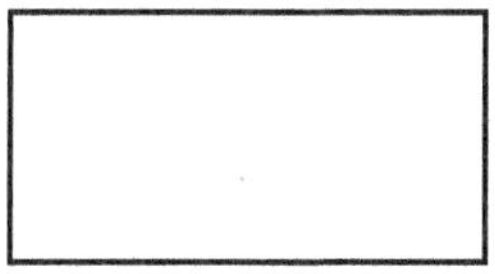

_____ pairs

b) 

_____ pairs

c) 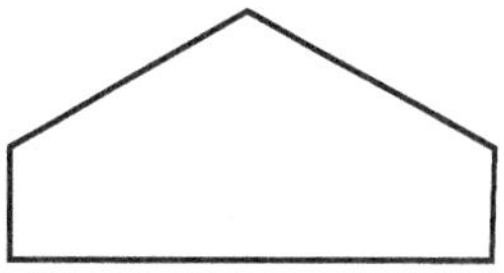

_____ pairs

d) 

_____ pairs

e) 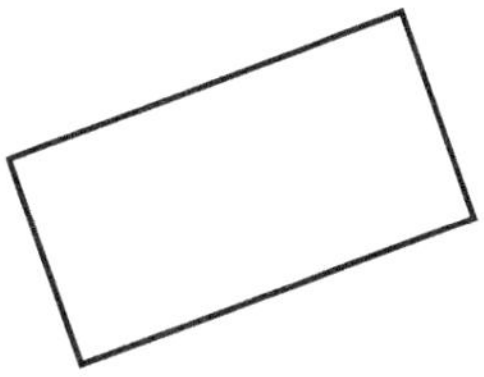

_____ pairs

f) 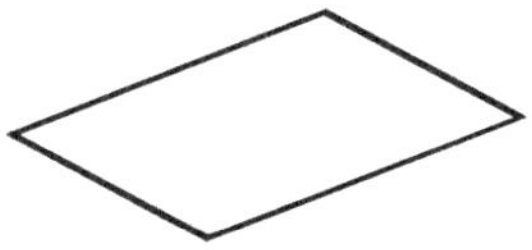

_____ pairs

g) 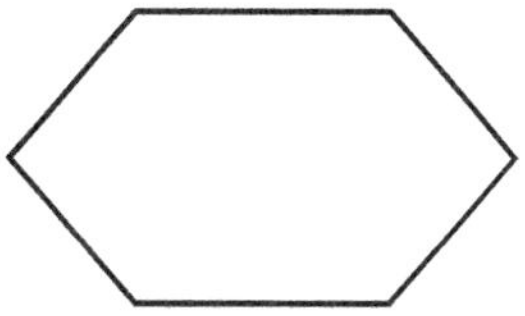

_____ pairs

BONUS ▶ 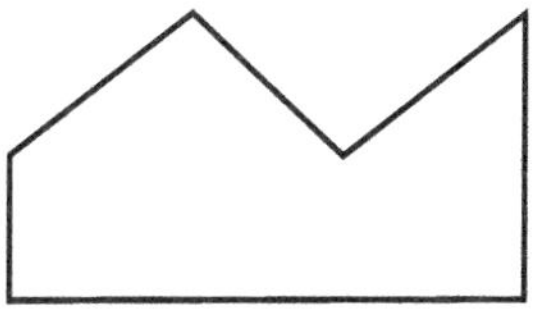

_____ pairs

G4-6 Quadrilaterals

REMINDER ▶ A quadrilateral is a polygon with 4 sides.

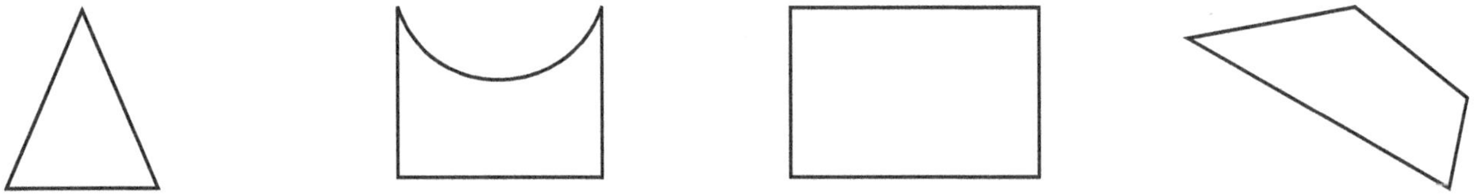

3 sides
not a quadrilateral

4 sides
not a polygon
not a quadrilateral

4 sides
quadrilateral

4 sides
quadrilateral

1. Sort the shapes into the chart below.

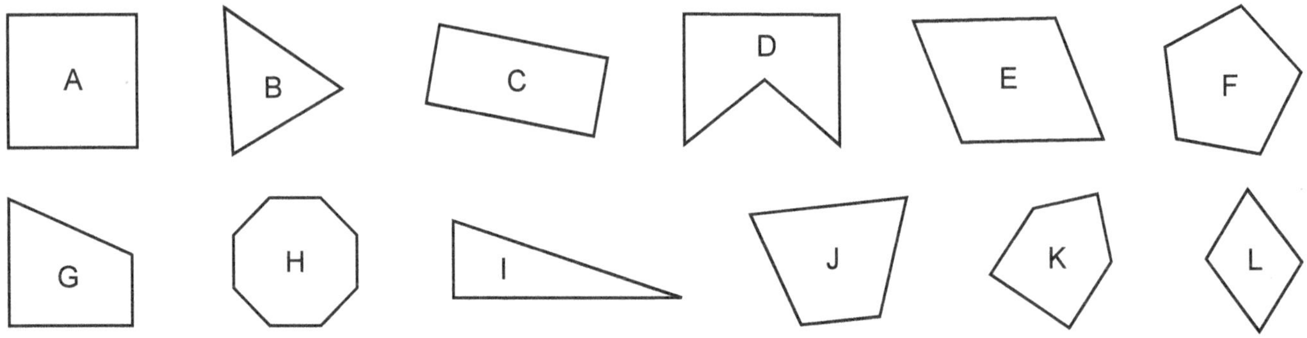

Quadrilaterals	*A,*
Not Quadrilaterals	

2.

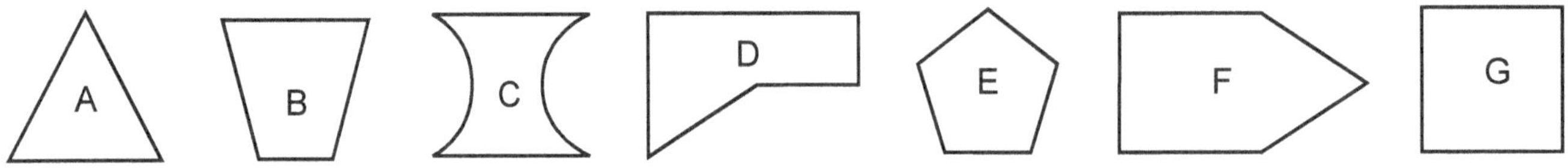

a) A polygon has only straight sides. Which shapes are polygons? ____________________

b) Which shapes have sides that are all the same length? (Check with a ruler.) ____________________

c) Which shapes have at least one curved side? ____________________

d) What do shapes B, C, and G have in common? ____________________

e) What do shapes D, E, and F have in common? ____________________

f) Which shape doesn't belong in this group: A, D, E, and F? ____________________

Explain. ____________________

g) Pick your own group of shapes and say what they have in common. ____________________

____

Properties of Shapes

Some quadrilaterals don't have any pairs of parallel sides. Some have one pair of parallel sides. Parallelograms have **two** pairs of parallel sides.

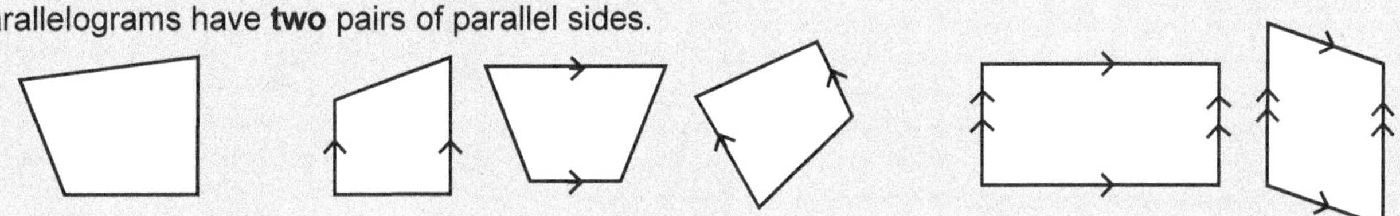

no parallel sides 1 pair of parallel sides 2 pairs of parallel sides

1. a) Mark the parallel sides with arrows. Mark the opposite sides that are not parallel with an ✕. Write how many pairs of sides are parallel.

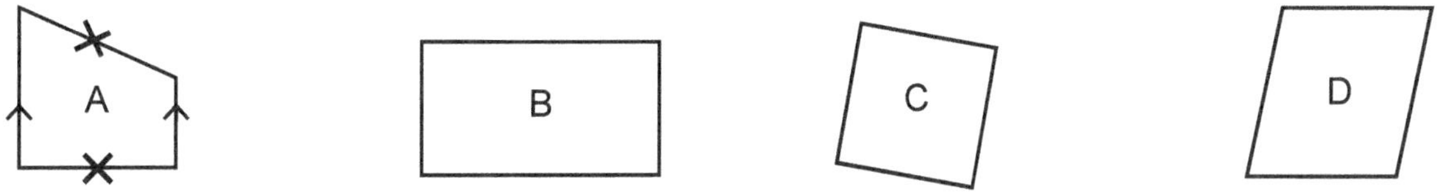

1 pair ______ ______ ______

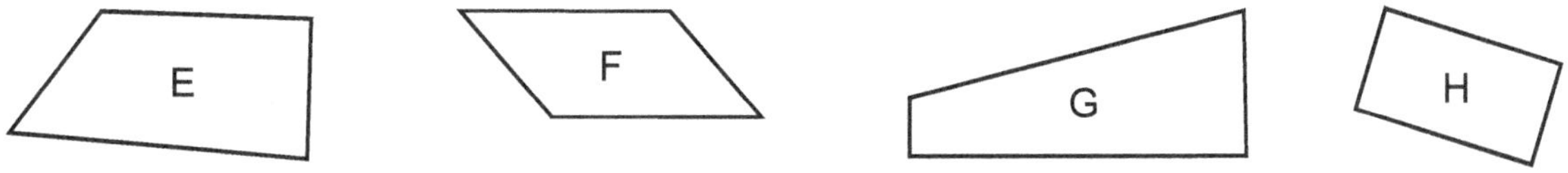

______ ______ ______ ______

b) Sort the shapes into the chart by writing the letter in the correct row.

No parallel sides	
1 pair of parallel sides	
2 pairs of parallel sides	

2. a) Mark the right angles and parallel sides in each figure.
b) Complete the two charts.

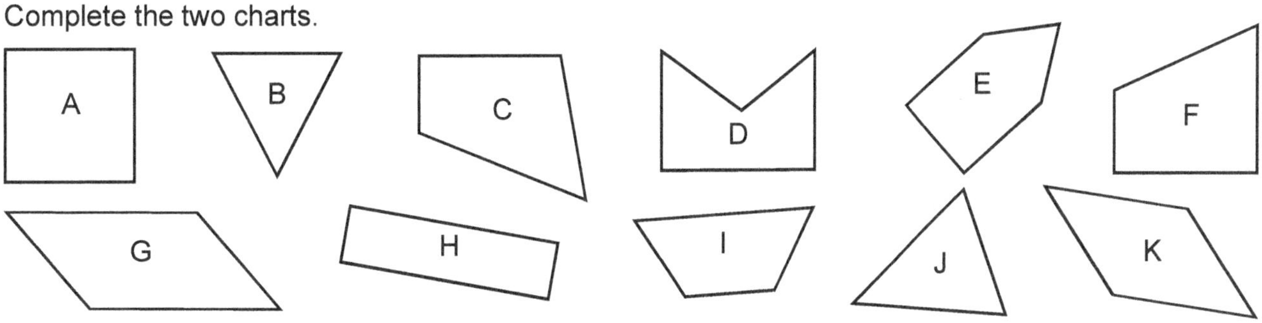

Property	Shapes with Property
No right angles	
1 right angle	
2 right angles	
4 right angles	

Property	Shapes with Property
No parallel sides	
1 pair of parallel sides	
2 pairs of parallel sides	

3. Use a ruler to measure the sides of the shapes below. Color the shapes that have all sides the same length.

a)

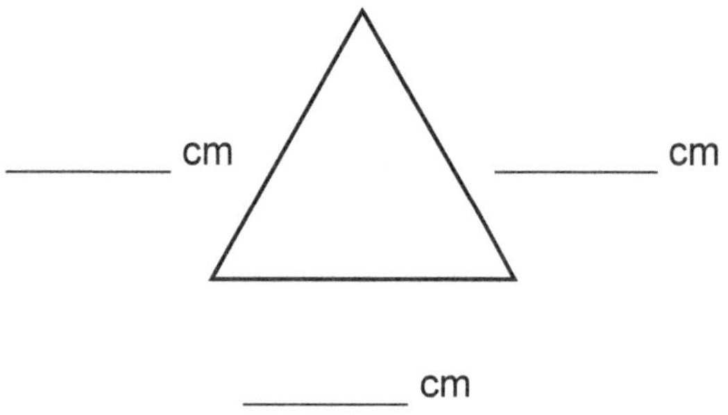

b)

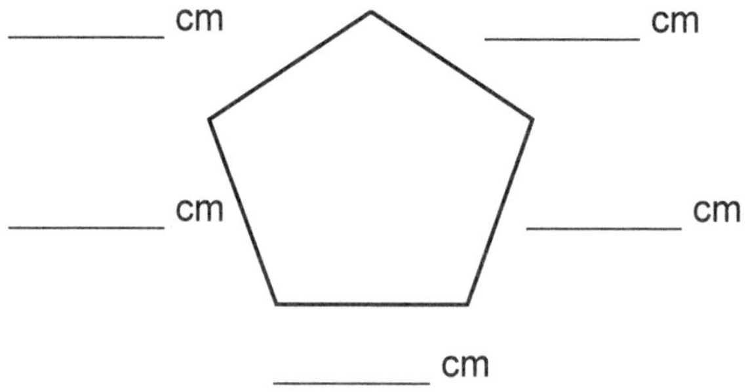

c)

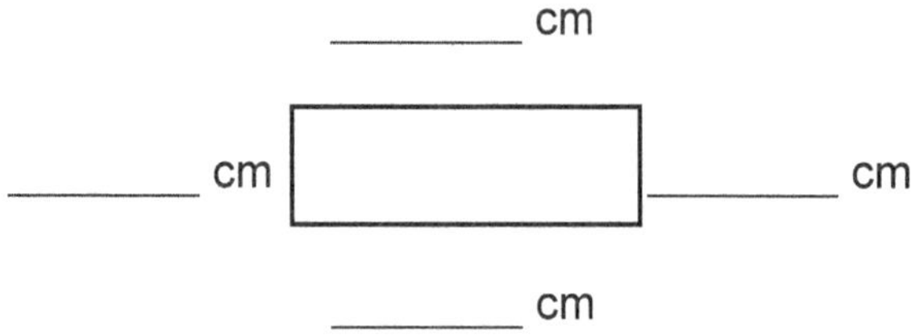

d)

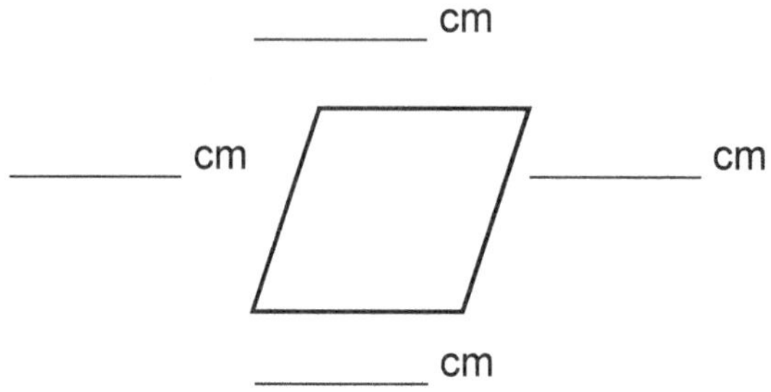

4. Use shapes A to J below to complete each chart. Hint: Mark the right angles and parallel lines in each figure. Use a ruler to check if sides are equal.

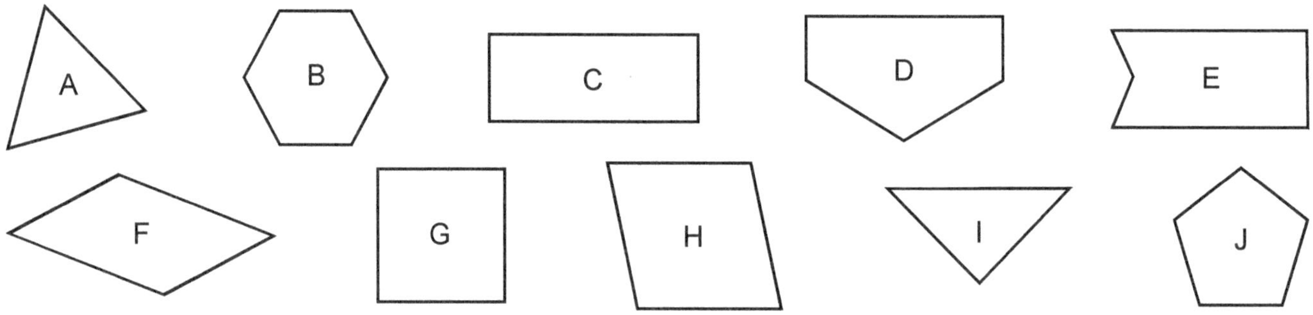

a)

Name	Shapes
Triangles	
Quadrilaterals	
Pentagons	
Hexagons	

b)

Property	Shapes with Property
No right angles	
1 right angle	
2 right angles	
4 right angles	

c)

Property	Shapes with Property
No parallel sides	
1 pair of parallel sides	
2 pairs of parallel sides	
3 pairs of parallel sides	

d)

Property	Shapes with Property
All sides are equal	
Some sides are not equal	

G4-8 Special Quadrilaterals

Some quadrilaterals (polygons with 4 sides) have special names.

A **parallelogram** is a quadrilateral with 2 pairs of parallel sides.

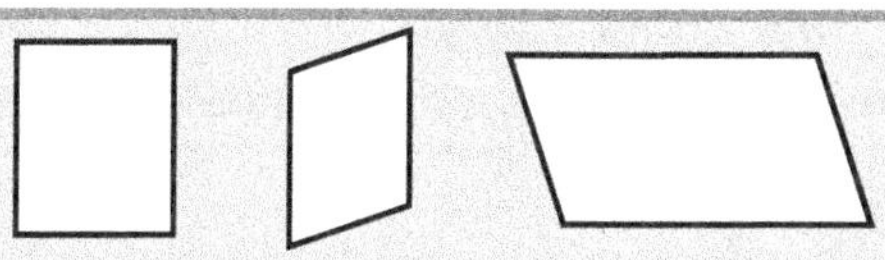

1. Circle the parallelograms.

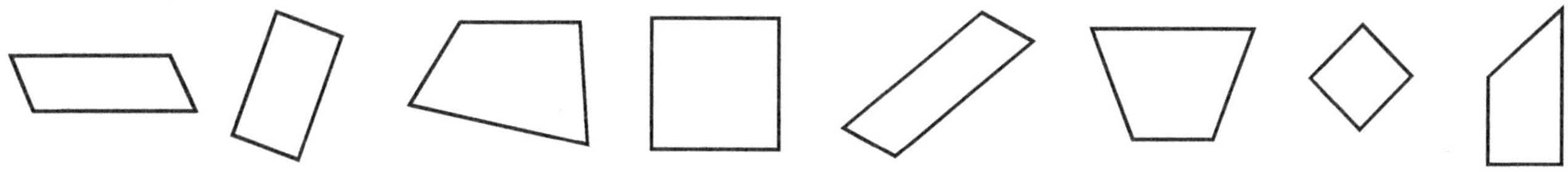

A **rhombus** is a parallelogram with 4 equal sides.

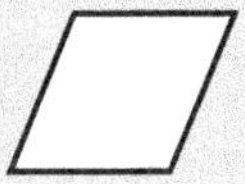

A **rectangle** is a parallelogram with 4 right angles.

A **square** is a parallelogram with 4 right angles and 4 equal sides.

A **trapezoid** is a quadrilateral with exactly one pair of parallel sides.

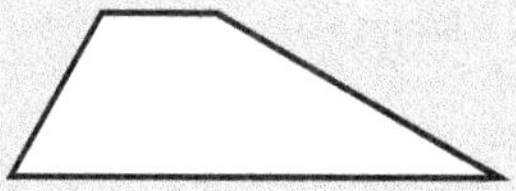

2. Mark all right angles in the quadrilaterals and measure the length of each side. Then choose the best (most specific) name for each quadrilateral.

a) ________ cm

________ cm 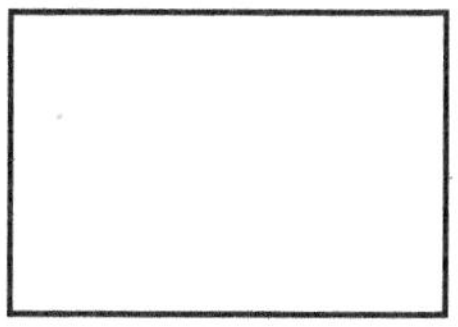 ________ cm

________ cm

Name ______________________________

b) ________ cm

________ cm 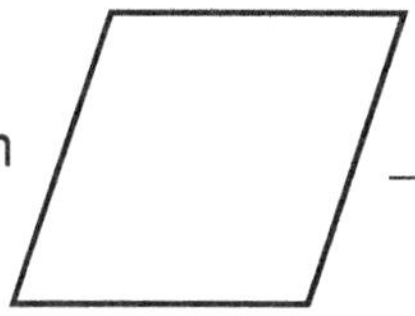 ________ cm

________ cm

Name ______________________________

3. Name the shapes. Use the words rhombus, square, parallelogram, and rectangle.

a) 

____

b) 

____

c) 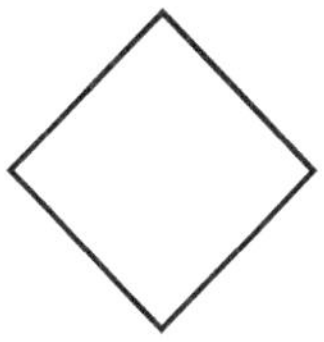

____

d) 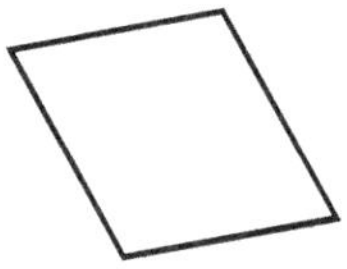

____

4. Mark all the right angles and parallel sides in each quadrilateral. Then name each quadrilateral.

a) 

____

b) 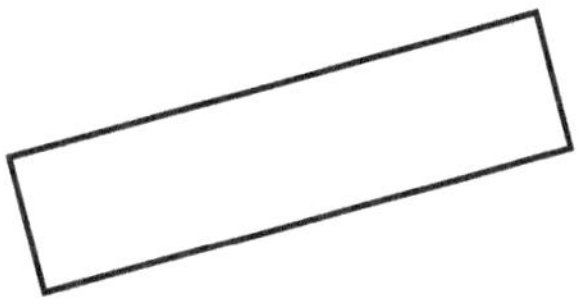

____

c) 

____

5. For each quadrilateral, write how many pairs of sides are parallel. Then name the quadrilateral.

a) 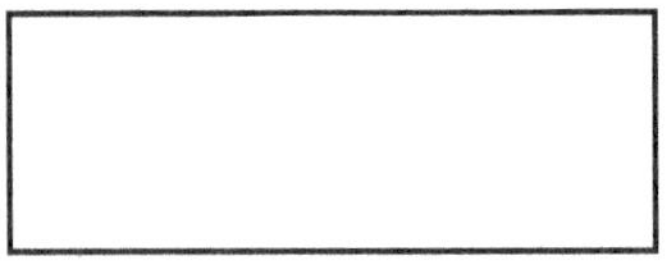

____

____

b) 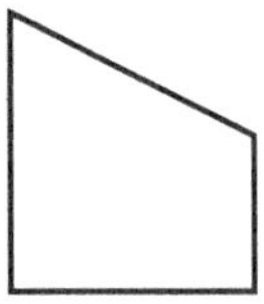

____

____

c) 

____

____

6. Draw a quadrilateral with ...

a) no right angle b) one right angle c) two right angles

7. Draw a quadrilateral with ...

a) no parallel sides b) one pair of parallel sides c) two pairs of parallel sides and no right angles

8. Write "all," "some," or "no" to make each statement true.

a) __________ squares are rectangles. b) __________ trapezoids are parallelograms.

c) __________ parallelograms are trapezoids. d) __________ parallelograms are rectangles.

9. a) A shape has four right angles. Which two special quadrilaterals might it be?
b) A quadrilateral has all equal sides. Which two special quadrilaterals might it be?
c) Write three different names for a square.

10. Describe any similarities or differences between ...

a) a rhombus and a parallelogram.
b) a rhombus and a square.
c) a trapezoid and a parallelogram.

G4-9 Symmetry

1. Each shape is divided into two parts. Are the parts the same size and shape?
Imagine folding the shape along the line. Do the parts match exactly?

a) 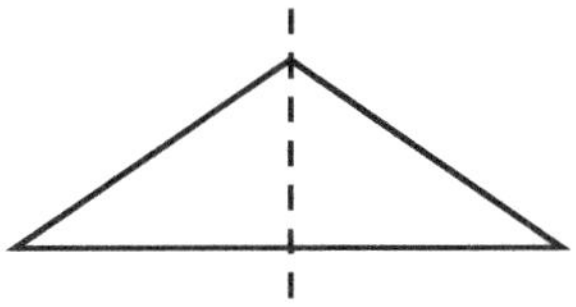

☑ same shape and size
☑ match exactly

b) 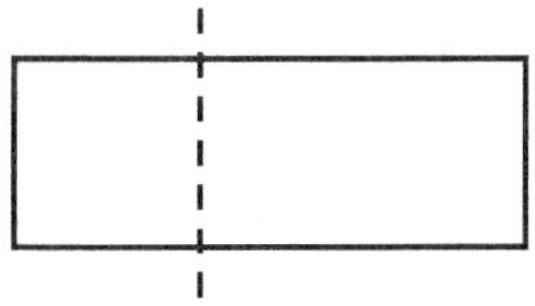

☒ same shape and size
☒ match exactly

c) 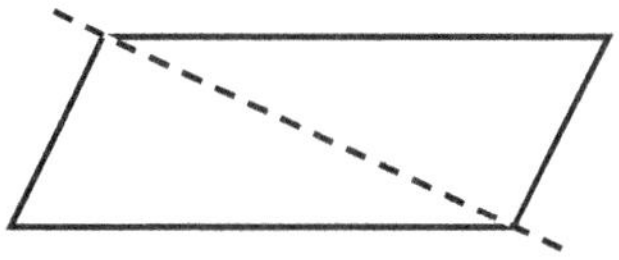

☑ same shape and size
☒ match exactly

d) 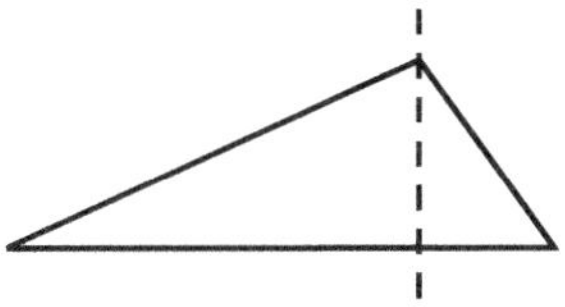

☐ same shape and size
☐ match exactly

e) 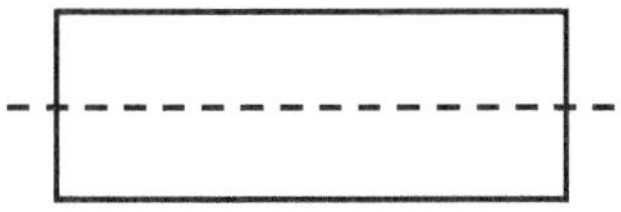

☐ same shape and size
☐ match exactly

f) 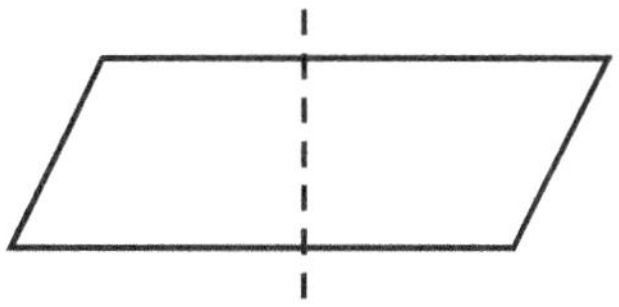

☐ same shape and size
☐ match exactly

g) 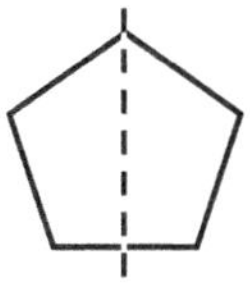

☐ same shape and size
☐ match exactly

h) 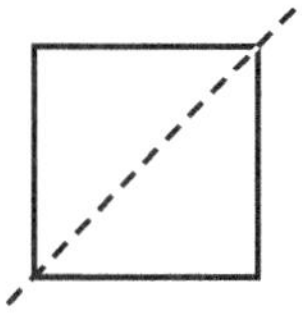

☐ same shape and size
☐ match exactly

i) 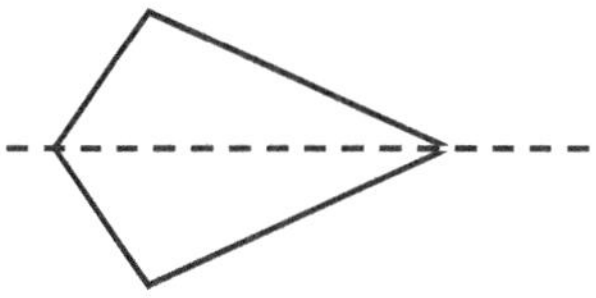

☐ same shape and size
☐ match exactly

Tina folds a shape along the dashed line.

If the parts of the shape match exactly, the dashed line is a **line of symmetry.**

A shape that has a line of symmetry is called **symmetrical**.

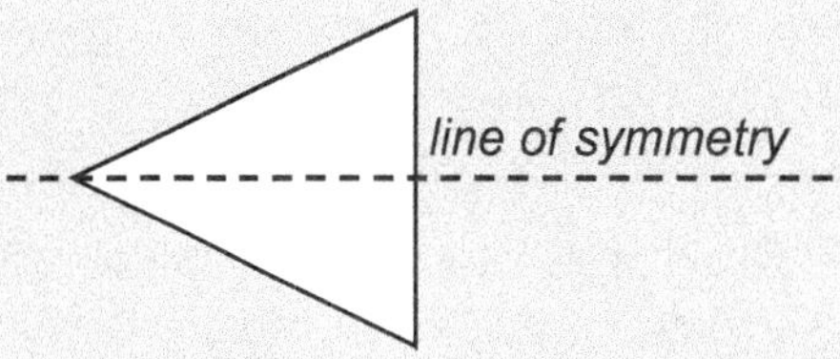

2. Circle the pictures that show a line of symmetry.

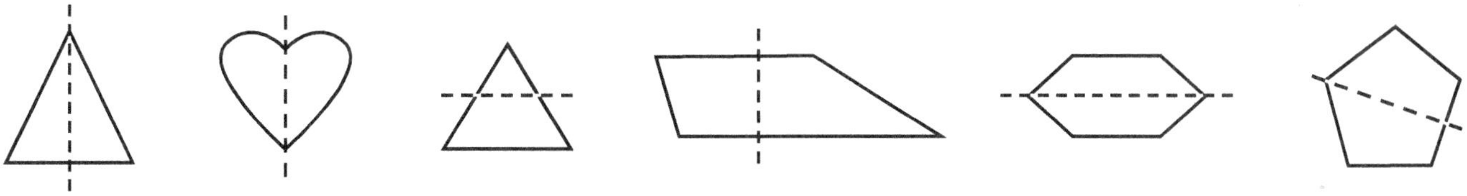

3. Sketch a line of symmetry.

Horizontal lines go side to side.

Vertical lines go up and down.

horizontal line | *vertical line*

4. a) Complete the picture so it has a horizontal line of symmetry. Then draw the line of symmetry.

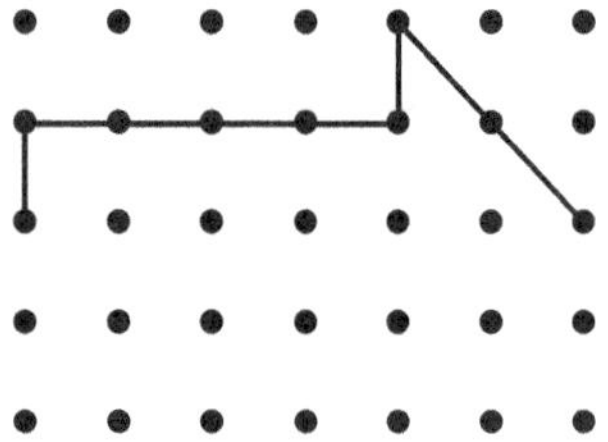

b) Complete the picture so it has a vertical line of symmetry. Then draw the line of symmetry.

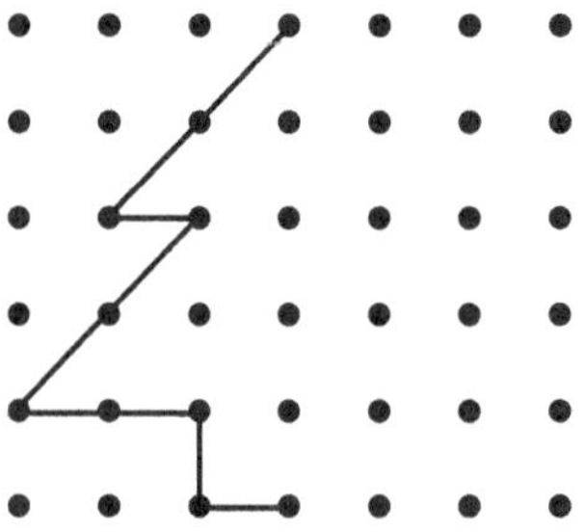

5. Draw a horizontal line of symmetry through each figure. Use a ruler.

a) 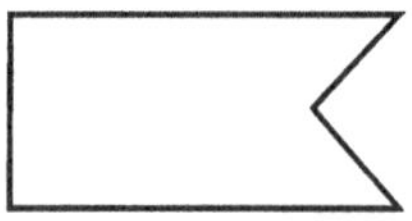

b) 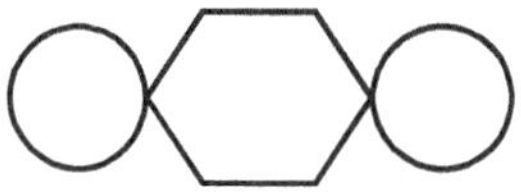

c) 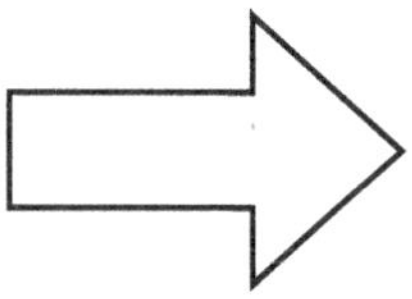

d) 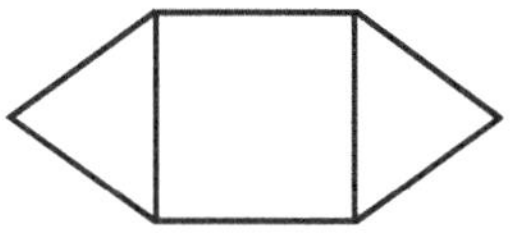

6. Draw a vertical line of symmetry through each figure.

a) 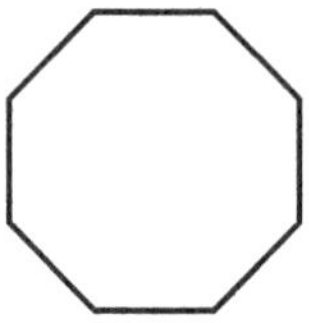

b) 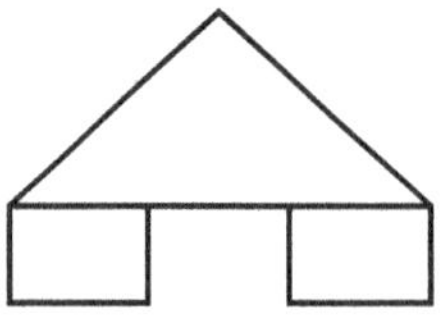

c) 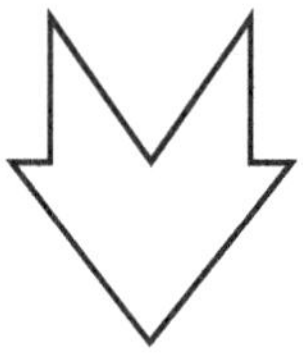

d) 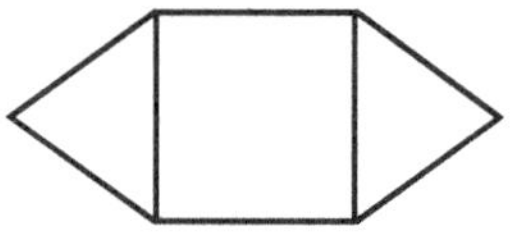

7. Draw lines of symmetry in the following figures.
Which figures have more than one line of symmetry? ________

a) 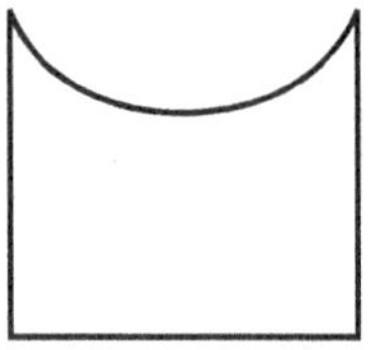

b) 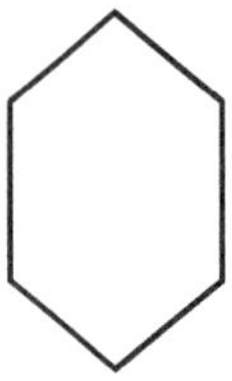

c) 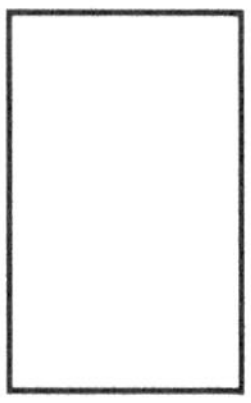

d) 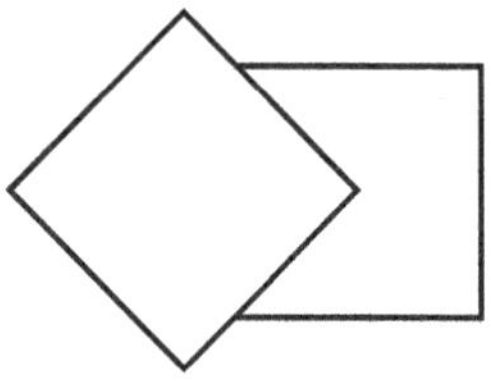

8. How many lines of symmetry does each figure have?

a) 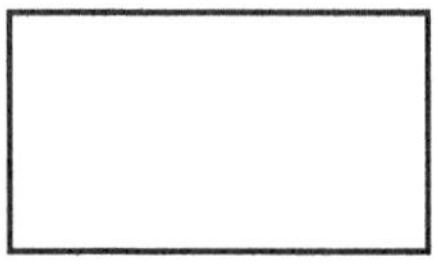
____

b) 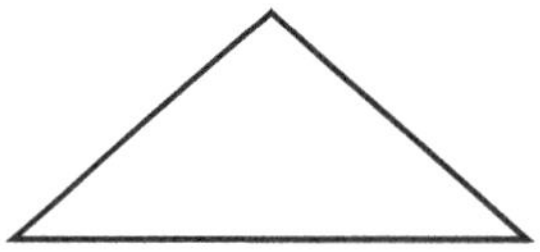
____

c) 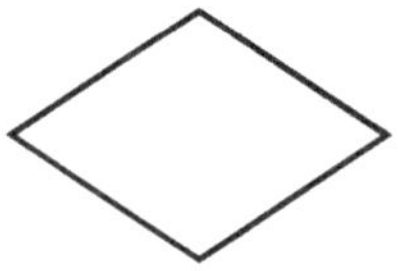
____

d) 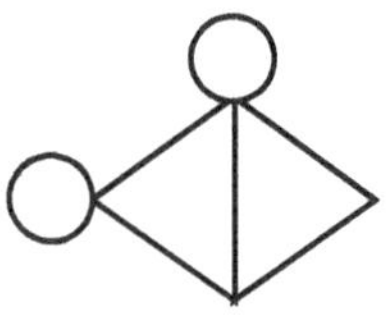
____

G4-10 More Symmetry

1. Cut out copies of the shapes shown below.

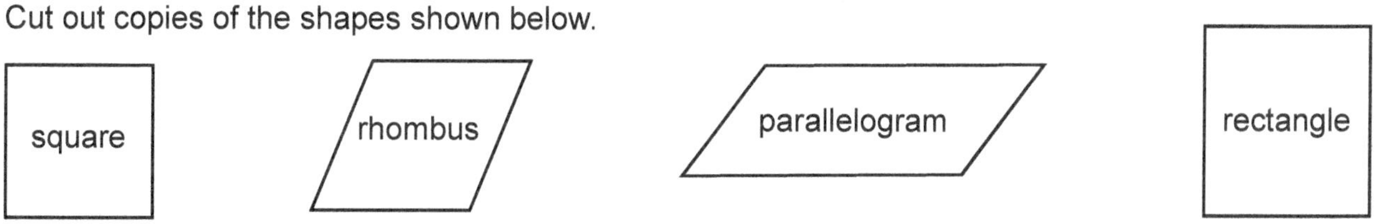

a) Predict how many lines of symmetry each shape will have.

Write your answers in the chart.

b) Fold your shapes to check how many lines of symmetry they have.

Draw the lines of symmetry onto the shapes above.

Then complete the chart.

Shape	Predicted number of lines of symmetry	Actual number of lines of symmetry
Square		
Rectangle		
Rhombus		
Parallelogram		

2. Draw a line of symmetry through each shape, parallel to line *A*.

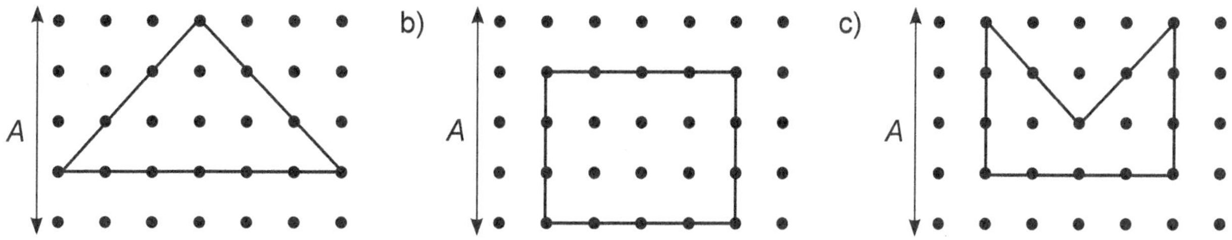

3. Draw a line through each shape that is parallel to line *B* but is *not* a line of symmetry.

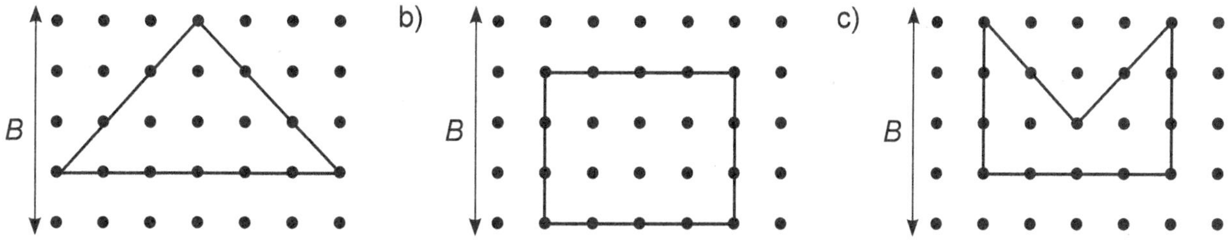

4. Many letters of the alphabet have lines of symmetry.

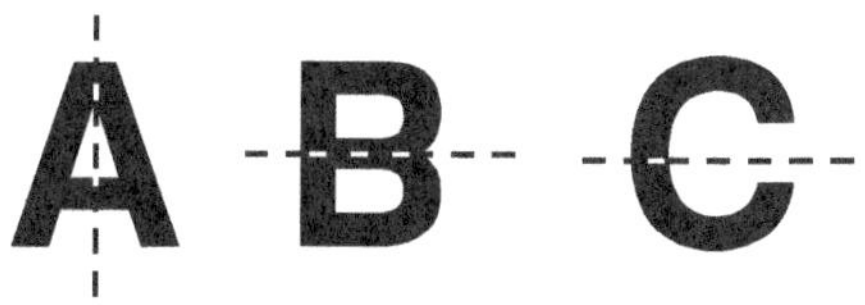

a) Draw at least 5 symmetrical letters of the alphabet and show their lines of symmetry.

b) How many letters with 2 or more lines of symmetry can you find?

5. Decode the words written in "mirror code" by filling in the missing half of each letter.

a) b) c)

G4-11 Comparing Shapes

1. a) Compare the two shapes by completing the chart below.

Shape 1

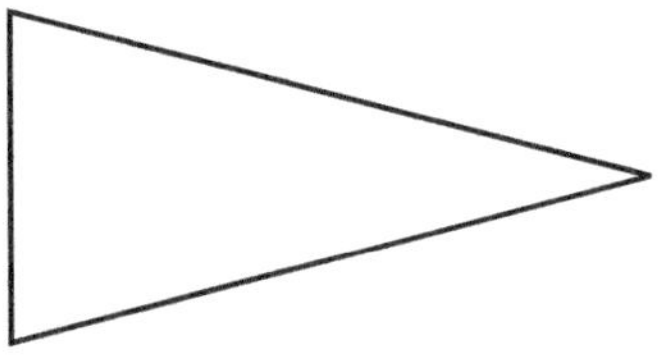

Shape 2

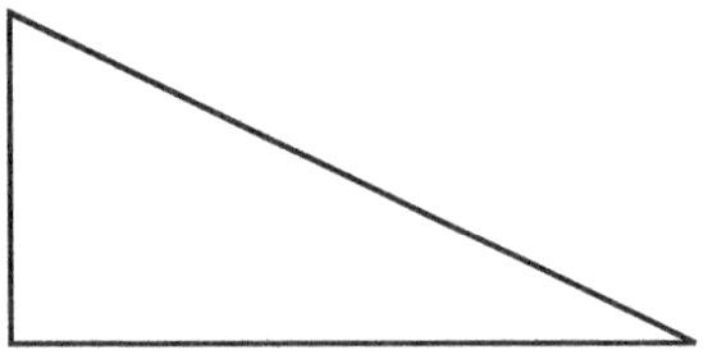

Property	Shape 1	Shape 2	Same?	Different?
Number of vertices	*3*	*3*	✓	
Number of sides				
Number of pairs of parallel sides				
Number of right angles				
Number of equal sides				
Number of lines of symmetry				

b) How are the shapes the same and how are they different?

Shape 1

Shape 2

Property	Same?	Different?
Number of vertices		
Number of sides		
Number of pairs of parallel sides		
Number of right angles		
Number of pairs of equal sides		
Number of lines of symmetry		

2. Draw two shapes and compare them using a chart.

3. Describe the similarities and differences between each two shapes.

Be sure to mention the following properties:

- The number of vertices
- The number of sides
- The number of pairs of parallel sides
- The number of right angles
- The number of lines of symmetry
- The number of equal sides or the number of pairs of equal sides
- Are both figures polygons?

a) Shape 1

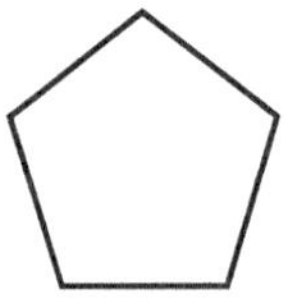

Shape 2

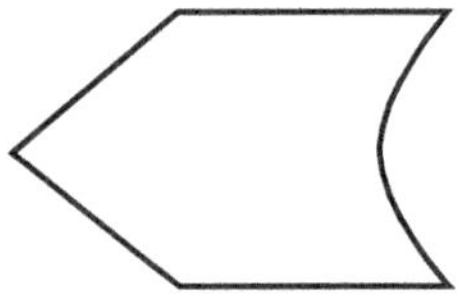

b) Shape 1

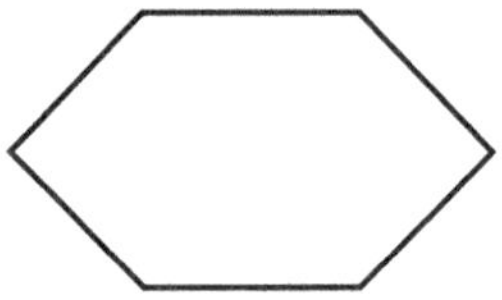

Shape 2

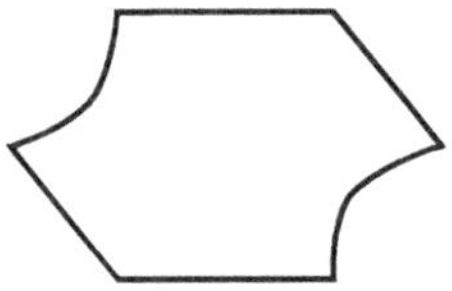

G4-12 Sorting and Classifying Shapes

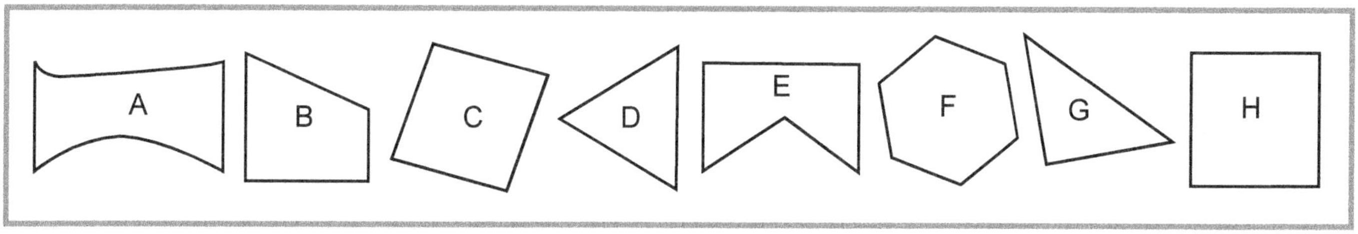

1. The shapes from the box were sorted by their properties.

Property	Shapes with this property
Quadrilateral	B, C, H
At least 2 right angles	B, E, H

Which shapes share both properties? __________

Use the information in the chart to complete the Venn diagram.

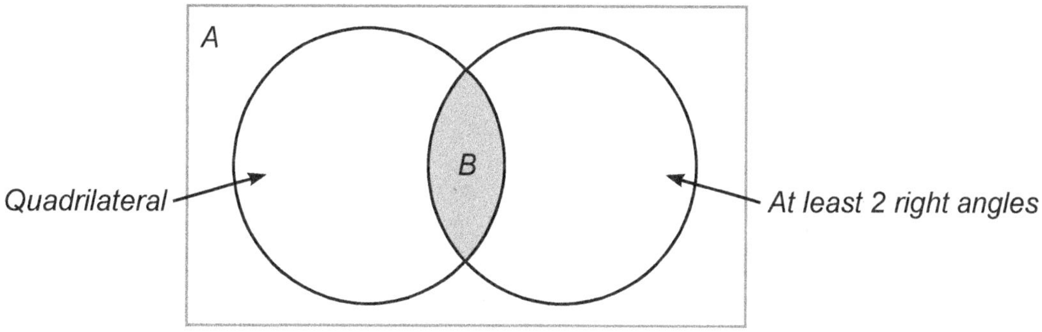

2. Use shapes from the box above to complete the charts and the Venn diagrams.

Property	Shapes with this property
Quadrilateral	
All sides equal	

Which figures share both properties? __________

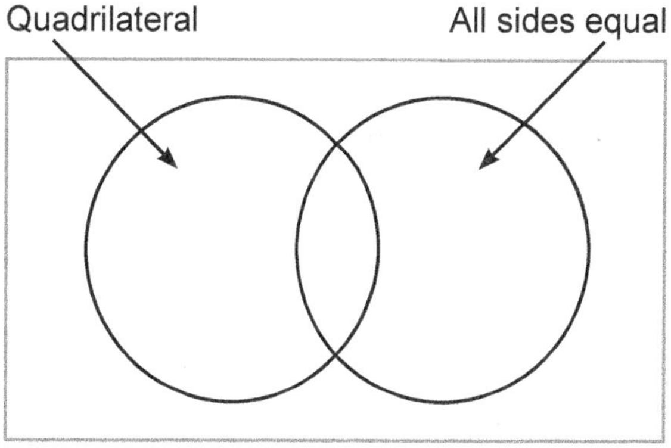

Property	Shapes with this property
4 or 5 vertices	
At least 1 right angle	

Which figures share both properties? __________

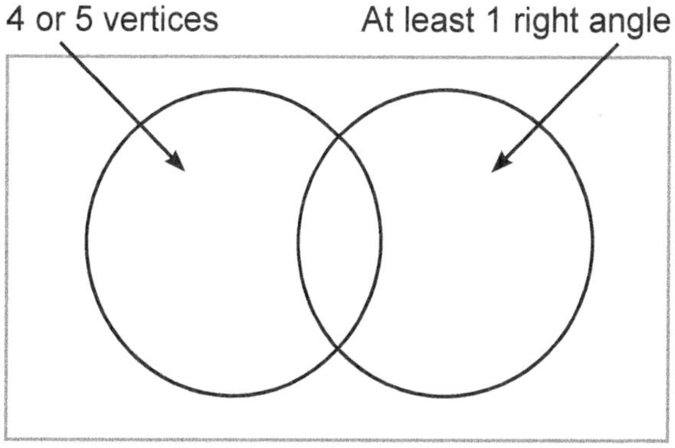

REMINDER ▶ Perpendicular sides make a right angle.

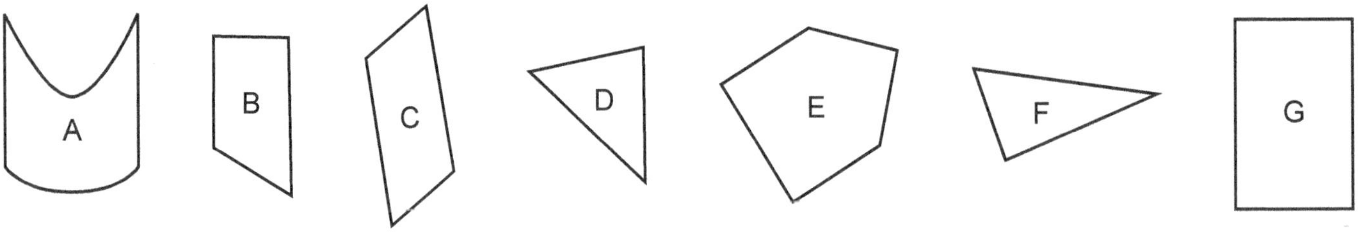

3. a) Sort the shapes above into the Venn diagram.

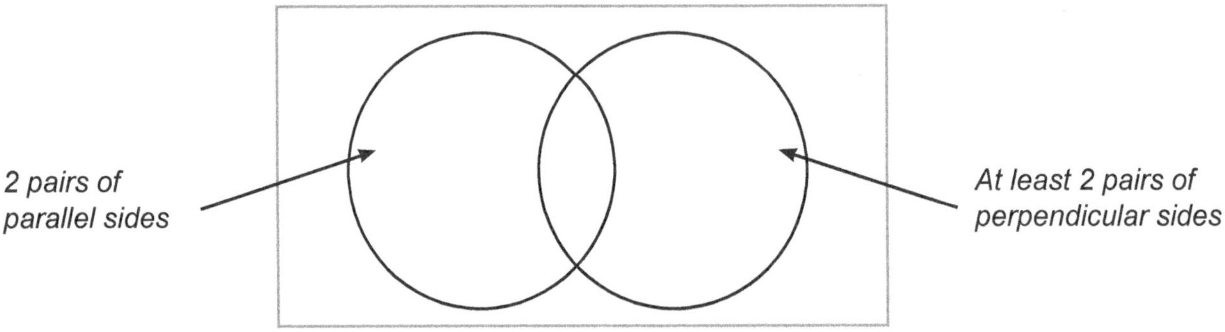

b) Choose two properties from the list below. Make a chart and a Venn diagram (as in Question 1) to sort the shapes above.

- At least 4 vertices
- 2 or more right angles
- 2 pairs of parallel sides
- Exactly 2 perpendicular sides
- Quadrilateral
- One pair of parallel sides
- At least one line of symmetry
- All sides equal

4. Describe each shape completely. Your description should mention these properties:

- Number of sides
- Number of vertices
- Number of pairs of parallel sides
- Number of right angles
- Number of lines of symmetry
- Are all the sides equal?

a) 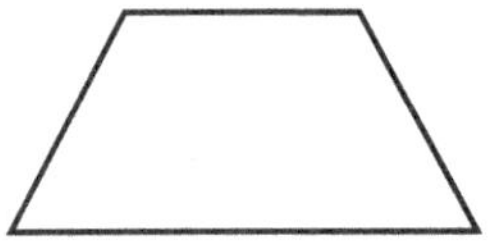 b) 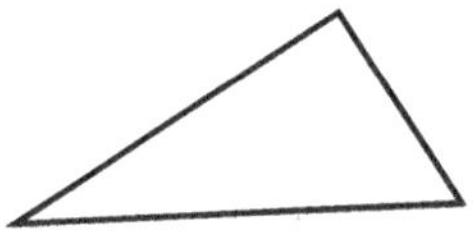 c) 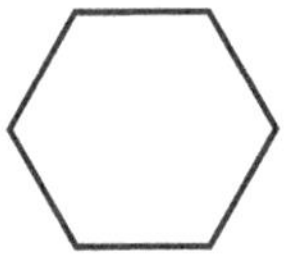

5. List all the properties shared by the shapes. Then list any differences.

a) 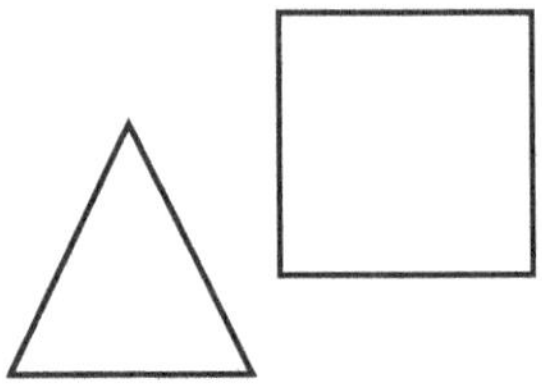 b) 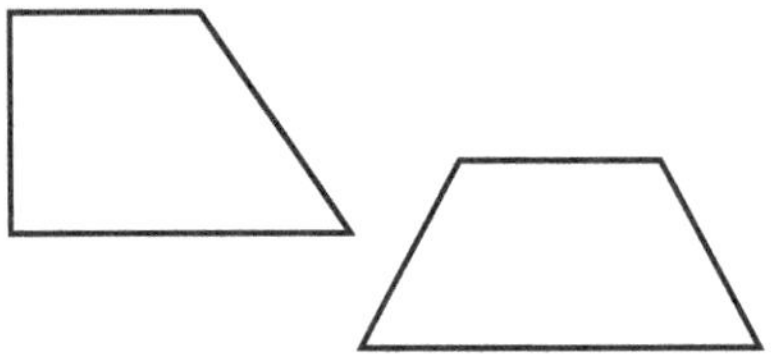 c) 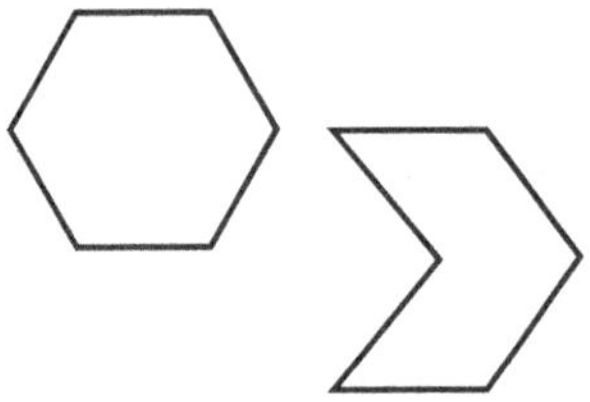

G4-13 Puzzles and Problems

1. Record the properties of each shape by writing "yes" or "no" in the corresponding columns.

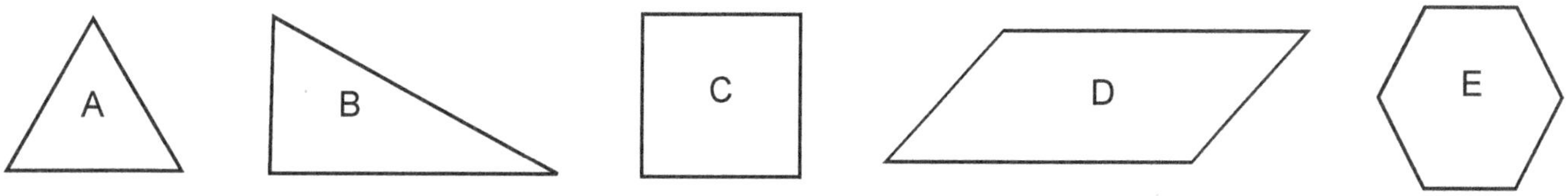

Shape	Quadrilateral	All sides are equal	Two pairs of parallel sides	At least one right angle
A				
B				
C				
D				
E				

2. Count the vertices and sides in the shapes. Mark right angles with a square. Mark pairs of parallel sides with arrows.

   Draw a check mark if both shapes share the property and draw an ✗ if they do not.

a) 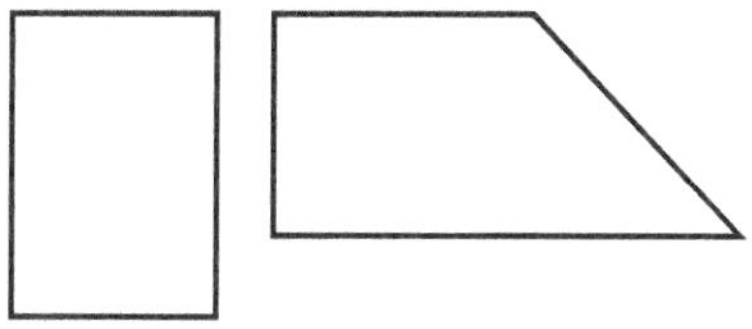

☑ 4 vertices ☒ 2 pairs of parallel sides

☐ 4 sides ☐ 2 right angles

b) 

☐ 3 vertices ☐ no right angles

☐ 5 sides ☐ all sides equal

c) 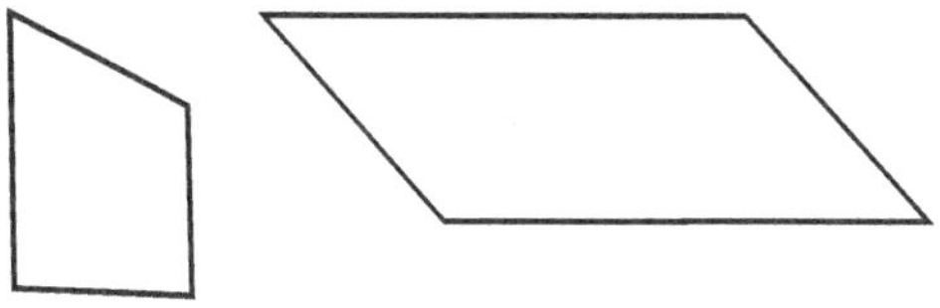

☐ quadrilateral

☐ 2 pairs of parallel sides

☐ at least 1 right angle

d) 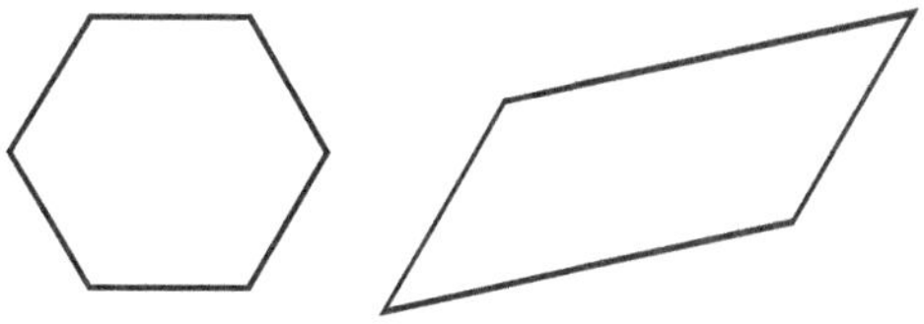

☐ 6 vertices

☐ no right angles

☐ at least 2 pairs of parallel sides

3. Name the shapes based on the descriptions.

a) I have four equal sides. All of my angles are right angles. I'm a ______________________

b) I have four equal sides. None of my angles are right angles. I'm a ______________________

c) I am a quadrilateral with two pairs of parallel sides. I'm a ______________________

4. Mark all the right angles in this figure.

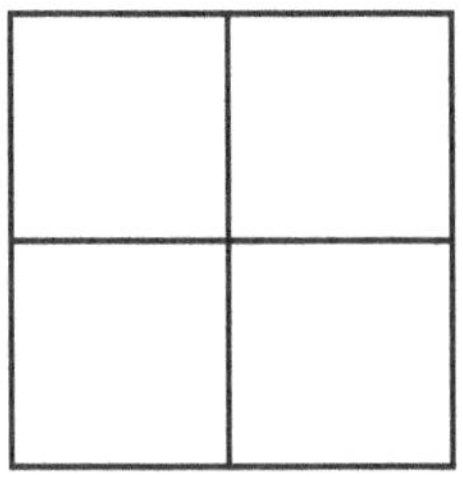

How many right angles are in this figure? ____________

How many squares are in this figure? ____________

How many rectangles are in this figure?
(Remember, a square is a rectangle too!) ____________

5. Name all the quadrilaterals in this picture.

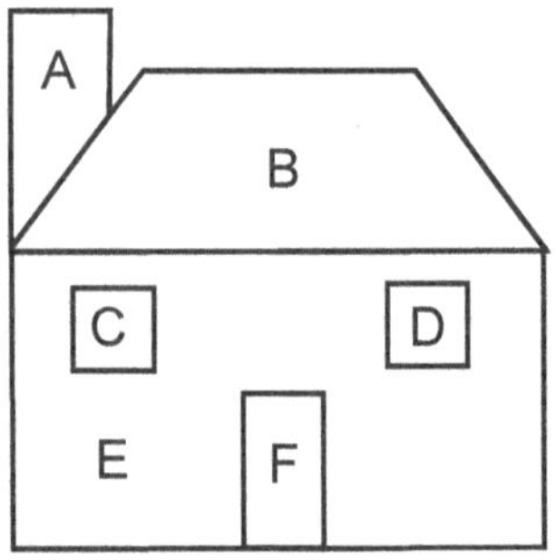

A ____________ B ____________

C ____________ D ____________

E ____________ F ____________

Which two special quadrilaterals are *not* in the picture?

____________ and ____________

6. Write as many names as you can for each figure.

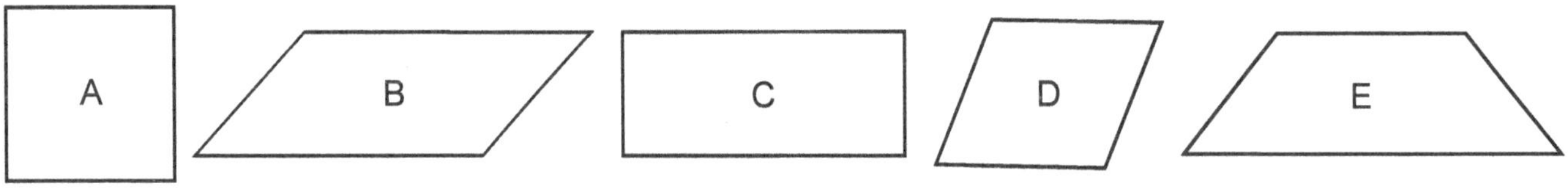

7. The shape on the grid is a trapezoid.

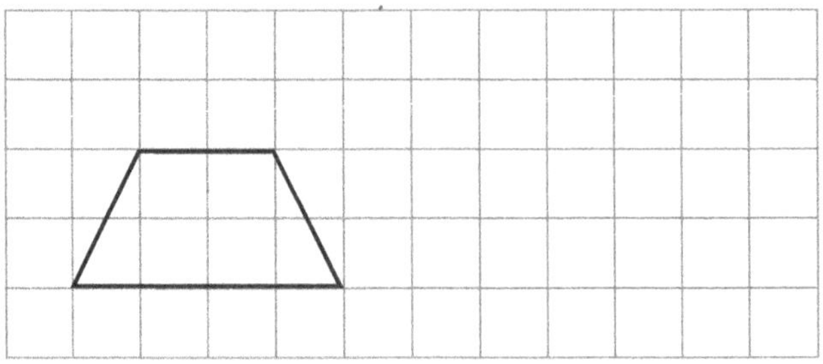

a) On the grid, draw a second trapezoid that has 2 right angles. Mark the right angles.

b) How do you know both shapes are trapezoids?

8. a) Why is a square a rectangle?
b) Why is a rectangle not always a square?
c) Why is a trapezoid not a parallelogram?

9. a) I have 4 equal sides, but no right angles. What am I?
b) I have 4 right angles, but my sides are not all equal. What am I?

BONUS ▶ I have exactly 2 right angles. Which special quadrilateral could I be? ____________